Study Guide

to accompany
*Money, the Financial System,
and the Economy*
Third Edition

Michael Redfearn
University of North Texas

 **ADDISON-WESLEY**

An imprint of Addison Wesley Longman, Inc.

Reading, Massachusetts ● Menlo Park, California ● New York ● Harlow, England
Don Mills, Ontario ● Sydney ● Mexico City ● Madrid ● Amsterdam

Study Guide to accompany *Money, the Financial System, and the Economy,* Third Edition

© 2000 Addison Wesley Longman, Inc.
Reprinted with corrections, December 2000

ISBN: 0-201-65728-7

2 3 4 5 6 7 8 9 10-BW-0403020100

Contents

PREFACE

This Study Guide is designed to help you master the material covered in the textbook *Money, The Financial System, and the Economy* by R. Glenn Hubbard. By reading through it and completing the exercises, you will deepen your understanding of the concepts presented in your money and banking course. No study guide can be a substitute for attending class and reading the course text, however. This study guide is designed to work in tandem with the Hubbard textbook, the Web site, and your instructor.

Given the rapid pace of change in the financial system, it is no longer enough to simply learn about the operations of financial institutions and the Federal Reserve System. Understanding the implications of ongoing changes in the system requires an appreciation of the economic theory influencing financial developments. The best way to develop this appreciation is through application of *the economic approach* to a number of different situations. A unique feature of this Study Guide is the large number of essay questions that stress applications of the concepts presented in the text. As you work through the essay questions, you will gain valuable practice in applying what you have learned to the economic world around you.

Useful Features

Each chapter of the Study Guide contains features that will help you better understand what you have read and will prepare you for taking the course examinations. Take a look at these features now before you begin.

Key Concepts

Each chapter opens with a summary of the material covered in the main text. This summary is designed to be read after you have read the main text. If after reviewing the summary you find that you are having problems with a concept, you can refer back to the main text.

Self-Test

Each chapter concludes with a set of exercises to help you test your understanding of what you have read. True-false, fill-in-the-blank, and multiple-choice questions review the text material. The essay questions amplify the main concepts of the course as they test your ability to apply the concepts. Coupled with the essay questions in the Hubbard text, these questions will give you extensive practice in applying *the economic approach* to real-world situations and events.

Examinations

There are four examinations at the end of the workbook—two exams which cover chapters 1 through 16 and two exams which cover chapters 17 through 28. These are designed to provide you with further review. They are a final check over your command of the material.

Using This Guide

The features of this guide may be used in a variety of ways, but they have been designed to work with the text in the following way.

- First, read the chapter in the Hubbard text without worrying too much about specific points *before* you attend the lecture on it.

- Next, read the Key Concepts section, referring back to the text as needed.

- Attend class and take good notes, then read the text chapter again, this time making sure that you understand the details and all calculations.

- At this point, you are ready to test yourself. Complete the Self-Test as if it were an actual exam, writing the answers to the essay questions, and making sure you understand the correct answer to the questions you miss.

- Visit the Web site (www.awlonline.com/hubbard) for additional multiple-choice and short-answer quizzes.

- After working through the Self-Test, the Web site, and reviewing relevant text sections, you should be well-prepared to answer the chapter-end questions from the main text.

- As you prepare for exams, use the Study Guide and the Web site to review and check your understanding of the main ideas.

Acknowledgements

I would like to thank Judean Patten for her assistance and encouragement during the preparation process. The editorial and technical staffs at Addison-Wesley-Longman also provided valuable assistance. I would like to thank R. Glenn Hubbard for providing timely answers to my questions. I also would like to thank the students in my *Money and Financial Institutions* classes who unknowingly tested many of the questions which appear throughout the Study Guide. Finally, I would like to thank Margie Tieslau, not only for her technical expertise and assistance, but also for her unfailing support and encouragement; I would not have been able to complete this project without her. As always, any remaining errors are completely my own.

1: INTRODUCING MONEY AND THE FINANCIAL SYSTEM

KEY CONCEPTS

This chapter serves as an introduction to money, banking, and the financial system. It provides an overview of the concepts and issues that will be discussed in detail in later chapters, and it introduces a number of important themes that will run throughout the course. The first major topic introduced in this chapter is the **financial system**, which is a network of **financial markets and financial institutions** that brings savers (those who have excess funds) together with investors (those who have uses for funds). The financial system is essential to a well-functioning economy because without a well-functioning financial system, many profitable investments would go unfunded. The financial system provides three key **financial services**:

- **Risk sharing**: Most people prefer less risk to more risk, all else being constant, so they seek to reduce risk through risk sharing. The financial system provides borrowers and lenders with risk sharing by pooling assets and through diversification.

- **Provision of liquidity**: The financial system creates liquidity services by providing a method for trading existing assets and by creating new, more liquid financial instruments.

- **Information services**: The financial system reduces information costs by taking advantage of economies of scale in the gathering and communicating of information.

How financial services can be most efficiently provided determines the structure of the financial system.

A second important concept that is set out for the first time in this chapter and returned to in more detail in later chapters is **money**. In the United States, the **Federal Reserve System** is responsible for regulating the money supply, which is the total quantity of money in the economy. The **money supply** is important because changes in money supply growth are associated with changes in other economic variables, such as the prices you pay and the interest you earn on your savings. Government policymakers set **monetary policy** so as to exploit the relationship between money and other economic variables. The investigation of the effect of the money supply on economic activity, interest rates, and prices is called **monetary theory**. Policymakers view monetary theory as important because it helps them to design more effective monetary policy. Monetary theory helps businesses and individuals to devise better strategies for coping with a changing economic environment.

A third major concept introduced in this chapter is the idea of **economic analysis**, which involves the following steps:

- The setting out of what is to be explained (the problem).

- The proposing of how the problem is to be explained (the theory).

- The examination of actual data in order to evaluate the theory.

Economic analysis is a powerful tool because it allows you to both *explain* current events and *predict* future developments.

Sometimes, economists differ as to what is the best theory for predicting and explaining the economy, so they have developed three criteria that are useful in deciding among theories:

- Are the assumptions of the theory reasonable?

- Does the theory generate predictions that you can verify with actual data?

- Do the data corroborate the predictions?

A theory for which the answer to the above three questions is "yes" is a theory that is useful in understanding the economy. However, there is no guarantee that this theory will be the only one that satisfies the above three criteria.

Check List

When you finish this chapter, you should be able to:

✔ Explain the role of the financial system in the efficient operation of the economy.

✔ Explain what a financial market is and give three examples.

✔ Explain what a financial institution is and give three examples.

✔ Describe the three key financial services that the financial system provides.

✔ Understand that differences among financial markets and institutions have evolved so as to provide financial services at low cost to diverse customers.

✔ Understand that there is a relationship among money, interest rates, prices, and economic activity.

✔ Understand the relationship between monetary policy and monetary theory.

✔ Understand the importance of being able to explain and predict the economy using economic analysis.

✔ Apply economic analysis in developing an economic theory.

✔ Apply the three criteria in deciding among competing economic theories.

Self-Test

True or False

1. The financial system is a network of markets and institutions that brings savers and borrowers together.   T

2. Most financial transactions are conducted through financial intermediaries.   T

3. The international capital market is an example of a financial intermediary.   F

4. Money is anything that a person accepts in payment for goods and services or to pay off a debt.   T

5. The central bank of the United States is the U.S. Treasury.   F

6. Monetary theory deals with the relationships among the money supply, economic activity, interest rates, and prices.   T

7. Monetary policy is the deliberate manipulation of the tax code to influence economic variables.   T

8. Although the economic approach is useful for explaining current events, it is of little use in predicting future developments.   F

9. Economists are in complete agreement about which theory best explains economic activity.   F

10. Economic analysis uses the following steps: (1) the setting out of what is to be explained (the problem), (2) the proposing of how the problem is to be explained (the theory), and (3) the examining of actual data to evaluate the theory.   T

Fill in the Blank

1. An example of a _____ _____ is a car loan, which is an asset to the bank but a liability to the borrower.

2. The three key financial services provided by the financial system are _____ _____, _____, and _____ services.

3. The financial system provides _____ _____ by providing savers and borrowers ways to reduce uncertainty.

4. An asset that can easily be converted into cash is _____.

5. In providing _____ _____, the financial system reduces the cost of gathering and processing information.

6. The _____ _____ _____ is the market for lending and borrowing across national boundaries.

7. Commercial banks, savings and loans, and insurance companies are examples of _____ _____.

8. _____ is anything that people are willing to accept in payment for goods and services or to pay off debts.

9. The _____ _____ _____ is responsible for the measurement of the _____ _____ and for the conduct of _____ _____.

10. That the Fed, in response to a rise in unemployment, increases the growth rate of the money supply is an example of _____ _____.

11. _____ _____ involves the development and testing of a theory's predictions to determine the theory's usefulness.

12. A _____ about interest rates, if confirmed by data, allows one to predict how interest rates will respond to changes in economic variables.

Multiple Choice

1. The financial system is
    a. unimportant for an efficient economic system.
    b. overdeveloped in the nations of the former Soviet Union.
    c. useful for transferring funds from lenders to borrowers.
    d. composed exclusively of commercial banks.

2. A well-functioning financial system is essential because
    a. those who have funds invested need to be able to borrow to finance productive investments.
    b. those who have excess funds are often not those who have productive investment opportunities.
    c. businesses need to borrow to pay workers.
    d. the financial system discourages wasteful consumer spending.

3. The international capital market
    a. involves the economies of Europe and the former Soviet Union but is not important in Japan and the United States.
    b. is not important for U.S. businesses because they depend on domestic markets for funding.
    c. is always the most expensive financing method to use for funding domestic projects.
    d. involves trading across national boundaries and has grown rapidly in recent years.

4. A higher interest rate might induce households to save _____ but businesses to borrow _____.
    a. more, less
    b. less, less
    c. less, more
    d. more, more

5. Which of the following is NOT an example of a financial intermediary?
    a. A commercial bank
    b. The bond market
    c. An insurance company
    d. A savings and loan association

6. Changes in the money supply are commonly associated with changes in which of the following?
    a. Interest rates
    b. Inflation rates
    c. Economic output
    d. All of the above

7. U.S. monetary policy is set by
    a. the U.S. Treasury.
    b. the Federal Reserve System.
    c. commercial banks.
    d. the U.S. Congress.

8. The activities of financial intermediaries can be explained by
    a. borrowers' and savers' desire for various financial services.
    b. the cost of providing financial services.
    c. political events that are generally not related to financial services.
    d. both (a.) and (b.) of the above.

9. Economic analysis involves
    a. developing theories to predict future events.
    b. calculating the relative return to actions.
    c. considering costs only.
    d. evaluating theories without regard for evidence.

10. Which of the following is NOT a criterion for determining the usefulness of a theory?
    a. Are the assumptions reasonable?
    b. Does it generate predictions that can be verified by actual data?
    c. Is the theory easy to understand?
    d. Are the predictions corroborated by real-world data?

11. You develop an economic theory that states that an increase in the growth rate of the money supply will result in higher inflation. What should be your next step?
    a. Begin making investment decisions based on the theory.
    b. Apply the three criteria for determining the usefulness of a theory.
    c. Modify the theory to make it easier to understand and apply.
    d. Modify the theory to account for all facets of the relationship between inflation and the money supply.

12. Fred says: "Economic theories are so simplistic that they are useless." How would an economist respond to this criticism?
    a. "Economic models are useful to the extent they explain current events and predict future events."
    b. "Economic models are not simplistic; they are very complicated."
    c. "The real world is simplistic so what do you expect?"
    d. "Hey, you think economics has problems? You should try mathematics."

13. Policymakers at the Federal Reserve are concerned about monetary theory because
    a. it helps them to understand the relationships between the money supply and other economic variables.
    b. it helps them to design fiscal polices that benefit the economy.
    c. it helps them to deflect criticism from academics about the policies they have adopted.
    d. both (a.) and (b.) of the above are true.

14. Understanding monetary theory can help you by allowing you to
    a. predict the actions of the Federal Reserve.
    b. understand how changes in monetary policy will affect interest rates and economic output.
    c. make financial decisions more efficiently.
    d. perform all of the above.

Essays

1. Give an example of when the financial system does not work efficiently. What negative consequences arise from this failure of the financial system?

2. Why is liquidity important to savers?

3. Why do you carry currency in your wallet even though it pays no interest?

4. Which debt instrument has greater information costs associated with it: U.S. Treasury securities or a loan to ABC Moving & Storage Company? Why?

5. Why bother with financial intermediaries when it is possible for borrowers and lenders to deal directly through financial markets?

6. Why does the financial system consist of such a wide array of different financial institutions?

7. What would likely happen if banks were prevented by the government from making credit card loans?

8. Under most circumstances, it is not possible to conduct controlled experiments to test economic theories. Does this fact help to explain why economists disagree about which economic theory is correct? Explain.

9. You develop a model that assumes that an increase in interest rates causes people to save more. The model predicts that lending will increase when interest rates increase because the supply of funds will increase when savings rise.
    a. Are the model's assumptions reasonable?
    b. If you wanted to test the model, what type of data might you want to collect?
    c. Suppose you found, after examining the data that an increase in interest rates *does not* lead to more lending. What conclusions might you draw?

10. Your boss has asked you to analyze the effect of changes in the money supply on the interest rates her business might have to pay.
    a. Develop a theory to explain the relationship between interest rates and the money supply.
    b. How might you test your theory?

ANSWERS TO SELF-TEST

True or False

1. True.
2. True.
3. False. The international capital market is an example of a financial market.
4. False. To be money, economic agents must generally accept an asset.
5. False. The Federal Reserve System is the central bank of the United States.
6. True.
7. False. Monetary policy deals with money supply not tax policy.
8. False. The economic approach is useful for *both* explaining current events and predicting future events.
9. False. There is considerable disagreement among economists about which economic theory best explains the economy.
10. True.

Fill in the Blank

1. financial instrument
2. risk sharing; liquidity; information
3. risk sharing
4. liquid
5. information services
6. international capital market
7. financial intermediaries
8. Money
9. Federal Reserve System; money supply; monetary policy
10. monetary policy
11. Economic analysis
12. theory

Multiple Choice

1.	c	2.	b
3.	d	4.	a
5.	b	6.	d
7.	b	8.	d
9.	a	10.	c
11.	b	12.	a
13.	a	14.	d

Essays

1. One example of a breakdown in the efficient operation of the financial system is the market for student loans. A consequence of this breakdown is underinvestment in education. (By the way, this is why the federal government provides student loan guarantees.)

2. Savers might incur unexpected expenses, which necessitates the conversion of an asset into cash.

3. Currency's liquidity compensates for the lack of interest payments.

4. U.S. Treasury securities are covered extensively by the media, so an investor can obtain information about them at low cost. ABC Moving & Storage Company would likely receive little media coverage, so getting information about it would be more difficult and costly.

5. Financial intermediaries can provide risk-sharing, liquidity, and/or information services at lower cost than can be achieved when individual savers and borrowers deal directly with each other.

6. Different types of financial markets and intermediaries have developed in response to the particular circumstances of their customers. For example, a well-known corporation such as General Motors can easily raise funds in the bond market. Your next-door neighbor, however, will have to rely on the local bank, where he or she can develop a personal relationship with a loan officer.

7. New restrictions on credit card lending by commercial banks would lead to financial innovation as competition caused the financial system to adapt to the changing financial environment.

8. Yes. Because economists typically depend on historical data to test theories, it is not possible to control confounding factors. This makes it difficult to determine which theory best explains the economy.

9. a. Because a higher interest rate means that savings will generate higher income for savers, it is reasonable that saving will increase if interest rates increase. Therefore, the model's assumptions seem reasonable.
    b. Data on lending volume could be obtained from flow-of-funds data that are collected by the Federal Reserve. Interest rate data could be gathered from *The Wall Street Journal*.
    c. The theory may be wrong, or changes in important variables other than interest rates may be confounding the results. One solution would be to include more variables, such as personal income.

10. a. There are a number of possible theories about the relationship between money supply and interest rates (several of which you will study later in the semester). One idea: an increase in money supply increases the supply of funds available for lending, causing interest rates to fall.

b. Of course, how you would test your theory depends on the theory you developed in your answer to (a.). For the idea that increased money supply increases the supply of loanable funds, you could look at the relationship between money supply and lending.

2: MONEY AND THE PAYMENTS SYSTEM

KEY CONCEPTS

This chapter discusses the role of **money** in the economy and how changes in technology, laws, and customs affect the payments system. Money refers to anything that is generally accepted as payment for goods and services or in the settlement of debts. That is, money is what economists call a **medium of exchange**. What serves as money depends on technology, law, and culture, and has varied through history. Money is used by all but the most primitive societies because money allows the economy to operate more efficiently by facilitating specialization. With **specialization**, each individual produces the goods or services for which he or she is relatively best suited. A society could use a method other than money to facilitate trade, but these alternatives involve **transactions costs (barter)** or ignore market forces **(government allocation)**.

The use of money avoids the transactions costs associated with barter while allowing trade to take place through markets. Money has four key features that make it the most efficient means of trade:

- **Medium of exchange**: Because money serves as a *medium of exchange*, money eliminates the need for a double coincidence of wants and hence reduces transactions costs arising from the search for trading partners.

- **Unit of account**: A *unit of account* is an asset, the value of which is used to keep track of other values. By using the medium of exchange as a unit of account, a single price can be quoted for each product in terms of the medium of exchange. This reduces information costs and facilitates trade.

- **Store of wealth**: By serving as a *store of wealth*, money reduces liquidity costs.

- **Standard of deferred payment**: Because individuals are willing to sell on credit today in exchange for money in the future, money can also serve as a *standard of deferred payment*. This facilitates trade over time.

The mechanism that an economy uses to settle transactions is called the **payments system**. The efficient operation of the payments system is important for the efficient operation of the financial system. The simplest payments systems involve the exclusive use of **definitive money**, but most payments systems are more complicated. Historically, traders used precious metals such as gold and silver as mediums of exchange. These physical goods were known as **commodity money**. In modern economies, paper money, issued by a **central bank** is used. Initially, paper money could be redeemed for commodity money. Currently, however, the payments system in the United States is a **fiat money** system. **Checks** have become an important part of a modern payments system because they are more convenient for large transactions and are less costly to transport than currency. However, transactions using checks require more steps to settle.

Electronic telecommunication breakthroughs have improved the efficiency of the payments system by reducing the time required to clear a transaction and by reducing paper flow.

Because money is an important determinant of economic activity, a measure of money is needed as a guide for policy. Which assets should be counted as money, however, is ambiguous. The definition that is used to measure money can be either narrow or broad, depending on how closely substitutable the assets included are for definitive money. A narrow measure of money would include only definitive money. A broader measure of money might also include checking or savings accounts. Because which assets should be included in money is ambiguous, no one measure of money is clearly superior. Recognizing this, the Fed has developed several different measures of money, called **monetary aggregates**.

- The narrowest Fed aggregate is the *M1* **aggregate**, which includes currency, traveler's checks, and checking account deposits.

- The *M2* **aggregate** is the next broader aggregate after *M1*. It includes all assets in *M1* as well as other short-term investment accounts.

- The *M3* **aggregate** is an even broader measure of money that includes the assets in *M2* and also some less liquid assets such as large time deposits.

- The broadest monetary aggregate defined by the Fed is the *L* **aggregate,** which is more a measure of total liquid assets than a measure of money. The *L* aggregate includes all the assets in *M3* as well as assets such as short-term U. S. Treasury securities and commercial paper.

Check List

When you finish this chapter, you should be able to:

✔ Define money.

✔ Explain the advantages of specialization and understand how specialization necessitates trade.

✔ Understand the disadvantages of using barter in trade.

✔ Understand the disadvantages of using government allocation.

✔ Explain how money promotes specialization by serving as a medium of exchange, unit of account, store of value, and standard of deferred payment.

✔ Describe the conditions under which an asset might serve as money.

✔ Explain the role of technology, law, and custom in the evolution of the payments system.

✔ Understand the distinction between narrow and broad definitions of money.

✔ Explain why the Fed measures money using several different definitions of money.

✔ Distinguish among *M1*, *M2*, *M3*, and *L*.

Self-Test

True or False

1. Money and wealth are synonymous because people who are wealthy also have lots of money.   F

2. Specialization necessitates the need for trade.   T

3. Barter involves the trading of one good directly for another.   T

4. A problem with government allocation is that it is insensitive to changes in market conditions.   T

5. Fiat money is intrinsically valuable apart from being money.   F

6. The U.S. Treasury is responsible for defining the assets included in each monetary aggregate (*M1*, *M2*, *M3*, and *L*).   F

7. Credit cards are included in the *M1* definition of money.   F

8. Vault cash held by banks is part of the money supply.   T

9. Currency is included in *M2*.   T

10. The *L* aggregate may be thought of as a measure of total liquid assets in the economy.   T

Fill in the Blank

1. The ease and speed with which an asset can be converted into money are referred to as _____.

2. Although money is a _____, income is a _____, which is measured over a period of time.

3. The three mechanisms that society has developed for the conduct of trade are _____, _____ _____ and _____.

4. Costs that arise as part of making a trade are _____ _____.

5. The _____ _____ is the mechanism by which society conducts transactions.

6. _____ _____ is money that does not have to be converted into a more basic type of money.

7. The purchasing power of money is reduced by _____.

8. During periods of _____, money's ability to serve as a store of wealth and as a standard of deferred payment is substantially reduced.

9. A government or quasi-government institution that is responsible for regulation of the money supply is the _____ _____.

10. A _____ definition of money would include only definitive money, whereas a _____ definition would also include assets that were substitutable for money.

Multiple Choice

1. Specialization improves economic efficiency by
   a. allowing for a double coincidence of wants.
   b. allowing the efficient production of individual goods and services despite the need for resources.
   c. allowing each individual to produce the goods and services for which he or she is relatively most skilled.
   d. eliminating transactions costs that would occur with barter.

2. For barter to take place, two traders would have to have
   a. a medium of exchange.
   b. a double coincidence of wants.
   c. several different goods in inventory.
   d. a common desire to trade the same good.

3. Of money's four functions, the one that defines money to be money is the
   a. medium of exchange function.
   b. unit of account function.
   c. store of wealth function.
   d. standard of deferred payment function.

4. An asset, the value of which is used to keep track of other values, is a
   a. medium of exchange.
   b. unit of account.
   c. store of wealth.
   d. standard of deferred payment.

5. People hold money during inflationary episodes, when other assets prove to be better stores of value. This is explained by the fact that money is
   a. liquid.
   b. unique.
   c. acceptable in exchange.
   d. durable.

6. The disadvantages of commodity money include
   a. lack of durability.
   b. lack of general acceptability.
   c. operation of mints by kings.
   d. difficulty of assessing purity.

7. Which of the following is an advantage of checks?
   a. The cost of processing checks can limit their liquidity.
   b. Information costs are associated with verifying that funds are sufficient cover the checks written.
   c. Checks may be written in any amount up to the total amount on deposit.
   d. Settling transactions with checks requires more steps than settling transactions with currency.

8. The payments system continues to evolve because
   a. laws have changed.
   b. of technological advances.
   c. of both a and b.
   d. of none of the above.

9. The *M1* aggregate includes those assets that are
   a. readily used as money but are not money.
   b. liquid, including short-term government securities.
   c. traditionally considered to be money.
   d. used as short-term investments such as time deposits.

10. The *L* aggregate includes those assets that are
    a. readily used as money but are not money.
    b. liquid, including short-term government securities.
    c. traditionally considered to be money.
    d. used as short-term investments such as corporate stock.

11. A disadvantage of government allocation as an option for the conduct of trade and exchange is that it
    a.   relies on an impersonal, faceless bureaucracy.
    b.   promotes specialization by individuals.
    c.   requires a double coincidence of wants.
    d.   ignores market forces in allocating goods.

12. The modern U.S. payments system is a fiat money system. What does that mean?
    a.   Only fiat money is used in trade and exchange.
    b.   Commodity money is convertible to fiat money.
    c.   Fiat money can be easily converted into gold.
    d.   Fiat money issued by the Fed is definitive money.

13. Which monetary aggregate do most economists and policymakers currently consider to be the best measure of the medium of exchange?
    a.   *M1*
    b.   *M2*
    c.   *M3*
    d.   *L*

14. Do different monetary aggregates move together?
    a.   Yes, they move broadly together, but there are significant differences at certain times.
    b.   Yes, they move together, making the choice of which aggregate to use unimportant to policymakers.
    c.   At times yes, at times no.
    d.   No, they do not move together.

15. The definitions of the monetary aggregates currently published by the Federal Reserve System
    a.   are the same ones that were used when the Fed was first created.
    b.   are well accepted by economists as explaining economic phenomena.
    c.   can be changed only by an act of Congress.
    d.   are changed periodically as financial innovation occurs.

Essays

1. By using money, a society reduces transactions costs and encourages specialization. Explain.

2. Why is money the most efficient method of exchange and trade?

3. How is it possible that an intrinsically worthless asset such as a dollar bill can serve as money?

4. The value of a dollar is how much it can buy. Explain.

5. How has technology influenced the payments system?

6. Why do we care what the definition of money is?

7. Why does the Fed find it necessary to define four different monetary aggregates?

8. If monetary aggregates move together, the aggregate that is used to measure inflation would not make any difference. Explain.

9. Suppose that you were the Fed official responsible for deciding into which monetary aggregate assets are to be classified. Use the information given below to decide into which monetary aggregate (*M1, M2, M3,* or *L*) each of the following (hypothetical) assets should be classified. Justify your choice.
    a. *K-posits*: These are issued by a large retail chain, and checks can be issued against them.
    b. *Gerniks*: Surveys reveal that consumers consider gerniks to be money. Although they are very liquid, you cannot write checks against them.
    c. *T-paper:* A new short-term security issued by the U.S. Treasury, T-paper is very liquid because it can be traded in the government securities market.
    d. *Coupon bills*: Issued by a well-known national stockbrokerage firm, these bills can be used to purchase items at grocery stores around the country. Surveys indicate that consumers think of them as being similar to traveler's checks, but many businesses are reluctant to accept them.

ANSWERS TO SELF-TEST

True or False

1. False. Although money is an asset, and therefore part of wealth, wealth does not consist just of money. Wealth is the total value of *all* assets.
2. True.
3. True.
4. True.
5. False. Fiat money is of value only because it is usable as the medium of exchange. It has no intrinsic value.
6. False. Credit cards are a means of borrowing. When you borrow you must repay the loan.
7. False. Credit card borrowing is debt.
8. False. Only currency in the hands of the public is considered part of the money supply.
9. True.
10. True.

Fill in the Blank

1. liquidity
2. stock; flow
3. barter; government allocation; money
4. transactions costs
5. payments system
6. Definitive money
7. inflation
8. hyperinflation
9. central bank
10. narrow; broad

Multiple Choice

1.	c	2.	b
3.	a	4.	b
5.	a	6.	d
7.	c	8.	c
9.	c	10.	b
11.	d	12.	d
13.	a	14.	a
15.	d		

Essays

1. If transactions costs are too high, trade will not be profitable and specialization will not be possible. By serving as a medium of exchange, money reduces search costs. By serving as a unit of account, money reduces information costs because all prices can be quoted in units of money. By serving as a store of wealth, money reduces liquidity costs. Finally, by serving as a standard of deferred payment, money facilitates credit transactions.

2. With barter, search costs are high because there must be a double coincidence of wants for a trade to take place. There is also no unit of account. Government allocation ignores market forces, thus reducing incentives for producers, and may leave consumers unhappy with the products allocated to them. The use of money avoids the costs of barter while retaining the benefits of the market.

3. Self-fulfilling expectations determine which asset will serve as money. A dollar bill is valued as money only if people believe that others will accept it as money.

4. Fiat money has no intrinsic value. People value the items that they can purchase with money; therefore it is what money can purchase that gives money value.

5. Technology, along with the legal system, is the primary determinant of the payments system. For example, the use of gold as commodity money requires the ability to smelt gold, the use of coins, the ability to mint, and so on. Technology created electronic transfer systems such as ATMs and debit cards.

6. Changes in money supply are associated with changes in other economic variables, such as interest rates, inflation, and economic activity. If monetary policy is to be used to influence these other variables, a valid definition of money must be developed.

7. Which assets are money and which assets are not money is ambiguous. Moreover, which monetary aggregate best measures money depends on the purpose for which the measure is being used.

8. If monetary aggregates moved together, it would not matter which definition of monetary policy was the focus of monetary policy. This is because a policy that is aimed at changing one aggregate would also affect all the other aggregates.

9. a. Because checks can be written against K-posits, they are best classified as part of *M1*.
   b. The *M2* aggregate includes those assets that are substitutable for money but are not as liquid as more traditional measures of money.
   c. Short-term government securities are included in *L*.

d.   More information is needed before a definitive answer can be given. Because
     consumers consider them to be similar to traveler's checks, coupon bills could
     be included in *M1*.   But if the lack of acceptance by businesses severely
     restricts coupon bills' liquidity, perhaps they should not be included in any
     aggregate. Balancing these two arguments might mean classifying coupon bills
     into *M2*, *M3*, or perhaps *L*. (By the way, coupon bills illustrate the ambiguities
     that face Fed officials in classifying assets.)

3: OVERVIEW OF THE FINANCIAL SYSTEM

KEY CONCEPTS

In Chapter 2, the role of money and the evolution of the payments system were discussed. This chapter provides an overview of the entire financial system. The **financial system** plays a crucial role in the economy by channeling funds to their most productive uses. Without a well functioning financial system, profitable investments would go unfunded. Moreover, the financial system promotes economic welfare by providing three key services to savers and borrowers:

- The financial system provides **risk sharing** by making it easier for savers to hold a diversified **portfolio** of assets. **Diversification** involves allocating wealth among different types of assets and reduces the overall risk faced by savers, as long as asset returns do not move perfectly together.

- Savers value **liquidity** because they may need to convert assets into cash. Financial markets and intermediaries provide trading systems for making assets more liquid.

- The financial system both gathers and communicates **information**.

There are two additional concepts that you need to master to fully understand the information services that the financial system provides.

- **Asymmetric information**: An asymmetric information problem exists when one party to a transaction is in a position to use information that is known to them, but not others, to their advantage. The minimization of the asymmetric information problem explains much of the structure of the financial system, and we will be returning to this topic several times during the course.

- **Informational role of prices**: Financial markets communicate information by incorporating information into the prices of financial assets. The easiest way to understand this is through an example. Suppose that new information becomes public about a government contract awarded to ABC Company. Market participants will evaluate the effect of the contract on ABC's future returns. If the stock is undervalued, the price will be bid up. Of course, the stock might have been overvalued (perhaps the contract was disappointingly small), in which case the price will be bid down. In either case, information about the new contract is incorporated into the stock's price.

By providing risk-sharing, liquidity, and information services, the financial system makes savers more willing to hold financial assets. This willingness in turn increases borrowers' ability to raise funds at low cost.

Financial Markets

Financial markets play a crucial role in the financial system by directly matching savers and borrowers. Markets can be classified in several non-mutually exclusive ways. One way to classify them is as primary or secondary markets. **Primary markets** are markets in which newly issued claims are sold to initial buyers by the borrower. It is in these markets that funds are raised. **Secondary markets** are where existing financial claims are traded. Borrowers do not raise any new funds in secondary markets, but secondary markets are very important for a smoothly functioning financial system.

- Secondary markets promote risk sharing by making it easier to hold a diversified portfolio.

- By providing a mechanism for trading existing financial claims, secondary markets promote liquidity.

- Secondary markets convey information by determining the price of financial instruments.

Secondary markets can be classified according to how assets are traded. With **auction markets**, competitive bidding by a large number of traders sets prices. The most common type of auction market is an **exchange**, which is a specific central location at which traders agree to meet. Well-known auction markets are the New York Stock Exchange, the American Stock Exchange, and the Tokyo Stock Exchange. **Over-the-counter (OTC) markets** have no centralized place for auction trading. Instead, OTC dealers buy and sell via computerized trading.

Another way to classify markets is by the time to maturity, or term of the securities traded. Short-term instruments, with a maturity of less than one year, are traded in **money markets**. Debt instruments with a maturity of more than one year are traded in **capital markets**. Equities, which are perpetual, with no fixed maturity, also are traded in capital markets. A final way in which financial markets can be classified is by whether the claims traded are an actual asset or are derivative. **Cash markets** are markets in which actual claims are bought and sold with immediate settlement; the buyer pays money to the seller in exchange for the asset. In **derivative markets**, trades are executed immediately, but settlement is made at a later date.

Financial intermediaries are another major component of the financial system. Intermediation adds an extra layer of complexity and cost to financial trades, so why do savers not just deal directly with one another through financial markets, bypassing the intermediary? The reason is that intermediaries are able to provide financial services at lower cost than can be achieved through financial markets.

- Banks and other intermediaries control large quantities of funds and have access to a variety of investments. Thus they can provide risk-sharing services at a lower cost by holding a diversified portfolio.

- Claims against intermediaries, especially bank deposits, are liquid.

- Because they act on behalf of many individual lenders, intermediaries can take advantage of economies of scale in collecting information about borrowers.

As in other industries, financial institutions compete with one another for market share through the provision of risk sharing, liquidity, and information services. When changes occur in either the cost of providing financial services or the demand for financial services, competitive forces cause financial intermediaries and institutions to adapt by altering their operations. This process of adaptation in response to market conditions is called **financial innovation**. Financial innovation has resulted in increased **financial integration** across regions and markets. A major development over the past two decades has been the increasing international integration of the financial system, a process referred to as **globalization**. **Government regulation** is another important factor in determining the structure of the financial system. Three categories of reasons account for most regulations:

- **Provision of information**: Unfortunately, firms may not be willing to truthfully reveal information that is needed to evaluate the financial securities they issue. To overcome this problem, the government requires issuers of financial instruments to disclose relevant information.

- **Maintenance of financial stability**: Most regulation of the financial system is concerned with the stability of the financial system. Specifically, because most financial assets are held by intermediaries, policymakers are particularly concerned about the financial soundness of intermediaries.

- **Advancement of other policy objectives**: Controlling money supply and encouraging home ownership are among the non-financial reasons that the government regulates financial markets.

Check List

When you finish this chapter, you should be able to:

✓ Explain the role of the financial system in transferring funds from savers to borrowers.

✓ Explain how a smoothly functioning financial system improves economic efficiency.

✓ Describe the three financial services and give examples of each.

✓ Explain how, by providing financial services at low cost, the financial system both encourages saving and promotes investment.

✔ Understand the role of debt and equity.

✔ Understand the role of asymmetric information and give three examples of how it influences the structure of the financial system.

✔ Understand how new information is reflected in financial asset prices and give an example.

✔ Categorize financial markets among primary and secondary markets, exchange and OTC markets, money and capital markets, and cash and derivative markets.

✔ Understand the crucial role that secondary markets play in providing the three financial services.

✔ Explain how using intermediaries can reduce the cost of providing financial services and give an example using each financial service.

✔ Understand the role of competition in shaping the financial system and give three examples of financial innovation.

✔ Understand the importance of financial integration and globalization.

✔ Explain the motivation for government regulation of the financial system.

✔ Describe the three sets of reasons for government regulation of the financial system.

Self-Test

True or False

1.   Money market mutual funds do not compete with banks for market share.   F T

2.   Treasury securities are traded in organized exchanges.   F

3.   The most common type of financial claim is a debt instrument.   T

4.   The New York Stock Exchange is an example of a secondary market.   It also is an example of an auction market and of a capital market.   T

5.   Financial markets in the United States are more fragmented today than they were 100 years ago.   F

6.   Two factors that are important in determining the efficiency of the financial system are the ability to provide liquidity and the degree of integration.   T

7. The Securities and Exchange Commission (SEC) was established by Congress in 1933 to regulate financial markets. T

8. The more liquid an asset, the higher its interest rate. F

9. The interest paid on a home mortgage loan and the interest paid on a car loan are both tax deductible. T

Fill in the Blank

1. The financial system provides a mechanism to transfer funds from individuals and groups who have _____ funds to individuals and groups who have _____ for those funds.

2. Borrowers are the _____ of funds, whereas savers are the _____ of funds.

3. The three key financial services are _____ _____, _____, and _____ services.

4. Financial instruments are _____ _____ for savers but _____ _____ for borrowers.

5. A bank lends you $200,000 to build an office building. The loan is an _____ to the bank and the building is an _____ to you.

6. The length of time before a debt instrument expires is called its _____ or _____.

7. Firms raise funds by selling new issues in _____ markets. Existing financial instruments are traded in _____ markets.

8. Debt instruments that have a maturity of more than one year are traded in the _____ market.

9. Financial futures and _____ are traded in _____ markets.

10. The splitting of wealth into many assets is known as _____.

11. _____ _____ refers to the degree to which regional financial markets are tied together.

12. _____ refers to the degree to which international capital markets are integrated.

13. The _____ is the agency that is primarily responsible for regulating financial markets in the United States.

14. A collection of assets is called a _____.

15. A retired individual wants a steady monthly income and asks you as his financial advisor whether he should invest in debt or equity. You should tell him to invest in _____.

16. Bonds that are denominated in a currency other than that of the country where they are sold are called _____.

Multiple Choice

1. Diversification reduces risk by
   a. spreading wealth over various assets, reducing the average risk.
   b. concentrating wealth in a few safe assets, reducing the average risk.
   c. spreading wealth over a number of assets, raising the average risk.
   d. concentrating wealth in a few assets that have a certain return, eliminating risk.

2. The type of market that is characterized by no centralized place for auction trading is a(n)
   a. secondary market.
   b. primary market.
   c. stock market.
   d. over-the-counter market.

3. The primary source of financial capital in the U.S. economy is
   a. capital markets.
   b. money markets.
   c. intermediaries.
   d. over-the-counter markets.

4. Financial futures
   a. require cash settlement today.
   b. require settlement at a specified future date for a price determined today.
   c. confer on the buyer the right to buy or sell within a specified time at a specified price.
   d. confer on the buyer the right to a cash settlement today at a specified price.

5. Financial options
   a. require cash settlement today.
   b. require settlement at a specified future date for a price determined today.
   c. confer on the buyer the right to buy or sell within a specified time at a specified price.
   d. confer on the buyer the right to a cash settlement today at a specified price.

6. Smoothly functioning secondary markets are important for a well functioning financial system because
   a. they provide risk sharing, liquidity, and information services.
   b. you can get rich trading in secondary markets, especially stock markets.
   c. wealthy businesspeople can use them to augment their assets.
   d. secondary markets are where businesses raise funds.

7. In less-developed countries, businesses depend more on intermediation than in developed countries. Why?
   a. Developed countries subsidize financial markets, artificially diverting business from banks.
   b. International lending organizations subsidize bank lending in less-developed countries.
   c. Less-developed countries depend more on foreign aid, which is channeled through banks.
   d. Less-developed financial markets are more fragmented, making information gathering more difficult.

8. During the 1980s, U.S. saving was inadequate to finance U.S. investment, yet the economy continued to grow. How?
   a. Increasing globalization of financial markets allowed foreign funds to fill the gap.
   b. Funds that were accumulated in the past were used.
   c. Ronald Reagan negotiated a secret deal with the Japanese to finance U.S. investment.
   d. The fall of the Berlin Wall allowed funds to flow into Western countries such as the United States.

9. Key services provided by the financial system to savers and borrowers include all of the following except
   a. collateral.
   b. risk sharing.
   c. liquidity.
   d. information.

10. Intermediate-term debt instruments have a maturity between one year and
    a.   5 years.
    b.   10 years.
    c.   15 years.
    d.   30 years.

11. You purchase a 10-year U.S. savings bond at your local bank. This would be an
    example of a _____ market instrument purchased in the _____
    market.
    a.   capital; primary
    b.   money; primary
    c.   capital; secondary
    d.   money; secondary

12. Financial futures would be most accurately classified as a
    a.   derivative claim
    b.   cash claim.
    c.   money market claim.
    d.   capital market claim.

13. Businesses raise external funds both from financial intermediaries and directly from
    financial markets. If we compare the amount raised from each source, the amount
    raised from financial intermediaries is
    a.   half as great.
    b.   about equal.
    c.   twice as great.
    d.   five times as great.

14. Two leading financiers who were prosecuted by the SEC in the 1980s were
    a.   James Baker and Steve Mills.
    b.   Claus Hammond and Buddy Rodgers.
    c.   Steve Paterson and Kurt Olson.
    d.   Ivan Boesky and Michael Milken.

15. Overnight loans between banks are called
    a.   bankers' acceptances.
    b.   discounts.
    c.   commercial paper.
    d.   federal funds.

Essays

1. The financial system provides three key services to savers and borrowers. Discuss
   each of these services briefly.

2. What does the statement "financial market prices reflect available information about the financial instruments" mean? Explain the process that is involved.

3. What has been the effect of increased financial integration and globalization on the cost of funds to borrowers? What implication does this effect have for economic growth and development?

4. What has been the effect of increased financial integration and globalization on the return to savers?

5. The interest rate that a business in Dover, New Hampshire is charged depends not just on local financial conditions or even on U.S. financial conditions, but also on financial conditions around the world. Explain.

6. What is the driving force behind financial innovation?

7. What restrictions did the government place on savings and loan associations lending prior to 1980? Many economists argue that these restrictions were counterproductive. Why?

8. Congress must now consider international competitiveness when enacting regulatory legislation. Why?

9. What is the effect on an asset's price if its return becomes more volatile relative to the market?

10. Suppose that Congress imposes a fixed tax on each purchase and sale of registered securities. That is, no matter how much is sold, the same tax is paid on every transaction, large and small. What implication would this action have for the ability of the financial system to provide liquidity?

11. Suppose that an investigation reveals that HiHopeCo's management has been engaging in insider trading. What is likely to happen to the price of the company's stock?

12. Classify each of the following transactions as involving the use of intermediaries or markets, and if a market is involved, classify it as a primary or secondary market and as a money or capital market.
    a. Prudential Insurance Company lends funds to IBM for construction of a new Factory.
    b. Thirty-year IBM bonds are traded.
    c. The U.S. Treasury conducts its quarterly T-bill auction.
    d. A local bank sells mortgages to a government-sponsored intermediary.
    e. Ricky Portillo sells shares in Apple Computer using an OTC market.

13. Recently, the World Bank and other international lenders have pushed developing countries to adopt new regulations requiring the disclosure of financial information by publicly traded companies. How might these policies aid economic development?

ANSWERS TO SELF-TEST

True or False

1. False. Money market mutual funds, which offer checkable deposits, compete directly with banks.
2. False. U.S. Treasury securities are traded over the counter.
3. True.
4. True.
5. False. Technology has allowed U.S. financial markets to become highly integrated.
6. True.
7. True.
8. False. Liquidity is desirable, so we would expect the interest rate to be lower.
9. False. The interest on a car loan is no longer tax deductible.

Fill in the Blank

1. excess; uses
2. demanders; suppliers
3. risk sharing; liquidity; information
4. financial assets; financial liabilities
5. asset; asset
6. maturity; term
7. primary; secondary
8. capital
9. options; derivative
10. diversification
11. Financial integration
12. Globalization
13. SEC
14. portfolio
15. debt
16. Eurobonds

Multiple Choice

1.	a	2.	d
3.	c	4.	b
5.	c	6.	a
7.	d	8.	a
9.	a	10.	b
11.	a	12.	a
13.	c	14.	d
15.	d		

Essays

1. *Risk sharing*: The financial system provides sharing of risk by allowing diversification.

   Liquidity: Financial markets and institutions provide a trading system for making assets more liquid.

   Information: Financial markets convey information through prices. Intermediaries collect information for many small savers.

2. The statement means that information about the future return on the financial instruments is reflected in the price. The process by which this is brought about works as follows: If new, favorable information about the financial instrument is learned by market participants, the price will be bid up. If unfavorable information is learned, the price is bid down.

3. The easy flow of capital among regions and across national boundaries helps countries to finance productive opportunities, even if the region or country's current resources are inadequate. Borrowers will be able to find funds to finance worthwhile projects at lower cost. Projects that would have gone unfunded before are funded, promoting economic growth and development.

4. Savers have earned higher returns because funds can flow to the project that promises the highest return.

5. Increased integration of financial markets and globalization mean that world financial conditions determine the availability of funds in local markets.

6. Competition for market share is the driving force behind financial innovation.

7. Savings and loan associations were restricted primarily to making home mortgage loans. Economists argued that these restrictions limited the ability of savings and loan associations to diversify, exposing them to increased risk.

8. Because of increased international financial integration, U.S. financial markets and institutions must compete more directly with foreign financial markets and institutions. If U.S. regulation makes the U.S. financial system less competitive, U.S. financial markets and institutions will lose business to foreign markets.

9. Because people prefer less risk to more risk, the price of the stock should fall.

10. The tax would limit the ability of the financial system to provide liquidity services, especially to small savers. The result would be a reduction in efficiency.

11. Insider trading reduces the ability of the financial system to provide information services with regard to HiHopeCo. The price of the stock will decline.

12.
   a. intermediary
   b. market; secondary; capital
   c. market; primary; money
   d. intermediary
   e. market; secondary; capital

13. By reducing the cost of providing information services, the cost of raising funds is reduced. Investors will be able to borrow at a lower cost, thereby encouraging economic development.

4: INTEREST RATES AND RATES OF RETURN

KEY CONCEPTS

We have completed the introductory part of the book and now move on to a more detailed examination of the financial system. This chapter begins that detailed discussion. We turn to the important issue of how to compare interest rates and rates of return across different financial instruments. This is an important topic because comparing rates on different **debt instruments** is a prerequisite in deciding among competing investment opportunities. There are four basic types of credit market instruments:

- **Simple loan**: The borrower receives from the lender an amount, called principal, and agrees to repay the principal plus an additional amount, called interest, at a given maturity date.

- **Discount bonds**: The borrower repays a specific face value at maturity while receiving a smaller amount initially.

- **Coupon bonds**: These require multiple payments of interest and a payment of a face value at maturity.

- **Fixed payment loan**: The borrower makes a regular periodic payment to the lender. Each payment includes interest and principal and is calibrated so that the entire loan is repaid at maturity.

In making financial decisions, both lenders and borrowers must evaluate different debt instruments. Yet directly comparing interest and principal payments on different credit market instruments is inappropriate because the timing of payments differ, and a dollar received earlier is worth more than a dollar received later (because the dollar received earlier can be invested to earn interest). To compare credit instruments, the **present value** of future payments must be calculated. Specifically, if the nominal interest rate is i, the present value of a dollar received n periods in the future is

$$\text{Present Value of \$1} = \frac{\$1}{(1+i)^n}$$

Another important concept is the **yield to maturity**, which is used to calculate interest rates of different credit instruments. The yield to maturity is the interest rate that equates the present value of a debt instrument with its current market value. Yield to maturity is important because using this concept allows direct comparison of interest rates across different credit market instruments. The instrument with the highest yield to maturity, all else being constant, is the best investment. There is an important relationship between a bond's price and the yield to maturity and between rate of return and yield to maturity.

- The yield to maturity and bond prices are inversely related. This is because discounting future payments at a higher rate reduces the present value of a bond's future payments and therefore the value or price of the bond today. Therefore, as yield to maturity rises, the bond's price must fall. Conversely, as the yield to maturity falls, the bond's price must rise. Understanding this relationship between interest rates and bond prices is crucial in making financial decisions.

- The yield to maturity and the rate of return are the same for a bond that is held to maturity. The rate of return, however, can be very different from the yield to maturity for bonds that are not held to maturity. The reason is that expected capital gains and losses during the holding period may differ depending on the length of the holding period. Indeed, if capital losses are large, the total rate of return can be negative, despite the yield to maturity being positive.

Borrowers and lenders, recognizing that inflation reduces purchasing power, would like to base their decisions on the **real interest rate**, which is adjusted for inflation, not on the **nominal interest rate**. Unfortunately, because the inflation rate is not known when a contract is entered, the real interest rate cannot be known. Instead, in making financial decisions, savers and borrowers use the **expected real interest rate**, which is the nominal interest rate less **expected inflation**. Generally, changes in expected inflation do not affect the real interest rate. The reason is that changes in expected inflation cause lenders to demand higher nominal rates to maintain their purchasing power. Borrowers are willing to pay the higher interest rate because, in terms of purchasing power, their payout is unchanged. The **Fisher hypothesis**, which states that nominal interest rates will increase point-for-point for each increase in the expected inflation rate, summarizes these ideas.

Check List

When you finish this chapter, you should be able to:

✔ Describe the four basic credit instruments.

✔ Understand the concepts of principal and interest.

✔ Calculate the simple interest rate on a simple interest loan.

✔ Calculate the yield to maturity for each of the four basic credit instruments.

✔ Understand the relationship between a bond's price and the yield to maturity and discuss its significance.

✔ Understand the relationship between the rate of return and the yield to maturity and discuss its significance.

✔ Understand the relationship between the nominal interest rate and the real interest rate.

✔ Discuss the significance of the Fisher hypothesis and describe the empirical evidence.

Self-Test

True or False

1. Credit market instruments and debt instruments are two terms for the same concept.

2. Present value is a method that allows comparison of credit market instruments with different streams of future earnings.

3. A discount bond gives a lump sum payment at maturity.

4. Bond prices and the yield to maturity are inversely related.

5. Long-term bond prices are less sensitive to changes in the yield to maturity.

6. The yield to maturity is a method for calculating the total rate of return on an asset.

7. According to the Fisher hypothesis, a rise in the expected inflation rate, *ceteris paribus*, should result in a point-for-point rise in the nominal interest rate.

8. A positive relationship normally exists between the inflation rate and the nominal interest rate. Therefore declining prices (deflation) should cause the nominal interest rate to be negative.

9. If the nominal interest rate is greater than 0%, the present value of receiving X will always be greater the closer the payment is to the present.

10. The greater the discount on a bond, the greater is the interest rate.

11. A coupon bond paying $100 a year forever (i.e., an infinite maturity), would have infinite value regardless of the interest rate, i.

12. If inflation rates in the future are expected to increase, this should cause the spread between short- and long-term bonds to widen.

Fill in the Blank

1. _____ _____ _____ require the borrower to make a periodic payment with no lump sum payment due at maturity.

2. With a _____ _____, borrowers receive a sum that is less than the face value.

3. With a _____ _____ the borrower receives an amount from the lender called the principal and agrees to repay the principal plus interest on a given maturity date.

4. _____ _____ require multiple payments of interest on a regular basis and a payment of a face value at maturity.

5. The process of earning interest on interest that has already been earned (as well as principal) is known as _____.

6. _____ _____ _____ is the interest rate that equates the current value of the obligation with the present value of its payments.

7. If you buy a stock for $1000 and sell it two years later for $1200, $200 is the

   _____ _____.

8. According to the Fisher hypothesis, for the actual real rate of interest to exceed the nominal rate, the _____ _____ would have to be negative.

Multiple Choice

1. You buy a one-year discount bond with a face value of $3000 issued by a local travel agency that is trying to raise money for expansion. If the yield to maturity is 8%, how much would you have to pay for this bond?
   a. $2777.78
   b. $3260.85
   c. $2760.00
   d. $3000.00

2. You buy a four-year $5000 certificate of deposit from a bank. The interest rate promised on the deposit is 6% compounded annually. At the end of four years, you should receive from the bank
   a. $5300.00.
   b. $6200.00.
   c. $6312.38.
   d. $3960.47.

3. A two-year discount bond with a face value of $20,000 that sells for $17,000 today has a yield to maturity of
    a. 17.65%.
    b. 10%.
    c. 8.47%.
    d. 9.48%.

4. If C is the coupon payment, F is the face value of the bond, and P is its current price, the coupon rate is
    a. P/F.
    b. C/F.
    c. F/C.
    d. F/P.

5. If interest rates fall, the current price of a coupon bond should
    a. fall.
    b. rise.
    c. remain constant.
    d. move in an unpredictable manner.

6. If the expected inflation rate is 4% and the expected real return on your investment is 5%, the nominal interest on that investment is
    a. 1%.
    b. 9%.
    c. −1%.
    d. 20%.

7. Suppose that you pay $2000 for a bond that has a coupon payment of $100. After one year, you sell it for $2150. What is your total rate of return on this bond?
    a. 5%
    b. 4½%
    c. 12½%
    d. 7½%

8. The total rate of return consists of
    a. the current yield and the rate of capital gain earned from holding the asset to maturity.
    b. the current yield and the yield to maturity earned during the holding period.
    c. the rate of capital gain only.
    d. the current yield and the rate of capital gain earned during the holding period.

9. You read that there has been a rally in the bond market. From this information, you might surmise that
   a. interest rates have fallen.
   b. corporate profits are higher.
   c. government budget deficits have increased.
   d. sales forecasts have been revised upward.

10. A rise in the nominal interest rate could have been caused by
   a. a rise in the expected interest rate or the capital gain rate.
   b. a fall in the expected inflation rate or the capital gain rate.
   c. a fall in the expected interest rate or the real interest rate.
   d. a rise in the expected inflation rate or the real interest rate.

11. If the interest rate remains a constant 6%, approximately how many years will it take until your initial investment doubles in value? (Assume compounding.)
   a. 5 years
   b. 12 years
   c. 17 years
   d. impossible to determine

12. A coupon bond with infinite maturity promises to pay $600 a year forever with the first payment in two years from now. What is the interest rate if the bond has a present value of $7442?
   a. 6%
   b. 7½%
   c. 9%
   d. 12%

13. Suppose that your friends, Alex and Evan, wish to borrow $2,000 from you to finance the purchase of a used car. You propose a two-year 8% installment loan with the first payment due one year from now and the second payment due two years from today. What are the two equal payments that Alex and Evan will make to you if they accept the loan?
   a. $1051.25
   b. $1101.37
   c. $1121.54
   d. $1505.76

14. A treasury security that has a maturity of 7 years is called a
   a. bond.
   b. bill.
   c. coupon.
   d. note.

Essays

1. Bond prices and market interest rates are inversely related. Why?

2. Why are long-term bond prices more sensitive to changes in interest rates?

3. Congratulations! You are the winning entry in the OSC Sweepstakes. As the lucky winner you receive the opportunity to receive one of the following three prize packages:

   (i) a $25,000 lump sum payment today;
   (ii) a $4,000 payment today and a $22,500 payment one year from now;
   (iii) a $9,000 payment at the end of this year and a $20,000 payment at the end of the next year.

   You may assume that all payments are quoted in after-tax dollars.

   a. Your financial advisor tells you to take the lump sum payment. If the interest rate is 7% and inflation is expected to be zero over the next two years, which of the above three options would you choose? Do you agree with your financial advisor? Explain.
   b. If the interest rate is actually 10%, which option would you choose? Would your choice be different than the choice you made in part (a.)? Explain in economic terms.

4. You make a fixed payment loan to your best friend. The fixed payment is $100 a year for three years with the first payment occurring one year from now.
   a. What is the present value of the loan if the market interest rate is 5%?
   b. Another friend offers to buy the loan from you for $250. Even though this is less than the present value of the loan, why might you still sell?

5. Your grandmother phones to tell you of the nice safe, steady, sensible long-term bond issued by a well-known corporation that her stockbroker has recommended. She brags about how the bond guarantees a steady coupon payment for the next 20 years. What should be your reaction?

6. Why is the yield to maturity the same as the total rate of return if the holding period is the same as the time to maturity?

7. What is the difference between the nominal interest rate and the real interest rate? Which interest rate is reported in *The Wall Street Journal*?

8. The Fisher hypothesis was first proposed almost a century ago.
   a. What is the Fisher hypothesis?
   b. Is it supported by empirical evidence?

9. Suppose that the market interest rate is 5%. Calculate the present value of
   a. a coupon bond with an annual coupon payment of $135 and a face value of $1500 that matures in five years.
   b. a discount bond with a face value of $5000 that matures in one year.
   c. a fixed payment loan with annual payments of $163 that matures in three years.
   d. a coupon bond with a coupon rate of 10% and a face value of $1000 that matures in five years.

10. How much will financial market participants be willing to pay for the discount bond described in essay 9(b.)? Why?

11. In each case, use the information provided to calculate the yield to maturity.
    a. A one-year simple loan with principal of $1243 and an interest payment of $93.22
    b. A coupon bond with an annual coupon payment of $100 and a face value of $1500 that matures in one year with a current price of $1350
    c. A discount bond that matures in one year, has a face value of $10,000, and is currently selling for $9543
    d. A discount bond that matures in four years, has a face value of $5000, and has a current price of $3500

12. Calculate the total rate of return for the following coupon bonds:
    a. Purchase price of $2130, coupon payment of $125, sold for $2005 after one year
    b. Purchase price of $2130, coupon payment of $125, sold for $2244 after one year
    c. Purchase price of $1649, coupon payment of $125, sold for $1649 after one year
    d. Purchase price of $2130, coupon payment of $125, sold for $2100 after one year

ANSWERS TO SELF-TEST

True or False

1. True.
2. True.
3. True.
4. True.
5. False. Long-term bonds are more sensitive to changes in interest rates because they are discounted over a longer period of time.
6. False. The yield to maturity and the rate of return are generally not the same because typically there is either a capital gain or loss.
7. True.
8. False. The interest rate should never go below zero. You could hold onto your money and get a zero percent interest rate.
9. True.
10. True.
11. False. The value of the bond would be $100/i$.
12. True.

Fill in the Blank

1. Fixed payment loans
2. discount bond
3. simple loan
4. Coupon bonds
5. compounding
6. Yield to maturity
7. capital gain
8. inflation rate

Multiple Choice

1.	a	2.	c
3.	c	4.	b
5.	b	6.	b
7.	c	8.	d
9.	a	10.	d
11.	b	12.	b
13.	c	14.	d

Essays

1. A rise in the market interest rate causes the yield on credit market instruments to become unattractive. If potential buyers are to be found, the price of the instrument will have to be lowered. Eventually, the price will fall far enough that the yield on the instrument is the same as the market interest rate. Thus the price is inversely related to the market interest rate.

2. Since long-term bonds are outstanding for a longer period, they are discounted by a larger factor. This makes them more sensitive to changes in interest rates.

3. a. When the interest rate is 7%, the present value of $4,000 today and $22,500 one year from now is $4,000 + 21,028.04 = $25,028.04. The present value of $9,000 one year from now plus $20,000 two years from now is $8411.21 + $17,468.77 = $25,879.98. You would prefer option (iii) to either options (i) or (ii). As long as you are assured that you will receive these payments, option (iii) has the highest present value. Thus, your calculations are at odds with the advice of your financial advisor.
    b. When the interest rate is 10%, the present value of options (ii) and (iii) are $24,545.55 and $24,710.74, respectively. Now the best choice in terms of present value is option (i). Remember, the higher the interest rate, the less income received in the future is worth today.

4. a. $272.32
    b. Savers value risk sharing, liquidity, and information services. Holding a single loan directly may not provide these services. Therefore, you may be willing to sell the loan for only $250 despite its higher present value.

5. Because your grandmother seems to value low risk, you should suggest that she not invest in long-term bonds, which are more sensitive to interest rate changes. You might also suggest that she find a new stockbroker!

6. The two components of the total rate of return are the current yield and the rate of capital gain during the holding period. The two components of the yield to maturity are the current yield and the capital gain rate from holding the bond to maturity. If the holding period is the time to maturity, the two returns are identical.

7. The real interest rate is adjusted for inflation. The real rate is the nominal rate minus the inflation rate. The nominal interest rate is the rate reported in newspapers.

8. a. The nominal interest rate rises or falls point-for-point with expected inflation.
    b. No. Although the nominal interest rate does rise and fall with expected inflation, the change is not point-for-point.

9. a. $1759.77
    b. $4761.90
    c. $443.89
    d. $1216.47

10. $4761.90, because that is the security's present value.

11. a.   7.5%
    b.   18.5%
    c.   4.8%
    d.   9.3%

12. a.   0%
    b.   11.2%
    c.   7.6%
    d.   4.5%

5: THE THEORY OF PORTFOLIO ALLOCATION

KEY CONCEPTS

This is the shortest chapter of the book, but the concepts that are covered are particularly important. It deals with the **theory of portfolio selection**, which predicts that savers decide which assets to include in their **portfolio** on the basis of five key factors: wealth, return, risk, liquidity, and information costs.

- As their **wealth** increases, people have more savings to allocate among assets, and so demand is greater for each individual asset. However, people do not increase the quantity of all assets demanded proportionally. As wealth increases, the demand increases more than proportionally for some assets and less than proportionally for others. The **wealth elasticity of demand** measures the responsiveness of asset demand to changes in wealth.

- Given a choice between two otherwise similar assets, investors will choose the one with the highest **expected return**. The correct measure of expected return is the after-tax *real* rate of expected return because savers care about the purchasing power generated from an investment.

- Most people are **risk averse**. Therefore, everything else being constant, an increase in the **risk** of an asset will reduce the quantity demanded of that asset.

- Greater **liquidity** increases the value of an asset held to smooth spending or for precautionary purposes. Thus an increase in liquidity of an asset increases the demand for that asset, all else being constant.

- Savers seek to lower the risk associated with an asset but want to do so without devoting time or resources to assessing creditworthiness or monitoring borrowers' actions. Some assets, such as Exxon stock or U.S. Treasury bills, have lower **information costs**. Other assets, such as loans to small businesses, have higher information costs. Higher information costs, all else being equal, decreases the demand for an asset.

Because returns on different assets do not move together perfectly, **diversification** can reduce the total risk of a portfolio. Diversification effectively allows investors to divide risk into smaller, less potentially harmful pieces. Unfortunately, diversification cannot eliminate **market risk** (also called systematic risk). This is because market risk arises from fluctuations of the market and hence affects all assets simultaneously. **Idiosyncratic risk**, or **unsystematic risk** is the part of risk that is unique to an individual asset. This kind of risk can be eliminated through diversification.

Check List

When you finish this chapter, you should be able to:

✓ Describe the five key factors affecting portfolio allocation.

✓ Explain the effect of changes in wealth, expected return, risk, liquidity, and informational costs on asset demand.

✓ Calculate the wealth elasticity of asset demand.

✓ Explain the role of taxes in determining asset demand.

✓ Explain how diversification reduces risk.

✓ Distinguish between market risk and idiosyncratic risk and give examples of each.

✓ Explain why it is possible to diversify away idiosyncratic risk but not market risk.

Self-Test

True or False

1. A luxury asset is one for which the wealth elasticity of demand exceeds 1.

2. An increase in the marginal tax rate should make municipal bonds less attractive, everything else being equal.

3. By diversifying, the risk on your portfolio's return can be reduced.

4. Through diversification, you can completely eliminate the risk on your portfolio.

5. Market risk can be reduced or eliminated through diversification.

6. The wealth elasticity of demand for a luxury asset is greater than that for a necessity asset.

7. A Treasury bond usually offers a higher return than a corporate bond.

8. The more highly correlated assets are, the greater the advantages of diversification.

Fill in the Blank

1. A collection of assets held by a saver is called a _____.

2. A necessity asset is one for which the wealth elasticity of demand is _____ _____ _____.

3. The ease with which an asset can be converted into cash at low cost is called _____.

4. Allocating savings among many different assets is known as _____.

5. Although savers want to lower their risks, they are not willing to incur high costs gathering _____ and _____ borrowers.

6. In comparing portfolio strategies for older versus younger savers, the author is of the opinion that the older saver would be more risk _____.

7. The arbitrage pricing theory was developed by _____ _____.

Multiple Choice

1. The wealth elasticity of demand equals

   a. $$\frac{\%\ \text{change in quantity demanded of an asset}}{\%\ \text{change in wealth}}$$

   b. $$\frac{\%\ \text{change in wealth}}{\%\ \text{change in quantity demanded of an asset}}$$

   c. $$\frac{\text{quantity demanded of an asset}}{\text{wealth}}$$

   d. $$\frac{\text{wealth}}{\text{quantity demanded of an asset}}$$

2. What is the after-tax return on a security that pays an interest rate of 8%? Assume that the marginal tax rate is 25%.
   a. 8%
   b. 25%
   c. 6%
   d. 10%

3.   Empirical evidence indicates that most investors are
     a.   risk loving.
     b.   risk craving.
     c.   risk averse.
     d.   risk neutral.

4.   Which of the following assets is most liquid?
     a.   a $10 bill
     b.   a plot of land
     c.   a Treasury bill
     d.   a share of stock

5.   Diversification will not reduce the risk on a portfolio of assets when
     a.   the assets are highly liquid.
     b.   the returns are perfectly negatively correlated.
     c.   the assets are highly illiquid.
     d.   the returns are perfectly positively correlated.

6.   Idiosyncratic risk refers to variations in return on
     a.   the entire market.
     b.   individual assets.
     c.   the total portfolio.
     d.   individual markets.

7.   All of the following are listed as determinants of portfolio choice by the author
     except
     a.   state of the economy.
     b.   wealth.
     c.   risk.
     d.   liquidity.

8.   You win the lottery, and as a result, your wealth increases from $500,000 to
     $1,500,000. With the additional $1,000,000, you decide to increase your stock
     holdings from $50,000 to $450,000. What is your wealth elasticity of demand for
     this asset?
     a.   0.40
     b.   1.75
     c.   2.50
     d.   4.00

9. An individual is in a 30% tax bracket and purchases a corporate security that is returning 10%. If the expected inflation rate is 4%, the after-tax real rate of return on the asset is
    a. 14%.
    b. 7%.
    c. 6%.
    d. 3%.

10. The expected after-tax real rate of return on a **tax-exempt** bond is 6%. Assuming a tax rate of 25% and a nominal interest rate of 12%, the expected rate of inflation is
    a. 0%.
    b. 3%.
    c. 6%.
    d. indeterminate.

11. Stock A has a beta value of 0.5 and a return of 8%. Stock B has a beta value of 1. Because of systematic risk, the most likely return for stock B would be
    a. less than 8%.
    b. more than 8%.
    c. 16%.
    d. 8%.

12. According to the capital asset pricing model, what would be the value of beta if the risk-free rate is 2%, the risk premium on the market portfolio is 8%, and the expected return on the asset is 12%?
    a. 0.5
    b. 1
    c. 1.25
    d. 2

Essays

1. What are the five determinants of asset demand? Discuss each briefly.

2. Municipal bonds have a lower interest rate than Treasury bonds. Why?

3. Mary Geronimo needs to raise funds to finance a glass-making factory that she wants to build. She goes to the local investment banker and asks advice on how to go about issuing securities so as to raise funds in financial markets. The investment banker refers her to the local commercial bank for financing. Why?

4. What are mutual funds, and why would they be particularly attractive to the small investor?

5. Consider two companies. One company is a retailer specializing in high-quality consumer goods such as expensive watches. The other company operates a multi-state grocery store chain. The stock of which company has the greater systematic risk? Why?

6. Why would a mutual fund that specialized in *cyclicals* (i.e., stocks that are more sensitive to overall business cycles than average) pay a higher expected return than would a typical mutual fund?

7. Biocon Corporation is a newly formed genetic engineering firm. Its president, Jose Murphy, a geneticist, was previously employed by a large pharmaceutical firm where he was responsible for the development of several new drugs. Dr. Murphy is considered by many to be a genius. He has staked the company's future on the development of a new genetic treatment for hay fever.
    a. Your stockbroker, trying to talk you into investing into Biocon, says: "High risk yes, but also high gain." Is she giving you good advice?
    b. Another stockbroker suggests that you invest in a large pharmaceutical firm that does research similar to Biocon's but simultaneously on many different products. The second broker says that even though the company engages in much high-risk research, the company itself is not high risk. Is he correct?
    c. Venture capital firms are intermediaries that specialize in funding new and emerging entrepreneurial companies. They typically hold a diversified portfolio of such companies. Do your answers to (a) and (b) suggest why a company like Biocon is typically financed by a venture capital firm? Explain.

8. Fine art is considered a luxury asset, while a savings account is not. When is an asset considered a luxury asset? Assume that your wealth increases from $1,000,000 to $1,600,000. How much would your ownership of fine art have to increase if at $1,000,000 you owned $80,000 of fine art?

9. Over the last 10 years, income tax rates have gone up. How should this affect the spread between municipal and Treasury securities?

ANSWERS TO SELF-TEST

True or False

1. True.
2. False. Municipal bonds would become more attractive because their tax-exempt status would take on greater significance.
3. True.
4. False. Through diversification, much of the risk can be eliminated. However, some market risk and idiosyncratic risk will remain.
5. False. Idiosyncratic risk can be reduced through diversification, but market risk cannot
6. True.
7. False. A Treasury bond would offer a lower return. The Treasury bond has lower risk and is also exempt from state and local income tax.
8. False. Diversification would not reduce the variability of the return by very much.

Fill in the Blank

1. portfolio
2. less than 1
3. liquidity
4. diversification
5. information; monitoring
6. averse
7. Stephen Ross

Multiple Choice

1.	a	2.	c
3.	c	4.	a
5.	d	6.	b
7.	a	8.	d
9.	d	10.	c
11.	b	12.	c

Essays

1. *Wealth*: The greater the wealth, the more savings there are to allocate among assets. Typically, however, we do not increase the quantity of all assets demanded proportionately. For example, a wealthier person may hold more stocks relative to cash than a poorer person.

Expected return: Given the choice between two similar assets, a saver will pick the one with the higher expected after-tax return.

Risk: Most investors are risk averse. They try to minimize variability in the return on their savings.

Liquidity: The more liquid it is, the more easily an asset can be converted to cash at low cost. Because savers want to maintain the option to convert assets to goods and services, savers prefer to have an asset that is more liquid.

Information: Savers want to hold assets with low information cost because they do not want to spend time and resources collecting information about a company.

2. Municipal bonds are exempt from federal income tax, and investors are concerned with after-tax returns when making investment decisions.

3. Since the return required by savers to compensate for information costs on a small business like Ms. Geronimo's is high, the cost of funds raised through a new security issue would be prohibitive. Therefore the investment banker cannot help her. Commercial banks, however, specialize in gathering information on little-known businesses. The commercial banker, therefore, is the appropriate person for her to contact.

4. In a mutual fund, investors buy shares in a diversified portfolio of assets. Mutual funds offer a way for savers to pool risk, they allow maintenance of liquidity through low transactions costs, and they provide information to investors about the portfolio of assets. In return for those benefits, investors sacrifice some of their expected return through payment of a management fee.

5. The first company, which sells high-quality consumer goods, has the greater systematic risk. This is because a downturn in the overall economy, which is usually associated with a market downturn, will have a greater effect on this company than on the grocery store. After all, people have to eat even during recessions, but they can put off buying expensive watches.

6. Cyclical stocks, by definition, are more sensitive to overall market fluctuations. That is, they are characterized by a greater degree of market risk that cannot be eliminated by diversification. This means that cyclical stocks are inherently more risky than other stocks. As a consequence, they must pay a higher return to compensate for risk.

7.   a.   Your stockbroker is giving you bad advice. Biocon has high risk, but the risk is idiosyncratic risk, not systematic risk. Therefore, someone holding a diversified portfolio would not view Biocon as particularly risky. There is a high chance that Biocon will fail, but its failure would be averaged out by other firms in the portfolio that succeed. Because Biocon has low systematic risk, it should not pay an unusually high expected return. (If Biocon is a success, it will pay a high return, but this is offset by the high probability of failure.)

    b.   The second stockbroker is providing you with correct information. Because the large pharmaceutical company is doing research on a large number of products, its research efforts are diversified. Although many of the research projects will come to nothing, the ones that succeed will compensate for the failures.

    c.   Because venture capital firms invest in a diversified portfolio of entrepreneurial businesses, they are able to diversify away idiosyncratic risk. Just as with the large pharmaceutical company, many of the research projects will fail, but the ones that succeed compensate for the failures. A venture capital firm could finance Biocon at low risk because the venture capital firm would hold Biocon as part of a well-diversified portfolio.

8.   A luxury asset has a wealth elasticity of demand that is greater than 1. Your ownership of fine art would have to increase by more than 60%, an amount exceeding $128,000.

9.   The spread should widen. You would expect municipals to have a lower rate because of their tax-exempt status. Raising the federal income tax makes municipals that much more attractive. If you were in the 30% tax bracket, a bond yielding 10% would have an after-tax return of 7%. If you were put into the 35% tax bracket as a result of the change in tax laws, your return would be 6.5%. At the new higher rate, you would be indifferent between a tax-free bond of 6.5% and a bond offering 10% that is taxed.

6: DETERMINING MARKET INTEREST RATES

KEY CONCEPTS

This chapter develops a demand and supply model and uses it to analyze the reaction of interest rates to market events. Although the model is similar to the models you have seen in other economics courses, there are differences. In particular, the factors that are important in financial markets differ somewhat from those in other markets.

There are really two ways to look at financial markets, depending on what we view as being the good traded:

- We can consider the bond to be a good, with the lender as the buyer of bonds and the borrower as the seller. In this case, the price paid is the bond price.

- We can consider loanable funds to be the good, with the borrower being the buyer and the lender being the seller. In this case, the interest rate is the price.

Which of these approaches is best to use depends on the type of analysis that is desired. When analyzing prices, the first approach is most convenient. When analyzing interest rates, the second approach is better.

The demand curve for bonds shows the relationship between a bond's price and the quantity that lenders are willing to buy. It is downward sloping because a lender is willing and able to purchase more bonds when the price of the bond is low than when it is high. An important but subtle point is that the demand curve for bonds is the supply curve of loanable funds. Recall that interest rates and bond prices are inversely related, so as the bond price falls, the interest rate rises, causing lenders to supply more funds. The supply curve for loanable funds is upward sloping.

The bond supply curve shows the relationship between a bond's price and the quantity that borrowers are willing to sell. The bond supply curve is upward sloping because as the price of a bond rises, the amount borrowed, *given that the face value that must be repaid*, increases, so borrowers are willing to sell more bonds. A key point to keep in mind is that bond supply is the same as the demand for loanable funds. The demand for loanable funds is downward sloping because borrowers are willing and able to buy more loanable funds when interest rates are low.

Equilibrium is determined by the intersection of the demand and supply curves. This is true whether the bond market or loanable funds market approach is used. Only at this point are both buyers and sellers simultaneously satisfied with both price and quantity. An important point to keep in mind is that the bond market and loanable funds market approaches are always consistent with one another. Anything that causes a change in the equilibrium of the bond market will cause a corresponding change in the equilibrium in the loanable funds market. The quantity that is transacted is identical in each market. A change in price will cause a corresponding change in the interest rate, so the interest rate is always the rate implied by the current market price. Anything that changes demand or supply will change the equilibrium quantity and price. There are five factors that affect demand for bonds (Chapter 5):

- **Wealth**: As aggregate wealth expands, the demand for bonds will rise; the demand curve will shift to the right.

- **Expected return and expected inflation**: As expected return increases relative to other assets, the demand for bonds will rise; the demand curve shifts to the right. If expected inflation rises, the real return falls and the bond demand curve shifts to the left.

- **Risk**: As the riskiness of a bond increases relative to other assets, demand decreases and the demand curve shifts to the left.

- **Liquidity**: The higher the liquidity, the greater is demand. An increase in liquidity shifts the demand curve to the right.

- **Information costs**: A rise in information costs of bonds, relative to other assets, decreases demand; the demand curve would shift to the left.

Keep in mind that anything that affects the demand for bonds must also affect the supply of loanable funds. For example, a rise in the relative expected return shifts both the demand for bonds and the supply of loanable funds to the right. There are four factors that are usually cited as affecting the supply of bonds.

- **Expected profitability of capital**: Higher expected profitability leads firms to want to borrow more to finance capital investment; the supply curve shifts to the right.

- **Business taxation**: Firms care about after-tax profits, so a rise in business taxation reduces bond supply; the supply curve shifts to the left.

- **Expected inflation**: A rise in inflation will reduce the purchasing power of funds used to repay a bond, increasing firms' willingness to supply bonds. The supply curve shifts to the right.

- **Government borrowing**: A rise in government borrowing, which is financed through the issuing of Treasury securities sold in the bond market, increases the supply of bonds. The supply curve shifts to the right.

Again, a shift in bond supply corresponds to a shift in loanable funds demand.

Check List

When you finish this chapter, you should be able to:

- ✓ Understand the relationship between the bond market and the loanable funds market.

- ✓ Describe the equilibrium in the bond market and relate it to the equilibrium in the loanable funds market.

- ✓ Understand that a change in either demand or supply will change the equilibrium price and interest rate.

- ✓ Describe the factors that affect demand and the factors that affect supply.

- ✓ Explain how a rise in government budget deficits can cause a rise in household saving.

- ✓ Use the demand and supply model to analyze the impact of recessions and changes in expected inflation.

- ✓ Distinguish between a small open economy and a large open economy and explain how interest rates are determined in each case.

Self-Test

True or False

1. As bond prices go up, the supply of loanable funds will also go up.

2. An individual who has all of his or her wealth tied up in bonds will suffer a decrease in wealth if interest rates rise because the value of the individual's existing bond portfolio will go down.

3. Higher expected inflation will shift the supply curve for bonds to the right and leave the demand curve unchanged.

4. The elimination of the investment tax credit will cause the demand curve for loanable funds to decrease and interest rates to fall.

5. Higher expected inflation affects both the supply curve and the demand curve for bonds.

6. In the early 1980s, the federal budget was running in the black; but over the last 10 years, it has had a deficit every year.

7. In an open economy, a small country such as Luxembourg would have little control over the expected real interest rate in that country.

8. In a closed economy, the amount of control a country has over the domestic interest increases as the size of the country increases.

9. Assuming that the U.S. is a net lender in the world capital market, U.S. bond prices would be higher if the U.S. became a closed economy.

Fill in the Blank

1. The demand for bonds is equivalent to the supply of _____
    _____.

2. As a result of higher real estate values nationwide, the wealth of Americans will
    _____. This will create an excess _____ of loanable funds and
    an eventual _____ in interest rates.

3. The life-cycle hypothesis argues that people in the _____ years of their
    lives save the most.

4. You see a bumper sticker that reads: "I am spending my children's inheritance." A
    person who is doing this is not engaging in _____ saving.

5. The expected real interest rate is the nominal interest rate less _____
    _____.

6. The periodic fluctuations in economic activity can be shown through the
    _____ _____.

7. In a(n) _____ economy, capital is mobile internationally.

Multiple Choice

1. The discount price of a one-year bond is $7000, and the interest rate is 6%. The face
    value of the bond would be
    a. $7420.
    b. $6580.
    c. $4200.
    d. $8000.

2. If there is an excess supply of bonds in the market, then the price of bonds is
    _____ the equilibrium price and the interest rate is _____ the
    equilibrium interest rate.
    a.   above; above
    b.   above; below
    c.   below; above
    d.   below; below

3. An increase in bond prices will cause
    a.   a decrease in the quantity of loanable funds supplied.
    b.   a decrease in the quantity of loanable funds demanded.
    c.   a leftward shift in the loanable funds supply curve.
    d.   a rightward shift in the loanable funds demand curve.

4. David Ortega is an investment banker with a reputation for predicting which junk
    bonds are likely to default. The junk bonds that he recommends will likely enjoy
    _____ demand because those bonds are characterized by _____
    _____.
    a.   higher; lower risk
    b.   higher; lower liquidity
    c.   lower; lower risk
    d.   lower; higher liquidity

5. During 1997, Ortega suffered several "black eyes" when junk bonds that he
    recommended subsequently defaulted. What will happen to bonds that he previously
    recommended?
    a.   Nothing, since those bonds have already been issued.
    b.   Market participants will view the bonds as now being more risky.
    c.   The secondary market price will decline.
    d.   Both b and c.

6. Businesses with stock trading on the New York Stock Exchange are required to
    make detailed financial disclosures. Why does the NYSE impose this requirement?
    a.   Risk is reduced, so the supply of loanable funds will rise.
    b.   Information costs are reduced, so the demand for bonds rises.
    c.   Information costs paid by businesses will rise, so supply will fall
    d.   Risk is reduced, so the demand for bonds will rise.

7. What would be the expected impact of the elimination of the investment tax credit in
    the 1980s on the bond market?
    a.   The bond demand curve will shift right, and interest rates will rise.
    b.   The bond supply curve will shift right, and interest rates will rise.
    c.   The bond supply curve will shift left, and bond prices will rise.
    d.   Both the bond supply curve and the bond demand curve will shift right, and the
         change in interest rates will be indeterminate.

8. Higher expected inflation should
   a. increase the nominal interest rate and the real interest rate.
   b. increase the nominal interest rate and decrease the real interest rate.
   c. increase the nominal interest rate, but its impact on the real interest rate is uncertain.
   d. decrease the nominal interest rate and increase the real interest rate.

9. The passage of a balanced budget amendment to the U.S. Constitution requiring the federal budget to be balanced each year would likely result in the bond _____ _____shifting to the _____.
   a. supply curve; right
   b. demand curve; right
   c. supply curve; left
   d. demand curve; left

10. In a small open economy, the domestic supply of loanable funds equals the domestic demand for loanable funds at the world interest rate of 6%. As a result of an improved economic outlook, we would expect the domestic demand curve for loanable funds to shift _____ and the equilibrium real interest rate to

    _____.
    a. right; increase
    b. left; decrease
    c. right; not be changed
    d. The supply curve, not the demand curve, will shift right, and the expected real interest rate will fall.

11. Suppose you read in the newspaper that the Attorney General has announced a stepped-up effort to enforce insider trading laws. What will happen to the value of bonds?
    a. Information costs will fall, demand will shift to the right, and bond prices will rise.
    b. Liquidity costs will fall, demand will shift to the left, and bond prices will rise.
    c. Information costs will rise, demand will shift to the left, and bond prices will fall.
    d. Relative expected return will decline, demand will shift to the left, and bond prices will rise.

Use the following information to answer the next three questions: Sophtwear is a small computer programming firm that specializes in software that operates cloth cutting machines used in apparel manufacturing. Recently, Amy Castillo, the company's CEO, decided to "bet the company" on developing a software package based on new nonlinear algorithms. If the new software is successful, the company will enjoy considerable profits. Otherwise, the company will go bankrupt.

12. A review in a trade journal gives Sophtwear's new program high marks. Why might the supply of Sophtwear bonds shift to the right?
    a. The risk of default is less.
    b. Expected profits from expanding operations is now greater.
    c. Because demand for Sophtwear bonds is now greater, liquidity will be greater.
    d. As the Sophtwear program becomes better known, information costs will decline.

13. Sophtwear's auditor gives the company a qualified opinion for fear that the firm will not be able to finance continued operations should the new software fail. Why might demand for Sophtwear bonds shift to the left?
    a. There is considerable risk of default.
    b. Higher expected profits will increase demand for Sophtwear bonds.
    c. As liquidity increases, bond demand increases.
    d. As the Sophtwear program becomes better known, information costs will decline.

14. In question 13, the yield on Sophtwear bonds will
    a. rise.
    b. fall.
    c. not change.
    d. change unpredictably.

Essays

1. Recent news out of Washington has led to increases in real estate values. Assume that the increase is expected to continue and that bonds and real estate are substitutes in one's portfolio. How should the expected increase in real estate affect bond prices and interest rates?

2. The author argues that the demand curve for bonds is the supply curve for loanable funds. Explain.

3. The stock market during 1998 and the first half of 1999 showed substantial strength.
   a. If the strong returns are expected to continue, how should this affect the supply of loanable funds?
   b. How might your answer change if one argues that overall wealth in the economy has increased substantially because of the higher stock prices?

4. In the late 1970s, it was argued that the low savings rate was largely attributed to the baby boomer generation, people born in the late 1940s and 1950s. Explain.

5. The large government deficits have increased the chance of default. At the same time, the government, in an attempt to sell bonds to finance these deficits, makes bonds easier to obtain. How should overall bond prices and interest rates be affected?

6. The most recent U.S. government report indicates that retail sales and personal income are growing at a healthy rate while inflation remains under control. How should this government report affect the bond market?

7. Assuming a small open economy, the central bank of a country will be helpless in changing the expected real interest rate in that country. Comment.

8. Looking at interest rates throughout the world, we see that they are quite different. But given what we have read in this chapter, we would expect them to be the same. Comment.

ANSWERS TO SELF-TEST

True or False

1. False. As bond prices go up, the interest rate goes down and lenders will be less willing to supply loanable funds. Borrowers would be more willing to borrow.
2. True.
3. False. The supply curve for bonds will shift to the right and the demand curve for bonds will shift left because the holding of bonds becomes less attractive.
4. True.
5. True.
6. False. In the early 1980s, the federal government was running at a deficit.
7. True.
8. False. In a closed economy, both the small country and the large country would have control over their domestic interest rate. In an open economy, the control would vary with the size of the country.
9. True.

Fill in the Blank

1. loanable funds
2. increase; supply; decrease
3. middle
4. bequest
5. expected inflation
6. business cycle
7. open

Multiple Choice

1. a   2. b
3. a   4. a
5. d   6. b
7. c   8. c
9. c   10. c
11. a   12. b
13. a   14. a

Essays

1. The demand for and price of bonds will fall, and the interest rate will rise. (Recall that individuals who are demanding bonds are the suppliers of loanable funds.)

2. If individuals are buying bonds, they are supplying loanable funds.

3. a. The supply of loanable funds will decrease as the demand for bonds falls because of the higher expected returns on stock.
    b. The increase in wealth would increase the demand for bonds and offset at least in part the decrease caused by the higher expected return on stock.

4. The baby boomers were in their early and middle twenties. According to the life-cycle hypothesis, people in that age group are not large savers.

5. The two events will affect bond prices and interest rates in opposite ways. The former will reduce bond prices and raise interest rates. The latter will raise bond prices and lower interest rates. Therefore, the overall effect is uncertain.

6. We would expect the supply of bonds to increase, shifting to the right, which means that the demand curve for loanable funds increases, shifting to the right. The equilibrium price of bonds should fall, and interest rate should rise.

7. If capital can move freely between countries, as is implied by an open economy, the home country would have little control over the real interest rate. If barriers on capital flows were imposed, then that country could control interest rates within its borders.

8. There are many explanations why interest rates are different: (1.) The interest rates we see in the paper are nominal not real. (2.) Capital flow restrictions do exist. (3.) Costs involved in international capital flows have to be considered. These are just three reasons. There are certainly many more.

7: RISK STRUCTURE AND TERM STRUCTURE OF INTEREST RATES

KEY CONCEPTS

Until now, the discussion has proceeded as though there were only one interest rate; in reality, there are many different interest rates. This chapter discusses why different assets pay different yields. The differences between yields on different assets of the *same maturity* are called the **risk structure of interest rates**. Several factors determine the risk structure:

- **Default risk**: The interest on a risky instrument must be higher than that on a **default-risk-free** instrument to compensate for losses when default does occur. Moreover, because savers are usually risk averse, the yield on risky assets must be even higher to compensate for risk bearing.

- **Liquidity**: A less liquid asset must pay a higher yield to compensate savers for sacrificing liquidity.

- **Information costs**: Instruments that are issued by borrowers for whom information is more difficult to acquire will pay a higher yield to compensate lenders for additional information costs.

- **Taxation**: Credit instruments that are taxed at a lower rate will have a lower yield.

The variation in yields among related instruments that differ only in maturity is known as **the term structure of interest rates**. The *yield curve* is often used to study the term structure. Any theory of the term structure must explain two facts about the yield curve:

- The yield curve usually slopes upward, so long-term yields are generally higher than short-term yields (although, at times, the yield curve has been flat or even sloped downward).

- Yields on default-risk-free instruments with different maturities typically move together, increasing and decreasing simultaneously.

Economists have advanced three theories to explain these facts:

- **Segmented market theory**: This theory holds that the yields on different maturities vary because they are traded in separate markets. Long-term yields are usually higher because the demand for long-term instruments is lower relative to supply than for short-term instruments. Because the segmented market theory cannot explain why yields move together, it is not a satisfactory theory of the term structure.

- **Expectations theory**: This theory is based on the assumption that savers view all maturities as perfect substitutes, given default risk, liquidity, information costs, and tax treatments. This view implies that the long-term bond rate should be an average of short-term rates. The expectations theory can explain why yields tend to move together. A change in short-term rates will cause long-term rates to change because long-term rates are an average of short-term rates. But the theory cannot explain why the yield curve usually slopes upward, so it is not a satisfactory theory of the term structure.

- **Preferred habitat theory**: With this theory, savers are assumed to care about both expected returns and maturities. That is, investors view instruments with different maturities as substitutes but not as perfect substitutes. The preferred habitat theory explains why yields move together and why the yield curve slopes upward. If the yield on long-term bonds were to rise, savers would shift from short-term to long-term instruments, increasing the yield on short-term securities. Therefore, yields on instruments with different maturities should move together. At the same time, savers prefer a shorter maturity, as in the segmented market theory, so the yield curve typically slopes upward. Because the preferred habitat theory can explain both major facts about the yield curve, it is the best theory of the term structure.

One final note of caution: Do not confuse the term structure with the risk structure. The risk structure applies to the *same* maturity. The term structure applies to *different* maturities.

Check List

When you finish this chapter, you should be able to:

✔ Distinguish between the risk structure and the term structure of interest rates.

✔ Explain how default risk, liquidity, information costs, and taxation affect the risk structure.

✔ Distinguish between the segmented markets, expectations, and preferred habitat theories of the term structure.

✔ Understand that the segmented markets theory is inadequate because it cannot explain why the yields on different terms to maturity tend to move together.

✔ Understand that the expectations theory is inadequate because it cannot explain why the yield curve is typically upward sloping.

✔ Distinguish between a buy-and-hold strategy and a roll-over strategy and explain how arbitrage ensures that the expected return to both strategies is the same.

✔ Calculate the n-period interest rate from a series of expected one period interest rates.

Self-Test

True or False

1. An increase in the risk premium could indicate that an asset is now considered to be more likely to default, or it could mean that it is now considered to be less liquid. _T_

2. A bond with a high rating, such as AAA, pays a higher yield than does a bond with a low rating, such as C. _F_

3. The variation in yields for related instruments that differ only in maturity is known as the term structure of interest rates. _T_

4. If the yield curve slopes upward, we would expect future short-term rates to be the same as current short-term rates according to the expectations theory of the term structure. _F_

5. According to the segmented market theory, investors view instruments having different maturity as perfect substitutes. _F_

6. The preferred habitat theory explains why the yield curve typically slopes upward. _T_

7. No one theory of the term structure can explain all the relevant facts of interest rate determination. _F_

Fill in the Blank

1. _____ _____ , _____ , _____ _____, and _____ are the four factors that affect the risk structure.

2. Another name for default risk is _____ risk.

3. A bond with a AAA bond rating has a _____ default risk than a bond with a B bond rating.

4. A saver who wants to shift funds to low-risk instruments because of a perceived increase in default risk is engaged in a _____ _____ _____.

5. The _____ _____ shows the relationship among bonds issued by the same company with different maturities.

6. _____ theory is based on the assumption that a long-term bond rate equals the average of short-term rates covering the same investment period.

7. _____ _____ assumption of the expectations theory implies that expected returns for a given holding period must be the same for bonds of different maturities.

8. To be induced to hold long-term securities, savers require a _____ _____.

9. A flight to quality would shift the _____ curve for a low-default risk bond to the _____.

10. _____ _____ distinguishes among interest rates of one maturity compared to another maturity.

Multiple Choice

1. Which of the following is NOT a factor in determining the risk premium?
    a. liquidity
    b. information cost
    c. expected inflation
    d. default risk

2. What is the risk premium on a 30-year corporate bond that pays 11% interest if a 30-year U.S. Treasury bond is yielding 7.2%?
    a. 7.2%
    b. 3.8%
    c. 11%
    d. 18.2%

3. Which of the following bonds should offer the lowest yield?
    a. B
    b. A
    c. AA
    d. BB

4. A financial instrument with high information costs also tends to have
    a. low liquidity.
    b. high liquidity.
    c. a low-risk premium.
    d. a high default risk.

5. Jennifer Burger is an investment banker who has been involved in 23 initial public offerings (IPOs) over the last five years. Yesterday, the SEC announced that it was investigating Ms. Burger in regard to potential fraud allocated with several IPOs. Investigations continue. What is the most important reason why the risk premium on IPOs recommended by Ms. Burger would increase?
    a.   decreased default risk
    b.   lower liquidity
    c.   lower information cost
    d.   higher expected inflation

6. The effective tax rate on capital gains relative to interest income is
    a.   higher because taxes on capital gains are deferred.
    b.   lower because taxes on capital gains are deferred.
    c.   lower because taxes on interest income are deferred.
    d.   the same.

7. After the October 1987 stock market crash, the New York Stock Exchange adopted *circuit breakers*, which required a halt in trading when stock prices fluctuated too much. Implementation of this policy would likely cause the risk premium to increase because of
    a.   higher liquidity risk.
    b.   higher information costs.
    c.   higher default risk.
    d.   both (a.) and (b.).

8. A yield curve will slope downward when
    a.   short-term rates are above long-term rates.
    b.   long-term rates are above short-term rates.
    c.   inflation rates are high.
    d.   none of the above. The yield curve never slopes downward.

9. Ali Niakoui believes that an important factor in deciding whether to expand his business is what the inflation rate will be over the next three years. How can he use the term structure to decide what inflation will be?
    a.   The slope of the yield curve indicates expected inflation.
    b.   A steep yield curve is associated with a higher expected inflation.
    c.   A flat yield curve is associated with a lower expected inflation.
    d.   All of the above are true.

10. Under the expectations theory, if the yield on a one-year, two-year, and three-year bond are 5%, 7%, and 7½%, respectively, we would expect the one-year rate in the third year to be
    a.   7½%.
    b.   7%.
    c.   8½%.
    d.   9½%.

11. With the preferred habitat model, the fact that the yield curve normally slopes upward indicates that
    a. expected inflation is higher than current inflation.
    b. people prefer longer-term securities.
    c. people's preferences have shifted toward long-term bonds.
    d. people prefer shorter-term securities.

12. The term premium is an element of the
    a. segmented market theory.
    b. expectations theory.
    c. preferred habitat theory.
    d. perfect substitutability theory.

Use the following information to answer questions 13 through 15.

Economic news coming out of Washington indicates that inflation may be heating up next year.

13. According to the segmented market theory, expected inflation should make the yield curve
    a. steeper.
    b. flatter.
    c. slope downward.
    d. Inflation should have no impact on the yield curve.

14. According to the expectations theory, expected inflation should make the yield curve
    a. steeper.
    b. flatter.
    c. slope downward.
    d. Inflation should have no impact on the yield curve.

15. According to the preferred habitat theory, expected inflation should make the yield curve
    a. steeper.
    b. flatter.
    c. slope downward.
    d. Inflation should have no impact on the yield curve.

Essays

1. What is meant by a risk premium, and what are its two components?

2. Economics news coming out of Washington indicates that the economy is growing at a healthier pace than originally was projected. What effects should this growth have on the spread between AAA and B rated bonds? Why?

3. Suppose that a profit-sharing plan has invested a substantial portion of your savings in your employer's bonds. A news story reports that your employer's auditor is issuing a qualified report because of the use of questionable accounting practices.
   a. Will the risk premium on your employer's bonds increase or decrease? Why?
   b. What will happen to the market value of your investment in your employer's bonds? Why?

4. a. What is a yield curve?
   b. Draw a typical example.

5. Fill in the following table:

Theory	Assumptions	Does the theory explain why yields move together?	Does the theory explain the typical slope of the yield curve?
Segmented markets			
Expectations			
Preferred habitat			

6. Use the expectations theory to calculate the yield on a three-year bond based on the following information.
   a. $i_{1t} = 7\%$; $i_{1t+1}^{e} = 6\%$; $i_{1t+2}^{e} = 5\%$
   b. $i_{1t+1}^{e} = 7\%$; $i_{2t}^{e} = 8\%$; $i_{1t+2}^{e} = 9\%$

7. Suppose that expectations are as described in question 6(a). If the preferred habitat theory is true, will the yield on a three-year bond be greater or less than 6%?

8. In deciding between the segmented market theory, expectations theory, and preferred habitat theory, we applied *economic analysis*. Explain how and why.

9. Suppose that you are the credit manager of a small clothing manufacturer. One important aspect of your job is to evaluate customers' creditworthiness. You are asked to recommend whether to extend credit to a new account, National Retailer Corp, which is a large department store chain. National Retailer issues long-term bonds. What might be an inexpensive way to assess National Retailer's creditworthiness?

ANSWERS TO SELF-TEST

True or False

1. True.
2. False. Bonds with higher ratings have lower default risk and so pay a lower yield.
3. True.
4. False. If short-term rates stay the same, the yield curve would be flat, not slope upward, according to the expectations theory.
5. False. The segmented market theory assumes that bonds with different maturities are imperfect substitutes.
6. True.
7. False. The preferred habitat theory explains the important facts about the term structure.

Fill in the Blank

1. Default risk; liquidity; information costs; taxation
2. credit
3. lower
4. flight to quality
5. term structure
6. Expectations
7. Perfect substitutability
8. term premium
9. demand; right
10. Term structure

Multiple Choice

1.	c	2.	b
3.	c	4.	d
5.	b	6.	b
7.	d	8.	a
9.	d	10.	c
11.	d	12.	c
13.	a	14.	a
15.	a		

Essays

1. The risk premium on a financial instrument is the difference between its yield and the yield on a default-risk-free instrument of comparable maturity. One component of the risk premium makes the expected returns on the investments with default risk equal to the certain returns from the default-risk-free obligation. The second component is that, because savers are risk averse, yields provide an extra premium for bearing risk.

2. The spread should narrow. The decrease in default risk will cause funds to be shifted from the AAA to B rated bonds, raising the rate on the low-risk AAA bonds relative to the high-risk B bonds.

3. a. The risk premium will increase because of increased information costs.
    b. You will suffer a capital loss. Remember that the yield is inversely related to the market price of an asset. By the way, this example illustrates why diversification is important—even when most saving is done through a profit-sharing plan.

4. a. A yield curve shows the yields to maturity on different default-risk-free obligations as a function of maturity.
    b.

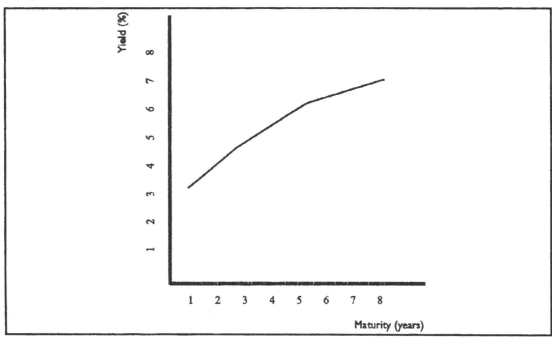

5.

Theory	Assumptions	Does the theory explain why yields move together?	Does the theory explain the typical slope of the yield curve?
Segmented markets	Different maturities are not substitutes.	No.	Yes.
Expectations	Different maturities are perfect substitutes.	Yes.	No.
Preferred habitat	Different maturities are imperfect substitutes.	Yes.	Yes.

6. a. 6%
    b. $8\frac{1}{3}\%$

7. Greater. Three-year bonds must pay a premium if the preferred habitat theory is correct.

8. Economic analysis involves the development and testing of a theory's predictions to determine the theory's usefulness. We used this approach for the three theories of the term structure. We then used the criteria outlined in Chapter 1 to decide among competing theories: Are the assumptions of the theory reasonable? Does the theory generate predictions that can be verified with actual data? Are the predictions corroborated by the data? We applied these criteria in determining that the preferred habitat theory best explains the term structure.

9. Since National Retailer has bonds outstanding, chances are that it is rated by Moody's or by Standard and Poor's. Therefore, you could check National's bond rating. If it is not rated, you could compare the yield on National Retailer's bonds and on U.S. Treasury bonds of the same maturity. The difference in these two yields represents the risk premium. However, keep in mind that the risk premium includes factors for liquidity and tax considerations in addition to default risk. (You care only about default risk.)

8: THE FOREIGN-EXCHANGE MARKET AND EXCHANGE RATES

KEY CONCEPTS

This chapter deals with the relationship between interest rates and exchange rates. Because nearly every country has its own currency, people must usually exchange currencies to buy foreign goods, services, or assets. Therefore, changes in exchange rates are an important determinant of international economic activity. However, the type of exchange rate that is the focus of economic analysis is somewhat surprising. While the **nominal exchange rate** is the exchange rate that is quoted in the newspaper and is the exchange rate that is familiar to most people, economists believe that the **real exchange rate**, which is adjusted for purchasing power, is in fact more important in determining international activity. When a country's real exchange rate appreciates, the country's products become more expensive in terms of the foreign country's products, so net exports decline. When the real exchange rate depreciates, the country's products become less expensive and net exports rise. Therefore, understanding fluctuations in real exchange rates is critical.

One theory of the determination of exchange rates in the long run is given by **purchasing power parity theory**. This theory is based on two assumptions. First, it assumes a version of the **law of one price**. Specifically, nominal exchange rates are assumed to adjust so that the prices of goods and services in one country are the same (on average) as the prices of goods and services in the other country. Second, the theory assumes that the real exchange rate is constant. From these two assumptions, it follows that changes in the nominal exchange rate arise from changes in the price level of one country relative to that of the other country. Unfortunately, purchasing power parity theory does not work well in practice. Actual exchange rate movements do not simply reflect differences in inflation. It appears that either one or both of the two assumptions underlying the theory do not hold in practice.

Purchasing power parity theory is used to explain fluctuation of exchange rates in the long run. To understand fluctuations in the short run, economists often rely on the **theory of interest parity**. This theory hypothesizes that currency arbitrage will ensure that the exchange rate will adjust so that the expected yield on foreign and domestic assets are identical. Specifically, the theory of portfolio choice (Chapter 5) says that if two instruments are denominated in the same currency, investors should prefer the asset with the higher yield. Comparing similar assets denominated in different currencies, however, requires consideration of expected changes in the exchange rate in addition to the yield. Suppose that the yield on, say, Japanese assets is greater than that on U.S. assets. In this case, arbitrators will sell U.S. assets to buy yen-dominated assets. The dollar will depreciate, and the yen will appreciate. But as the yen appreciates, *the expected future* depreciation of the yen will increase. As expected depreciation increases, the yield on yen-denominated assets will decrease until the yield on U.S. and Japanese assets equalizes. Therefore expected nominal returns on foreign and domestic assets will equalize after allowance for risk, liquidity, information costs, *and expected* *changes in exchange rates.* Anything that affects the expected relative return to domestic assets compared to foreign assets affects exchange rates.

- A rise in the domestic interest rate increases the expected return causing demand for the domestic currency to buy domestic assets to increase and the domestic currency appreciates.

- A rise in expected inflation has two effects. First, an increase in expected inflation causes the nominal interest rate to increase, which causes the domestic currency to appreciate. Second, higher expected inflation means that the purchasing power of the domestic currency is reduced, resulting in a decrease in the expected appreciation of the domestic currency. This decrease increases the expected foreign rate of return and the demand for foreign assets. Empirical evidence shows that the second effect dominates, so a rise in expected domestic inflation causes a net depreciation.

- If the foreign interest rate increases, the return to foreign assets will rise. This condition leads to an increased demand for foreign currency to buy the foreign asset, which results in depreciation of the domestic currency.

- If the expected future exchange rate increases, expected appreciation of the domestic currency must also increase. This results in an increase in the expected return to domestic assets compared to foreign assets, causing the demand for domestic currency to increase and the domestic currency to appreciate.

Check List

When you finish this chapter, you should be able to:

✔ Explain how changes in exchange rates affect a country's net exports.

✔ Distinguish between nominal and real exchange rates.

✔ Distinguish between spot market transactions and forward transactions.

✔ Explain the relationship among changes in nominal exchange rates, real exchange rates, and the difference between foreign and domestic inflation.

✔ Explain the role of profit opportunities for ensuring that the law of one price will hold.

✔ Describe the two assumptions underlying the theory of purchasing power parity.

✔ Understand that purchasing power parity is not very successful at explaining actual exchange rate fluctuations.

✔ Explain how the existence of international differences in products, nontraded goods, or fluctuations in the real exchange rate might lead to a failure of purchasing power parity.

✔ Explain how changes in tastes, changes in relative rates of productivity growth, and trade barriers can cause real exchange rates to fluctuate and discuss the implications of each for the theory of purchasing power parity.

✔ Explain the role of interest rates in the theory of interest rate parity.

✔ Distinguish between nominal interest rate parity and real interest rate parity.

✔ Describe the role of international capital mobility in achieving interest rate parity.

✔ Use graphs to illustrate the determination of exchange rates in financial markets.

✔ Explain how changes in domestic interest rates, domestic expected inflation, foreign interest rates, and changes in expected future exchange rates affect exchange rates.

Self-Test

True or False

1. Most currency transactions occur to finance the buying and selling of goods and services.

2. When the French franc appreciates, more French tourists would visit Florida.

3. According to the purchasing power parity theory of exchange rate determination, if a country experiences very rapid inflation, the country's currency should appreciate relative to other countries' currencies.

4. A compact disc costs $10 in New York and the same disc costs ¥1500 in Tokyo. If the exchange rate is $1 = ¥117, then according to the Law of One Price, the yen is undervalued.

5. An increase in one country's productivity relative to that of other countries causes its nominal but not its real exchange rate to appreciate.

6. Comparing two assets denominated in different currencies requires consideration not only of the yield on each asset but also of possible changes in exchange rates.

7. High inflation rates in the home country should cause the domestic currency to depreciate.

8. Nominal interest rate parity implies that interest rates are identical in all countries.

9. The real exchange rate is the nominal exchange rate adjusted for inflation.

10. A decrease in the real exchange rate will occur if the nominal exchange rate is fixed and foreign prices are rising faster than domestic prices.

11. The real exchange rate cannot be less than 1.

12. Assume that the exchange rate between the dollar and peso are determined by supply and demand and that goods can flow freely from one country to another. We would expect both the real and nominal exchange rates to change if the inflation rate in the U.S. were lower than that in Mexico.

13. Exchange rates are more closely tied to real interest rates than to nominal interest rates.

Fill in the Blank

1. Most foreign-exchange trading takes place in London, New York, and
    _____.

2. The _____ _____ _____ is reported in the media,
    but the _____ _____ _____ is adjusted for
    purchasing power.

3. Changes in the nominal exchange rate reflect changes in the real exchange rate,
    domestic inflation, and _____ _____.

4. A _____ _____ _____ is settled immediately,
    whereas a _____ _____ _____ is settled at some
    future date.

5. The _____ _____ _____ _____ says that
    if two countries produce an identical good, profit opportunities should ensure that its
    price is the same, regardless of which country produces the good.

6. Financial markets are characterized by considerable _____
    _____ _____, which means that investors can move funds
    easily among international asset markets.

7. A _____ _____ indicates investors' collective preferences for
    financial instruments denominated in one currency relative to those denominated in
    another currency.

8. The currencies of Denmark and Hungary are the krone and forint, respectively. If 6 krone equal $1 and 153 forint equal $1, an item costing 74 krone would cost _____ forint.

9. The author lists four factors that affect long-run exchange rate trends. They are price level differences, preferences for domestic and foreign goods, trade barriers, and _____ _____.

10. A strict adherence to the law of one price would have the real exchange rate numerically equal to _____.

11. Assuming that capital is mobile internationally and the interest rate in the U.S. is 7% while the interest rate in a comparable Italian security is 8%. If the exchange rate currently between the dollar and the lira is $1 = 1550 lire, we can conclude that the exchange rate one year from now would be $1 = _____ lire.

12. The European Community converted to a common currency called the _____ in 1999.

Multiple Choice

1. If the dollar appreciates against the mark, German goods become
    a. more expensive to Americans.
    b. less expensive to Americans.
    c. less expensive to Germans.
    d. more expensive to Germans.

2. If the dollar appreciates against the mark, U.S. exports should
    a. rise.
    b. fall.
    c. remain unchanged.
    d. change unpredictably.

3. The exchange rate is important because
    a. the political power of the United States depends on the dollar's value.
    b. Japanese trade deficits will decline if the yen appreciates.
    c. domestic political considerations make them important, even though they have little meaning.
    d. changes in exchange rates affect the value of U.S. goods, services, and assets.

4. A high domestic inflation rate will cause a(n)
    a. appreciation of the domestic currency against foreign currencies.
    b. depreciation of the domestic currency against foreign currencies.
    c. depreciation of the foreign currencies against domestic currencies
    d. increased purchasing power for the domestic currency.

5. The law of one price would be LEAST likely to hold for which of the following
    goods?
    a. haircuts
    b. wheat
    c. gold
    d. computer chips

6. Rene Bueler, arbiter of all things fashionable, announces that all things Japanese are
    out and all things French are in. The French franc should
    a. appreciate.
    b. depreciate.
    c. not change.
    d. change in an unpredictable manner.

7. Rally, a U.S. firm, and Fugai, a Japanese firm, are agricultural businesses that sell
    wheat at the wholesale level. Rally sells wheat in the United States for about 45%
    less than Fugai sells wheat in Japan. What might explain this phenomenon?
    a. Purchasing power parity does not apply to services.
    b. Trade barriers could prevent the sale of low-cost U.S. wheat in Japan.
    c. Japanese farmers may produce superior wheat compared to that of U.S. farmers.
    d. Purchasing power parity does not hold in practice.

8. When U.S. interest rates are high compared to French interest rates, people will
    _____ U.S. securities causing the dollar to _____.
    a. buy; appreciate
    b. sell; appreciate
    c. buy; depreciate
    d. sell; depreciate

9. A German asset is offering a 7% yield. A comparable U.S. asset is offering a 5%
    yield. If capital is highly mobile, what is the expected dollar appreciation or
    depreciation rate? (Assume that there is no currency premium.)
    a. 2% appreciation
    b. 5% depreciation
    c. 7% appreciation
    d. 5% depreciation

10. A U.S. security yields 4%, and a comparable German security yields 3%. If the U.S.
    dollar is expected to depreciate 1% against the mark, the currency premium would
    be
    a. 3%.
    b. 0%.
    c. 1%.
    d. 2%.

11. The amount of U.S. exports in 1995 as a percentage of U.S. output is approximately _____ what it was in 1915.
    a. half
    b. equal to
    c. twice
    d. four times

12. A Rado watch costs $700 in New York City and 812.50 Swiss francs in Zurich. If 1.25 Swiss francs equal $1, then the real exchange rate is approximately
    a. 1.16.
    b. 1.08.
    c. 1.00.
    d. 0.86.

13. In question 12, the real exchange rate would be 1 if the price of the watch in New York City were
    a. $650.
    b. $700.
    c. $812.50.
    d. $1,015.63.

14. Differences among countries in _____ is a barrier to single currency in Europe.
    a. per capita income
    b. international trade volume
    c. population density
    d. interest rates

Essays

1. When the dollar appreciates, U.S. net exports decline. Why?

2. A currency depreciation harms consumers but benefits businesses selling abroad. Explain.

3. If the spot exchange rate is $1 = FF65 on March 16, 1993 and the 180-day forward exchange rate is $1 = FF84, would this change mean that investors expect the dollar to increase or decrease against the French franc? What effect should this have on U.S. exports to France, everything else being equal?

4. What do we mean when we say that the foreign-exchange market is over-the-counter?

5. Suppose that you own a small playground equipment manufacturing company in Denton, Texas. You are about to sign a contract to deliver a shipment to Hamburg, Germany, three months from now. The contract specifies payment on delivery in marks.
   a. Are you more or less likely to accept the contract if exchange rates are volatile? Why?
   b. As a businessperson, might you favor government intervention in foreign-exchange markets to stabilize or even fix exchange rates?
   c. If you want to lock in the dollar value today of the future contract, what might you do?

6. The theory of purchasing power parity of the exchange rate states that changes in the nominal exchange rate arise from differences in inflation rates among countries.
   a. Use economic analysis to evaluate purchasing power parity theory.
   b. How might the purchasing power parity theory be modified so that it better explains exchange rate changes?

7. If the yield on German securities is 8%, the current exchange rate is $1 = DM5, and the expected exchange rate one year from now is $1 = DM5.1, what is R_f?

8. Suppose that the yield on a U.S. asset is 8% and the yield on a comparable Japanese asset is 6%. If the expected depreciation rate of the dollar is 4%, what will happen?

9. What is the effect of an increase in domestic inflation on the exchange rate?

10. Use the exchange rate diagram to illustrate what will happen in each of the following cases.
    a. A decrease in the domestic interest rate
    b. A decrease in the foreign interest rate
    c. A decrease in the expected domestic inflation rate
    d. A decrease in tariffs on imports

11. You have been given the responsibility of deciding between building sites located in two different countries. The expected nominal return in the local currency from building a plant in the first country is 15%. The nominal return in the second country is 25%. What additional information do you need before deciding between the two sites?

12. The U.S. economy is growing faster than that of Japan. The faster growth rate in the United States should cause the value of the dollar to depreciate against the yen, everything else being equal. Explain.

13. A one-year Japanese security is currently yielding 5%. Furthermore, it is expected that the exchange rate between the dollar and the yen is going to go from 98 yen to the dollar to 95 yen to the dollar over the next year. To invest in U.S. Treasury securities rather than the Japanese security, you would need a return at least equal to what value?

14. What does the nominal interest rate parity condition state? Would the condition be violated if nominal interest rates in the domestic and foreign country were different on two securities that were identical in all respects? A currency premium would lead to a modification of the nominal interest rate parity condition. Why?

ANSWERS TO SELF-TEST

True or False

1. False. Most foreign-exchange transactions are to finance the purchase of foreign assets.
2. True.
3. False. The country's currency should depreciate relative to the other country's currency because the currency now has less purchasing power.
4. False. The dollar is undervalued. The exchange rate should be $1 = ¥150. The $10 buys 1 CD in New York but only 0.78 CD in Tokyo.
5. False. Both the nominal and real exchange rates will appreciate.
6. True.
7. True.
8. False. Assets that have different risk, liquidity, and information costs, which are denominated in currencies with different expected depreciation rates, will have different yields.
9. False.

$$\text{The real exchange rate} = \frac{\text{Nominal exchange rate} \times \text{domestic price}}{\text{Foreign price}}$$

10. True.
11. False.
12. False. The nominal exchange rate would change, while the real exchange rate would not. The nominal exchange rate would adjust to keep the real exchange rate unchanged.
13. True.

Fill in the Blank

1. Tokyo
2. nominal exchange rate; real exchange rate
3. foreign inflation
4. spot market transaction; forward market transaction
5. law of one price
6. international capital mobility
7. currency premium
8. 1887
9. productivity differences
10. one
11. 1565.5
12. Euro

Multiple Choice

1.	b	2.	b
3.	d	4.	b
5.	a	6.	a
7.	b	8.	a
9.	a	10.	b
11.	c	12.	b
13.	a	14.	a

Essays

1. First, U.S. products become more expensive, reducing U.S. exports. Second, foreign products become less expensive, increasing U.S. imports.

2. When the domestic currency depreciates, foreign goods, services, and assets become more expensive, which harms consumers. But domestic goods and services become more competitive with foreign products, helping businesses that sell abroad.

3. The dollar is expected to appreciate. U.S. exports to France should decline.

4. There is no single physical location at which traders gather to exchange currencies.

5. a. Because production costs are in dollars but revenue is in marks, fluctuations in the dollar/mark exchange rate exposes your company to risk. As long as you are risk averse, you will be less likely to accept the contract.
    b. Yes. Attempts by the government to stabilize or even fix the exchange rate, if successful, would reduce the risk of international transactions.
    c. Enter into a futures contract in which you sell marks for delivery in the future, when your playground contract is completed. This way, you guarantee today the exchange rate at which you obtain dollars. By the way, to help businesses and consumers avoid exchange rate risk is why currency futures markets exist.

6. a. Using the criteria for evaluating a theory: (1.) *Are the assumptions of the theory reasonable?* Yes. (2.) *Does the theory generate predictions that you can verify with actual data?* Yes. (3.) *Are the* predictions *corroborated by the data?* No, differences in inflation rates do not do a good job of explaining exchange rate movements.
    b. The theory can be modified to allow for changes in preferences, productivity, nontraded goods, and trade barriers.

7. The expected depreciation rate is 2%. Thus $R_f = i_f - \Delta Ex/Ex = 8\% - 2\% = 6\%$.

8. R is only 8%, whereas R_f is 6% − (−4%) = 10%, so the demand for the dollar will be weak and the demand for the yen will be strong. The dollar will depreciate relative to the yen. As the dollar depreciates *today*, expected *future* depreciation will decline (expected future exchange rates being held constant). This condition causes R_f to decline until $R = R_f$.

9. Increases in domestic expected inflation affect exchange rates. First, an increase in expected inflation causes the nominal interest rate to increase, which causes the currency to appreciate. Second, higher expected inflation means that the purchasing power of the domestic currency is reduced, resulting in a decrease in the expected appreciation of the domestic currency. This decrease increases the expected foreign rate of return and the demand for foreign assets which causes a depreciation of the domestic currency. Studies show that the second effect is larger than the first. Hence, an increase in expected domestic inflation leads to a depreciation of the domestic currency.

10. a. A decrease in the domestic interest rate:

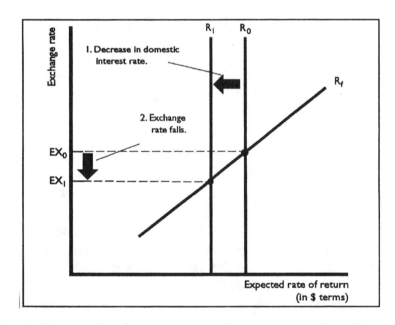

10. b.   A decrease in the foreign interest rate:

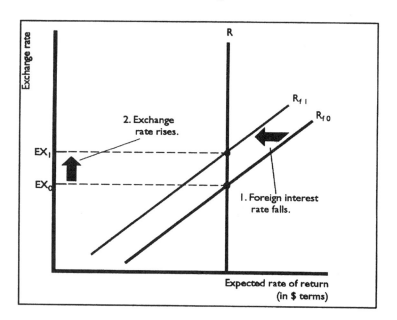

c.   A decrease in the expected domestic inflation rate:

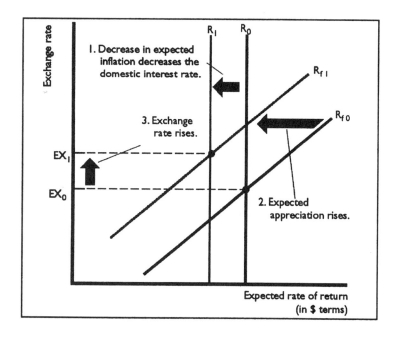

d. A decrease in tariffs on imports.

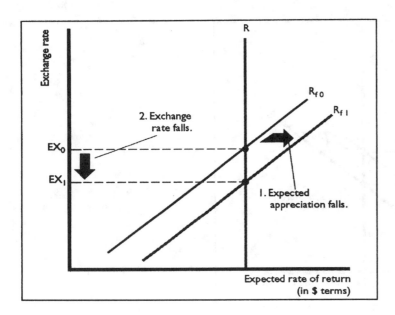

11. You would need to know the expected depreciation rates of the two countries' currencies.

12. U.S. demand for Japanese goods will be rising faster than Japanese demand for U.S. goods. Faster income growth in the U.S. will create more demand for goods and services, both foreign and domestic. Because of this increased relative demand for Japanese goods, the demand for yen will increase relative to the demand for dollars, causing the value of the dollar to fall against that of the yen.

13. $1 + i > 1 + i_f$ – expected appreciation of the dollar
    $1 + i > 1 + 0.05 - (-0.031)$
    $i > 0.081$

14. The nominal interest rate parity condition states that when domestic and foreign assets have identical risk, liquidity, and information characteristics, their nominal returns (measured in the same currency) also must be identical. The condition would not be violated because capital need not be highly mobile between the two countries, and the condition holds only after the conversion is made to the same currency. The currency premium would consider investors' preferences for financial instruments denominated in a particular currency. Therefore the currency premium would have to be considered in looking at the returns on securities in different countries.

9: DERIVATIVE SECURITIES AND DERIVATIVE MARKETS

KEY CONCEPTS

So far, the chapters in Part II have dealt with the financial system in detail. This chapter extends that discussion to **derivative markets**. Generally, **derivative assets** involve **forward transactions**, in which savers and borrowers undertake a transaction now but execute, or settle, the transaction in the future. There are two basic types of forward contracts:

- **Futures contracts**: These are agreements that specify the delivery of a commodity or financial instrument at a *future date* but at a *currently* agreed upon price.

- **Options contracts**: These contracts confer the right to buy or sell an asset at a predetermined price by a predetermined time.

With a futures contract, the buyer and seller have symmetric obligations. The buyer assumes the **long position**, which is the right and obligation to receive the underlying asset. The seller assumes the **short position**, which is the right and obligation to deliver the underlying asset. The price of the contract is set when the contract is sold. By locking in the price today, both buyer and seller can protect themselves from unanticipated price fluctuations.

With an options contract, the buyer and seller have asymmetric rights. The seller has the obligation to perform, but the buyer is not so obligated.

- With a **call option**, the *buyer of the option* obtains the right to buy the underlying asset; the *seller of the option* is obligated to sell at the buyer's request.

- With a **put option**, the *buyer of the option* obtains the right to sell the underlying asset; the *seller of the option* is obligated to buy at the buyer's request.

Because the sellers of options contracts are obligated under the option contract to transact at the **strike price (exercise price)**, they are in effect providing insurance to the buyer of the option against adverse price fluctuations. They receive a **premium**, or payment, as compensation for providing this service.

Like any other financial instrument, demand and supply determine the prices of derivative assets. However, special features of futures and options contracts must be considered when you attempt to understand their prices. For futures, on the delivery date, the future price and **spot price** are identical. So the expected spot price on the delivery date will influence the potential capital gains or losses on the futures contract. Thus, one determinant of the future price is the expectation of the spot price on the date of delivery. Any factor that influences the expected spot price will affect the future price. For options, the most important determinant of the option premium is the chance that the option will be exercised. Factors that affect the probability of exercising the options contract affect the contract price.

By agreeing to a price in advance, buyers and sellers use forward transactions to reduce the risk from price fluctuations. **Hedging** through futures contracts has three key advantages:

- the ability to spread risk from price fluctuations between hedgers and speculators,

- the promotion of liquidity by trading derivative instruments through organized exchanges, and

- the reduction of information costs through the introduction of organized exchanges.

Unfortunately, futures contracts cannot eliminate all risk.

- If market participants have anticipated changes in future spot prices, those changes will already be incorporated into current futures prices. Therefore, using the futures contract to hedge against anticipated price changes is not possible.

- The spot price and future price may not move together perfectly. This imperfect correlation is called **basis risk**.

Options contracts share the advantages of futures contracts; but because they operate more like "insurance" than a futures contract, options contracts do not share the disadvantages of futures contracts. Since the issuer of the options contract is paid a premium, however, options cost more to use. That is, although options are a better hedge, they are more expensive.

Before we leave the topic of derivative markets, a word of warning. The terminology that is introduced in this chapter can be confusing. When discussing futures, be careful to distinguish between the future price, which is the price promised on the delivery date, and the spot price, which is the price at which the underlying asset is currently trading. When discussing options, do not confuse the option premium, which is the price of the options contract, with the strike price, which is the price specified in the contract for the underlying asset. Similarly, be careful to differentiate between the buyer and seller of the derivative contract and the buyer and seller of the underlying asset specified in the contract. For example, the buyer of a put option is the seller of the underlying asset.

Check List

When you finish this chapter, you should be able to:

✓ Define a derivative asset.

✓ Explain the importance of derivative markets in reducing risk.

✓ Distinguish between a futures contract and an options contract.

✓ Distinguish between the long position and the short position.

✓ Distinguish between put and call options contracts.

✓ Understand the relationship between the expected spot price on the delivery date of a futures contract and the current price of the futures contract.

✓ Understand the concept of marking to market.

✓ Explain how options can serve as insurance against changes in price.

✓ Describe the factors that influence the price of call and put options.

✓ Describe the four factors that influence the probability that an option will be exercised.

✓ Explain the relationship of hedgers and speculators.

✓ Describe the advantages and disadvantages of using futures and options as hedges.

Self-Test

True or False

1. The buyer of a call option is obligated to purchase an asset on a specified future date.

2. In a futures contract, the person holding the short position promises to deliver the asset on a future date.

3. In the futures market, gains and losses are settled each day.

4. You can use a futures contract to limit risk from a price fall but not from a price rise.

5. The more distant the expiration date, the higher the option premium is.

6. You can use a put option to limit the risk of a price fall but not a price rise.

7. The more volatile the share price, the lower the premium is.

8. The buyer of an option contract assumes less risk than does the purchaser of a futures contract.

Fill in the Blank

1. Forward transactions reduce the _____ associated with price fluctuations.

2. A _____ option involves the obligation to sell, whereas a _____ option involves the obligation to buy.

3. Under an options contract, the price at which an asset is bought or sold is called the _____ price.

4. A put option is said to be _____ _____ _____ when the market price of the underlying asset is less than the strike price.

5. Futures trading traditionally has been dominated by markets located in _____.

6. Futures and options markets allow those who want to avoid risk to transfer risk to _____.

7. In December 1994, the biggest municipal bankruptcy of all time occurred in _____ County, California.

Multiple Choice

1. Which of the following statements is true?
    a. A spot transaction is settled immediately.
    b. A forward transaction is settled immediately.
    c. Both spot and forward transactions are settled immediately.
    d. Both spot and forward transactions are settled in the future.

2. A call option contract involves asymmetric rights and obligations because
    a. the option seller is obligated to buy the underlying asset.
    b. the option seller is obligated to sell the underlying asset.
    c. the option buyer is obligated to buy the underlying asset.
    d. the option buyer is obligated to sell the underlying asset.

3. Speculators are important for smoothly functioning derivative markets because they
    a. shift risk to issuers of futures.
    b. undertake risk and provide liquidity.
    c. reduce liquidity, thereby increasing information flows.
    d. buy and sell futures and options in a way that reduces risk.

4. In 60 days, you will be leaving for a vacation in France. Your budget is tight, but at the current exchange rate, you can just afford the trip. A friend then points out to you that exchange rates are subject to change. If the dollar falls relative to the franc, you will have to cancel your trip. What might you do to protect your vacation?
   a. Sell a call option on francs
   b. Sell a put option on francs
   c. Buy a call option on francs
   d. Buy a put option on francs

5. Suppose that the President is thinking of imposing regulations to restrict speculation in futures markets. Why is this a bad idea?
   a. Speculators shift risk to other market participants.
   b. Speculation is a profitable activity.
   c. Speculators are large campaign contributors.
   d. Speculators increase market liquidity.

6. Futures trading has been dominated by markets in which city?
   a. New York
   b. Los Angeles
   c. Miami
   d. Chicago

7. A lender who is worried that the cost of its funds might rise during the term of a loan it has made, can hedge against this rise by
   a. buying futures contracts on Treasury bills.
   b. selling futures contracts on Treasury bills.
   c. buying call options on Treasury bills.
   d. increasing the amount of money that it lends.

8. Basis risk is the risk
   a. that a borrower might default on a bank loan.
   b. that well known corporations will be unable to payoff its maturing commercial paper issue.
   c. that owners of a corporate bond will be unable to sell the security when desired.
   d. that arises from a change in the spread between the rate on the hedged instrument and the rate on the instrument actually traded.

9. Which of the following regulates options on securities?
   a. The Securities and Exchange Commission
   b. The Federal Reserve System
   c. The Federal Deposit Insurance Corporation
   d. The Commodity Futures Trading Commission

10. The Benedicts are corn farmers whose crop will be harvested in August. Between now and then, they are worried about a fall in price. What strategy could they adopt to limit their risk?
    a. Purchase a put option
    b. Purchase a call option
    c. Enter into a futures contract
    d. Both a and c

11. Shelly West is a miller. She is afraid that corn prices will rise between now and August. What strategy could she adopt to limit her risk?
    a. Purchase a put option
    b. Purchase a call option
    c. Enter into a futures contract
    d. Both b and c

Use the following information to answer questions 12 through 15:

A put option for 100 shares with a strike price of $45 and a premium of $10 is issued. The current market price is $50.

12. What is the profit to the issuer of the option?
    a. −$10
    b. $10
    c. $490
    d. −$490

13. What is the profit from the contract to the holder of the contract?
    a. −$10
    b. $10
    c. $490
    d. −$490

14. If the price falls to $40 a share, what is the profit to the issuer of the option?
    a. −$10
    b. $10
    c. $490
    d. −$490

15. If the price falls to $40 a share, what is the profit to the holder of the contract?
    a. −$10
    b. $10
    c. $490
    d. −$490

Essays

1. What is the difference between a futures contract and an options contract?

2. Buying an options contract is like buying insurance. Comment.

3. Without speculators, derivative markets could not exist. Comment.

4. What are the costs and benefits of standardization?

5. Mr. Clinton buys a futures contract on six-month U.S. Treasury bills for $985,000 issued by Mr. Bush for delivery in 90 days. The face value of the Treasury bills is $1,000,000. (Remember that U.S. Treasury bills are discount bonds.) The current interest rate on these six-month bills is 3%. If the future spot rate turns out to be 4½% annualized, who will gain and who will lose on the transaction? By how much?

6. Suppose that you are the vice-president of a bank. A major industrial customer of the bank will be breaking ground on a new manufacturing plant in three months. The bank has agreed to lend $1,000,000 at an interest rate of 9.8% to finance the plant. However, the bank's board of directors worries that interest rate fluctuations between now and the effective date of the loan will expose the bank to risk. What can you do to reassure the board?

7. Describe the basic attributes of a swap contract. What are the two most often used types of swaps?

8. Many people believe that the stock market is subject to more extreme swings in price today than it was a few years ago. How should this increased volatility affect the options premium? Explain.

ANSWERS TO SELF-TEST

True or False

1. False. The seller of an option is obligated.
2. True.
3. True.
4. False. With futures contracts, the price is set for both buyer and seller.
5. True.
6. True.
7. False. The premium is higher because the likelihood of the share price rising above the strike price increases.
8. True.

Fill in the Blank

1. risk
2. call; put
3. strike (or exercise)
4. in the money
5. Chicago
6. speculators
7. Orange

Multiple Choice

1.	a	2.	b
3.	b	4.	c
5.	d	6.	d
7.	b	8.	d
9.	d	10.	d
11.	d	12.	b
13.	a	14.	d
15.	c		

Essays

1. A futures contract involves symmetric obligations of both buyer and seller. The seller has both the right and the obligation to deliver the underlying asset at the specified date and price. The buyer has both the right and the obligation to receive the underlying asset at the specified date and price. An options contract involves asymmetric rights. The seller is obligated to carry out the contract, but the buyer has the right to cancel the contract.

2. An option must be exercised only in the event that the price moves above (call) or below (put) the strike price. Thus the option provides insurance against price movements.

3. The statement is not necessarily true. For example, a farmer and a meat-packing plant could enter a futures contract in which the farmer agrees to sell pigs and the meat packer agrees to buy them in 90 days. Such a contract reduces the risk faced by both the farmer and the meat-packing plant. For another example, a person who did not want to speculate could issue two offsetting contracts—one a put and one a call. The issuer would collect the premium but would face no risk. Although the two examples involve no speculation, this does not mean that speculators are not useful. By standing ready to trade, they increase the liquidity of the market. They also assume risk when there is a mismatch between buyers and sellers of futures contracts or between put and call options contracts.

4. Standardization increases liquidity but reduces traders' flexibility.

5. If the rate rises to 4½%, the value of the Treasury bills will fall to $1,000,000/1.0223 = $978,186. (Use 1.0223 instead of 1.045 because the Treasury bills are for six months.) This means that Mr. Clinton loses $6,814 and Mr. Bush gains that amount. Despite his losses, Mr. Clinton might still be happy with the futures contract because he reduced his risk. After all, interest rates could have fallen instead of risen.

6. There are several possible answers, two of which are: (a.) Issue futures contracts on CDs that specify the interest rate that will be paid. (b.) Buy a call option on U.S. Treasury bonds.

7. A swap is an agreement between two or more parties to exchange sets of cash flows over some future period. The cash flows are generally related to the value of the underlying financial instruments. Interest rate swaps and currency swaps are the most often used forms of swaps.

8. The options premium will increase. The greater volatility increases the probability that the asset price will rise above the strike price.

KEY CONCEPTS

In this chapter, we return to the discussion of the informational role of prices in the financial system. The importance of prices in coordinating economic activity cannot be overstated, so whether financial markets efficiently incorporate information into prices is of vital interest. The **efficient markets hypothesis** holds that when market participants have **rational expectations** and transactions costs are low, an asset's price will reflect all available information. How this comes to pass can probably be best understood through an example. Suppose you are considering how much of Rose Valley Telephone stock you should hold in your portfolio. On the basis of all the information currently available to you about the company, the industry, and the economy, you believe that Rose Valley Telephone stock is worth $40. The current market price is $39. You (and others like you) will therefore buy the stock, bidding the price up to $40. As a consequence, the price of Rose Valley Telephone stock will come to reflect the information that you and other market participants have about the stock. The process would also work in reverse. Had Rose Valley Telephone been valued at $41, you would have sold the stock, bidding its price down. Thus, by trading on the basis of their best prediction of future price, market participants ensure that the current price reflects all available information.

That the price of an asset is based on all available information does not mean that prices do not change. In an **efficient financial market,** the price of an asset is the asset's **fundamental value**. Therefore, anything that affects the asset's fundamental value will cause its price to fluctuate:

- Changes in market interest rates affect the present value of future income flows (i.e., the asset's fundamental value).

- For stocks, important sources of price fluctuations are changes in expected future dividends.

Prices constantly change to reflect news about changes in fundamental value. News about short-term fluctuations in prospects change stock prices only slightly. Large changes in stock prices are possible in response to changes in a stock's long-term prospects.

The efficient markets hypothesis can be used to formulate strategies for portfolio allocation:

- In an efficient market, all above-normal profit opportunities should be eliminated. Therefore, a risk-averse saver should not risk all his or her saving in a single asset. Instead, the risk-averse saver should hold a diversified portfolio. (*Hint*: Do not confuse "no above-normal profit opportunities" with "no profit opportunities." Even in an efficient market, you can still earn normal profits.)

- Because there are no above-normal profits, active trading will only generate commissions for stock brokers. Individual savers should follow a buy-and-hold strategy.

- Financial analysis that uses past prices to try to predict future prices will not work because past prices do not reflect all available information. Similarly, published tips are unlikely to be useful because these tips will already be reflected in the price.

- Trying to predict future prices is not helpful because today's price is already based on the best forecast. Only unexpected announcements (true news) will affect the price.

Some analysts are skeptical about whether the stock market is efficient. They point to three factors that indicate that the stock market is not efficient:

- Stock markets are characterized by pricing anomalies, which are trading strategies that allow an investor to systematically earn abnormal returns. Such anomalies are not consistent with an efficient market. Two such anomalies are the *small-firm effect* and the *January effect*.

- Asset prices should not be predictable from currently available information. Nevertheless, stocks experiencing high returns today tend to have lower returns in the future, a phenomenon known as *mean reversion*.

- In an efficient market, prices reflect the fundamental value of the asset. Prices therefore should not fluctuate more than the fundamental value. Yet they do.

Unfortunately, inefficient markets can impose substantial costs on society. With inefficient markets, there are excessive price fluctuations and increased information costs. Much of government regulation of the financial system is aimed at promoting an efficient market.

Check List

When you finish this chapter, you should be able to:

✔ Describe the assumptions underlying the efficient markets hypothesis.

✔ Understand the importance of rational expectations.

✔ Explain the mechanism by which prices come to incorporate information.

✔ Distinguish between the effects of anticipated events and unanticipated events on financial prices.

✔ Explain how the price of an asset comes to reflect fundamental value.

✔ Explain why above-normal profit opportunities are eliminated in an efficient market.

✔ Understand the significance of the efficient markets hypothesis for designing an investment strategy.

✔ Indicate the significance of no above-normal profits, diversification, the buy-and-hold strategy, published tips, and technical trading.

✔ Explain the significance of price anomalies, mean reversion, and excessive price volatility. Give examples of each.

✔ Describe the events surrounding the 1987 stock market crash.

✔ Discuss the three leading explanations of the 1987 stock market crash and explain the significance of each of the following: noise trader, fads, bubble, greater fool, circuit breaker, and program traders.

✔ Identify the costs arising from inefficient markets.

Self-Test

True or False

1. Another name for the present value of the sum of expected future returns on an asset is *fundamental value*.   T

2. As long as transactions costs are high, efficient markets will have no unexploited profit opportunities.   F

3. The decline in the market value of equities was greater in the stock market crash of 1929 than in the crash of 1987.   F

4. The bubble in stock market prices can be explained by the "greater fool" theory.   T

5. If the margin requirement is 40%, a saver is allowed to borrow 40% of the purchase price of shares   F

6. The major source of funds for most businesses is current and accumulated profits rather than the stock and bond market.   T

Fill in the Blank

1. In an efficient financial market, all information that is available to market participants is reflected in market _____.

2. Information that is not available to the general public is known as _____ information.

3. The tendency for stocks with high returns today to experience low returns in the future and for stocks with low returns today to experience high returns in the future is called _____ _____.

4. A period when a stock price increases above its fundamental value is referred to as a _____.

5. If the price of a financial asset is less than the current value of its expected future returns, savers will _____ the asset, putting _____ pressure on the price.

6. The stock market crash of 1987 caused many economists to question the _____ _____ hypothesis.

7. The halting of stock market trading when prices or order volumes reach certain levels is referred to as a _____ _____.

8. In the United States, the largest participants in financial markets for bonds, stocks, and other financial instruments are not individual savers and borrowers but _____ _____.

Multiple Choice

1. An increase in wealth should cause the price of financial securities to
   a. rise.
   b. fall.
   c. remain unchanged.
   d. change unpredictably.

2. Which of the following is NOT an assumption of the efficient markets hypothesis?
   a. Market participants have rational expectations.
   b. There are no unexploited profits.
   c. Technical analysis is effective.
   d. Markets are characterized by low transactions costs.

3. If financial markets are efficient, a reasonable investment strategy would be to
   a. buy and hold a diversified portfolio.
   b. actively trade securities in response to news releases.
   c. engage in extensive research before carefully choosing which security to purchase.
   d. exploit insider information so as to consistently beat the market.

4. The assumption that participants use all available information in the pricing of financial assets is known as the
    a.   theory of one price.
    b.   rational expectations hypothesis.
    c.   theory of capital markets.
    d.   fundamental value.

5. The income that you receive from a bond is the
    a.   interest you receive.
    b.   dividend you receive.
    c.   interest you receive plus the dividend while you hold the bond.
    d.   interest you receive plus the expected future capital gain (or loss).

6. Microswift stock is currently paying a dividend of $4 per share. The growth rate of its dividend is revised upward from 3% to 4% on the basis of its latest earnings report. For a discount rate of 7%, the value of the stock should increase by
    a.   35%.
    b.   7%.
    c.   0%.
    d.   5%.

7. The existence of unexploited profits indicates
    a.   that markets are efficient.
    b.   that markets are not efficient.
    c.   nothing about markets.
    d.   that markets need regulation.

8. Studies show that rates of return on stock have been abnormally high during
    a.   December.
    b.   October.
    c.   June.
    d.   January.

9. Which of the following is NOT a market anomaly?
    a.   the January effect
    b.   exploited profits
    c.   mean revision
    d.   excessive volatility

10. Stocks that are traded in the Lilliputian stock exchange tend to revert to a long-term trend value over time. This would indicate that the Lilliputian stock exchange is characterized by
    a.   excessive volatility.
    b.   price anomaly.
    c.   mean revision.
    d.   rational expectations.

11. Stocks that are traded in the Utopian stock exchange vary considerably relative to changes in their underlying fundamental value. This would indicate that the Utopian stock exchange is characterized by
    a. excessive volatility.
    b. price anomalies.
    c. mean revision.
    d. rational expectations.

12. Stocks that are traded in the Frutopian stock exchange have prices that reflect the underlying fundamental value of the stock. This would indicate that the Frutopian stock exchange is characterized by
    a. excessive volatility.
    b. price anomalies.
    c. mean revision.
    d. rational expectations.

13. Stocks that are traded in the Ecotopian stock exchange tend to appreciate in price each Wednesday. This would indicate that the Ecotopian stock exchange is characterized by
    a. excessive volatility.
    b. price anomalies.
    c. mean revision.
    d. rational expectations.

14. Which of the following is NOT an explanation for the 1987 stock market crash?
    a. noise traders
    b. bubbles
    c. trading mechanism
    d. the small-business effect

15. Program trading is
    a. computer based.
    b. stock market based.
    c. TV based.
    d. bond market based.

Essays

1. The author lists three ways in which financial market prices convey information. What are they?

2. Big Blue Company stock is currently offering a dividend of $3 per share. The dividend is expected to grow at a constant rate of 5% per year. If the discount rate is 8%, what should be the share price of Big Blue Company stock under the efficient market hypothesis?

3. What three factors may impair the efficiency of the stock market?

4. Your friend Karla claims that she has proof that markets are not efficient. "Why, just yesterday," she says, "GM announced increased profits, yet its stock price fell." Is her example proof that markets are inefficient?

5. What are noise traders and bubbles, and how are they related?

6. At 7 a.m., you read in today's *Wall Street Journal* that Exxon has discovered large new oil reserves in Montana.
   a. If markets are efficient, what would you do to profit from Exxon's discovery?
   b. If you believe that many market participants are noise traders who overreact to news, what would you do?

7. What is the significance of the small-business effect?

8. You are a hog farmer. If markets are efficient, how might you determine the value of your hogs next August, when you plan to sell your livestock?

9. Suppose that you are the credit manager for a small clothing manufacturer. Your main responsibility is deciding to whom your company should extend credit. Respond to the following questions.
   a. Dull's Department Store, Inc., is a large publicly traded corporation that issues commercial paper. How can you inexpensively access its creditworthiness?
   b. Will the strategy in (a.) work as well if markets are inefficient?

ANSWERS TO SELF-TEST

True or False

1. True.
2. False. High transactions costs make trading more expensive, so some unexploited profit opportunities might remain.
3. False. In the 1929 crash, the market fell by 13%. In 1987, the decline was 23%.
4. True.
5. False. Savers may borrow 60%.
6. True.

Fill in the Blank

1. prices
2. inside
3. mean reversion
4. bubble
5. buy; upward
6. efficient markets
7. circuit breakers
8. financial intermediaries

Multiple Choice

1.	a	2.	c
3.	a	4.	b
5.	d	6.	a
7.	b	8.	d
9.	b	10.	c
11.	a	12.	d
13.	b.	14.	d
15.	a		

Essays

1. The three ways listed by the author are the following: (1.) Prices represent expectations of future value, (2.) long-term bond yields provide information about expected future short-term yields, and (3.) differences in interest rates in various countries reveal information about expected changes in exchange rates.

2. $PV = \$3.00 \times 1.05/(0.08 - 0.05) = \$105$.

3. *Pricing Anomalies*: Analysts have found strategies by which stock trading can result in above-normal returns.

   Mean Reversion: High-return stocks today tend to have lower returns in the future.

   Excess Volatility: The price of an asset equals the market's best estimate of its fundamental value. Fluctuations in its value should therefore be no greater than the fluctuations in the underlying fundamental value. Shiller found that this was not the case. He found that actual market price fluctuated much more than his estimates of fluctuations in fundamental value.

4. No. GM's profits, though increased, might have been less than expected, so GM's stock price fell.

5. Noise traders are traders who, by overreacting to good or bad news, can push the price of a share of stock down or up by more than would be suggested by the change in fundamental value. Bubbles are speculative episodes wherein the price of an asset is more than its fundamental value. Noise traders and bubbles were used to explain the stock market crash of 1987.

6. a. If markets are efficient, Exxon's oil discovery is already reflected in the price of Exxon stock. The best strategy is to do nothing, thereby avoiding brokerage commissions.
   b. Because noise traders overreact to news, you would want to sell Exxon stock.

7. The small-business effect is an example of a financial market anomaly. It refers to the unusually high returns that are earned historically on small business stocks. Because efficient markets should have no unexploited profit opportunities, the small-business effect (along with the January effect) is often used as evidence against the efficient markets hypothesis.

8. If markets are efficient, current market prices reflect all relevant information. Therefore, hog prices as printed in *The Wall Street Journal* or as reported on the morning Farm Report would be the best indicator of the true economic value of your livestock.

9. a. Compare the yield on Dull's commercial paper to the yield on a risk-free U.S. Treasury security with a similar maturity. Both of these yields can be found in *The Wall Street Journal*. The difference in the yields represents the risk premium.
   b. No. If markets are not efficient, the difference will not reflect all relevant information and will not be as good a signal of Dull's creditworthiness. (Of course, comparing returns is still a very inexpensive method for assessing creditworthiness and might still be a preferred approach to take.)

11: Reducing Transactions Costs and Information Costs

KEY CONCEPTS

In this chapter, we turn to a discussion of markets and intermediation. The first issue that we deal with is **financial structure**, which refers to how funds are raised. It is the determination of the mix of equity and debt used to finance investment and of the source of funds—direct finance through markets or indirect finance through intermediaries. As it turns out, both **transactions costs**, and **information costs** are important in determining optimal financial structure. By varying the mix of debt and equity, and by varying between financial markets and intermediaries, the financial system minimizes transactions costs and information costs. In so doing, the financial system allows funds to be channeled to their best use at low cost.

In the absence of transactions costs, all financial transactions would be made through markets. However, when transactions costs are substantial, it is often more efficient to use financial intermediaries because intermediaries can reduce transactions costs by taking advantage of *economies of scale*.

In Chapter 3 we introduced the concept of **asymmetric information**. Here, we return to that topic. If there were no information costs, asymmetric information would not be a problem. But information costs mean that it might not be practical to discover all relevant information. This leads to two problems:

- **Adverse selection** occurs when distinguishing a good risk from a bad risk is not possible prior to a transaction. An example would be a chronic drunk driver purchasing auto insurance meant for a safe driver.

- **Moral hazard** occurs when, after an agreement is made, one party engages in activities that are not in the best interests of the other party. An example is borrowing money from a bank to remodel your kitchen and then using the money to take a cruise around the world.

Adverse selection and moral hazard are ubiquitous in financial transactions, and much of the structure of the financial system can be explained by attempts to overcome these problems.

Adverse selection can lead to a breakdown in the financial system called **credit rationing**. This situation occurs when lenders, unable to distinguish between good and bad risks, limit the credit available to all borrowers, forcing firms to rely on internal funds. To prevent credit rationing, the financial system has developed several mechanisms.

- **Direct disclosure**: Private firms, such as Moody's and Standard and Poor's, collect information on individual borrowers and sell the information to savers. However, such private disclosures may not be adequate because of the **free-rider problem** and because firms have an incentive not to disclose adverse information about themselves. Government regulation, which requires that information be disclosed, can overcome these problems in some cases.

- **Collateral and net worth**: A poor risk will be less likely to borrow if its own assets are at risk. Therefore, lenders often require borrowers to provide **collateral** so as to discourage bad risks from applying for loans. Because **net worth** can be seized by lenders if default occurs, it works much like collateral in limiting adverse selection.

- **Financial intermediaries**: Financial intermediaries, especially banks, can be used to overcome adverse selection problems. Banks are able to do so by specializing in gathering information on default risk. They then use their superior information to direct the funds raised from depositors to the best risks. Banks are able to avoid the free-rider problem by holding the loans they make, thereby retaining all benefit from information they gathered. This explains why unknown small and medium-sized businesses depend on banks for financing.

Moral hazard, like adverse selection, is a very common problem in financial transactions. It often arises in the context of the **principal-agent problem**. In equity markets, shareholders (principals) own the net worth of the firm. Managers (agents) control the assets of the firm. Managers may pursue their own agenda at the expense of the shareholders. Managers might not have the same incentive to maximize the value of the firm as the owners do. Shareholders benefit from an increase in the price of stock, but managers might not and hence may not act to maximize the share price.

The financial system has developed a number of ways to cope with moral hazard:

- **Equity stake**: Often, managers are required to have equity stakes in the firm. That way, the managers' interests would be more in line with the interests of other shareholders.

- **Audits**: Another solution to the moral hazard problem involves audits to determine whether management is using corporate funds efficiently.

- **Debt finance**: With debt financing, the lender does not care about the profits of the firm and so does not need to monitor the firm's activities (unless the borrower defaults).

- **Financial Intermediaries**: **Venture capital firms** are financial intermediaries that specialize in emerging or growing entrepreneurial firms. Venture capital firms are able to get around the free-rider problem by holding large equity stakes and by limiting the marketing of shares in the firms they own. Thus, the venture capital firm avoids the free-rider problem because other investors are unable to buy shares in firms that they monitor. **Corporate restructuring firms** operate in a manner similar to venture capital firms but specialize in mature firms.

Check List

When you finish this chapter, you should be able to:

✔ Identify the elements of financial structure.

✔ Describe the role of transactions costs in shaping the financial system.

✔ Explain the role of economies of scale.

✔ Give three examples of how intermediaries take advantage of economies of scale.

✔ Describe the role of information costs in shaping the financial system.

✔ Describe the role of the free-rider problem and give three examples of how intermediaries help to overcome it.

✔ Distinguish between adverse selection and moral hazard.

✔ Explain how the free-rider problem makes asymmetric information problems worse.

✔ Give three examples of how financial intermediaries help to overcome asymmetric information problems.

✔ Discuss the significance of credit rationing and describe three ways the financial system responds to this problem.

✔ Discuss the significance of the principal-agent problem and describe three ways the financial system responds to this problem.

✔ Discuss the special role that banks play in lending to individuals and small businesses.

Self-Test

True or False

1. Financial intermediaries reduce adverse selection costs in financial markets. *T*

2. Most industrialized countries require information disclosure by firms before the firms can sell securities in financial markets. *T*

3. Equity financing instead of debt financing would reduce the moral hazard problem.

4. A common restrictive covenant requires the borrower to maintain a certain minimum level of net worth.

5. The need for financial intermediaries increases as monitoring costs increase.

6. A restructuring in which external equity is replaced by debt is called a *financial buyout*.

7. A greater use of debt financing relative to equity financing increases the firm's default risk.

Fill in the Blank

1. _____ _____ _____ occur when transactions costs per dollar of investment decline as the transaction's size increases.

2. Usually, small- and medium-sized businesses depend on _____ when they need external funds, whereas large, well-known corporations have access to _____ _____ _____ markets.

3. An individual who is able to obtain and use information for free from a service that is provided to others at a charge is called a _____ _____.

4. Assets pledged by a borrower that are forfeited if the borrower defaults are called _____.

5. In the early 1990s, U.S. corporations shifted from a reliance on _____ financing to _____ financing, reversing the trend of the 1980s.

6. The situation in which a group of shareholders buys a controlling interest in the firm, reshaping the board of directors and even replacing managers, is called a _____.

Multiple Choice

1. Difficulties encountered by lenders in monitoring how borrowers spend the proceeds from their loans are called
    a. moral hazard.
    b. adverse selection.
    c. hedging.
    d. speculation.

2. Which of the following is an example of the lemons problem?
   a. Sellers of good cars withdraw from the market because the average price of cars is too low.
   b. Depositors fail to monitor banks adequately because of federal deposit insurance.
   c. Banks lend to risky borrowers because of federal deposit insurance.
   d. Risky drivers buy auto insurance at a rate that is appropriate for safe drivers.

3. Credit rationing occurs when
   a. banks restrict lending rather than raising interest rates.
   b. the Fed restricts lending by banks to cool the economy.
   c. business cycles lead banks to reduce lending even to their best customers.
   d. All of the above.

4. Which of the following private agencies promotes uniform accounting principles?
   a. The Securities and Exchange Commission
   b. The Financial Accounting Standards Board
   c. The Federal Banking Authority
   d. The New York Stock Exchange

5. Direct disclosure of information is not adequate to overcome adverse selection because
   a. economies of scale are quickly exhausted.
   b. young companies may not have an adequate track record.
   c. high risk firms will attempt to report information in the best possible manner.
   d. both (b.) and (c.).

6. Banks avoid the free-rider problem by
   a. charging customers for gathering information provided to credit references.
   b. retaining loans so as to profit from information gathered.
   c. selling credit reports through Equifax and Dun & Bradstreet.
   d. refusing to make loans at any interest rate.

7. Venture capital firms overcome the free-rider problem by
   a. restricting trading in shares of the companies they invest in.
   b. requiring a fee up front from the companies they manage.
   c. shrewdly investing in firms that need restructuring.
   d. using banks and other intermediaries instead of the market.

8. The principal-agent problem is an example of
   a. adverse selection.
   b. moral hazard.
   c. the lemons problem.
   d. credit rationing.

9. Assuming no default, debt reduces monitoring cost by
    a. eliminating the need to conduct costly audits of profits.
    b. reducing the cost of capital.
    c. allowing the legal system to enforce contractual requirements.
    d. all of the above.

10. Which of the following is NOT a way to reduce information costs?
    a. lending to all those seeking to borrow
    b. government-required information disclosures
    c. free riding on others' information
    d. subscribing to information services

11. Banks are the main source of external funds for businesses because banks
    a. have access to funds that are not available to other intermediaries.
    b. are generally more profitable than other businesses.
    c. provide liquidity to depositors.
    d. specialize in gathering information.

12. Debt financing reduces information costs by
    a. guaranteeing repayment of a fixed amount.
    b. imposing restrictive covenants on borrowers.
    c. eliminating the need to audit except in default.
    d. providing lenders with a fixed share of profits.

13. SW and WS borrow $150,000 from Polar Bank to purchase a new home. As part of the loan contract, Polar Bank requires that SW and WS put up their new house as collateral. The use of collateral by Polar Bank
    a. reduces the principal that SW and WS need to borrow.
    b. increases the tax liability of SW and WS.
    c. reduces the asymmetric information advantage of SW and WS.
    d. reduces the asymmetric information advantage of Polar Bank.

14. The difference between a firm's cash receipts and cash disbursements, including payments to equityholders and debtholders, is called
    a. accounting profit.
    b. free cash flow.
    c. marginal return.
    d. net worth.

15. A form of restructuring by which a firm's managers acquire a greater stake in the firm by buying shares from shareholders is known as
    a. a marketing buyout.
    b. equity claiming.
    c. stock claiming.
    d. a management buyout.

Essays

1. Briefly discuss adverse selection in bank loans.

2. How does adverse selection inhibit growth in the economy?

3. What is the principal-agent problem in the context of the corporation? In your answer, indicate who are the principals and who are the agents.

4. Suppose that you want to start a new business. You go to your rich Uncle Oscar and ask for a loan. Uncle Oscar offers to lend you half of what you need, but only if you can borrow the other half from the bank. Is Uncle Oscar wise to force you to borrow from the bank? Why or why not?

5. A key element of financial structure is the choice between debt and equity.
   a. How does the use of debt reduce information costs?
   b. How does high debt induce borrowers to undertake undue risks?
   c. What are some ways to overcome principal-agent problems with debt?

6. The savings and loan crisis in the 1980s was in part due to the principal-agent problem. Explain.

7. Suppose that you are the credit manager for a small clothing manufacturer. Your main responsibility is deciding to whom your company should extend credit. Respond to the following questions.
   a. Why might you be willing to pay for credit reports on your customers?
   b. What is a good reference to contact directly to find out about a new potential customer called Joe's Suits, which is a small retailer?
   c. Why might Joe's Suits' bank NOT be willing to give you information?

ANSWERS TO SELF-TEST

True or False

1. True.
2. True.
3. False. Just the opposite is true. Debt financing reduces moral hazard.
4. True.
5. True.
6. False. It is called a financial takeover.
7. True.

Fill in the Blank

1. Economies of Scale
2. banks; stock and bond
3. free rider
4. collateral
5. debt; equity
6. takeover

Multiple Choice

1.	a	2.	a
3.	a	4.	b
5.	d	6.	b
7.	a	8.	b
9.	a	10.	a
11.	d	12.	c
13.	c	14.	b
15.	d		

Essays

1. The lender does not have enough information to adequately assess a borrower's creditworthiness. Without the knowledge they need, lenders have to set the terms of all loans to reflect the likelihood that they are financing some bad risks. Under these circumstances, borrowers who are bad risks are more likely to accept a loan than are borrowers who are good risks.

2. Because lenders do not have enough information to adequately assess creditworthiness, firms that are good risks have difficulty in obtaining funds at low rates. They are forced to grow by obtaining funds from other sources, which may be limited. The firms that are most affected usually are in dynamic, emerging sectors of the economy. Therefore, the opportunities for economic growth are restricted.

3. Principals are shareholders; they own the firm's net worth. Agents are the managers; they control the firm's assets. The principal-agent problem arises because managers do not own much of the firm's equity and therefore do not have the same incentive to maximize the firm's value as owners do.

4. Yes. Uncle Oscar is trying to free ride on information gathered by the banks. He figures that if the bank is willing to lend to you, you are creditworthy. Moreover, to protect its investment, the bank will monitor your actions on an ongoing basis, so Uncle Oscar will not have to.

5. a. As long as the debt is repaid, lenders do not have to monitor the borrower closely. (Of course, if the debt is not repaid, costly collection procedures have to be used.)
    b. Borrowers are more likely to undertake a project that promises a big payoff at high risk because debtholders bear the costs in default and borrowers gain the benefits in success. In effect, borrowers transfer the risks of failure to the lender while retaining the benefits of success for themselves. Therefore, the borrowers' incentives are to undertake greater risks than the lender would prefer—an example of a principal-agent problem.
    c. Requiring collateral or net worth would mean that borrowers have their own wealth at risk, reducing their incentive to undertake risk. Restrictive covenants reduce the scope for moral hazard by the borrower but at the cost of increased monitoring costs.

6. The managers of many savings and loan associations had limited ownership in their S&Ls. The interests of managers, shareholders, and regulators were therefore not closely aligned. Moreover, depositors, knowing that their deposits were insured, did not closely monitor S&Ls. Therefore, savings and loan associations suffered principal-agent problems and engaged in excessively risky lending.

7. a. A credit bureau (such as Dun & Bradstreet) is able to provide information at lower cost by taking advantage of economies of scale.
    b. Because banks specialize in gathering information on small, relatively unknown businesses, Joe's Suits' bank would be a good reference to contact.
    c. The bank does not want you to free ride on its information. (Of course, banks also want their customers to prosper, so most banks do release information on their customers to other creditors.)

KEY CONCEPTS

In Chapter 11, we discussed why borrowers choose between financial markets and financial intermediaries. This chapter turns to a discussion of the types of intermediaries that form the financial system. Financial institutions fall into five broad categories: securities market institutions, investment institutions, contractual saving institutions, depository institutions, and government financial institutions. Of these, securities market institutions are not intermediaries; rather, they help financial markets to function more smoothly (thus promoting liquidity). The other four categories of institutions are intermediaries in that they borrow from savers and lend to borrowers. We now turn to a discussion of each of the five categories.

Securities market institutions help securities markets to function smoothly by channeling funds from savers to borrowers. There are several different types of securities market institutions:

- **Investment banks** help businesses to raise new capital in primary markets. They also advise businesses on the best way to raise capital: issuing stocks or bonds and, if bonds, what type—short-term or long-term. Investment banks also earn income by **underwriting** new issues. By putting its reputation behind a new issue, the underwriting investment bank lowers information costs. By underwriting, the investment bank also reduces the risk faced by the issuing firm.

- **Brokers** promote liquidity in secondary markets by matching buyers and sellers in particular markets.

- **Dealers** promote liquidity in secondary markets by standing ready to buy or sell a security.

The second category of financial institutions is **investment institutions**. These raise funds to invest in loans and securities.

- **Mutual funds** are financial intermediaries that convert small individual claims into diversified portfolios by pooling the resources of many small savers. They obtain funds by selling shares and use the funds to purchase a diversified portfolio. Mutual funds reduce transactions costs by allowing savers to buy a diversified portfolio with only one transaction. They also provide risk sharing by holding a diversified portfolio. Mutual funds promote liquidity by guaranteeing to buy back a saver's shares quickly. Mutual fund managers provide information services through financial analyses.

- **Money market mutual funds** specialize in high-quality, short-term assets, such as Treasury bills. The underlying instruments have short maturities, which are not subject to much interest rate risk. Holding low-risk assets allows money market mutual funds to provide liquidity services by offering checking privileges.

- **Finance companies** raise funds through the sale of commercial paper or other securities and use funds to make small loans to households and businesses. As do banks, finance companies must invest in gathering and monitoring information about borrowers' default risk. However, finance companies do not accept deposits.

The next type of financial intermediary is **contractual savings institutions**. They offer contracts that require individuals to make payments in a disciplined manner over time. There are two major types of contractual savings institutions:

- **Insurance companies** specialize in writing contracts to protect their policyholders from the risk of financial loss associated with particular events.

- **Pension funds** invest contributions of workers and firms into stocks, bonds, and mortgages so as to provide pension benefits during the worker's retirement.

Depository institutions are the most important type of financial intermediary. They differ from other intermediaries in that they both accept deposits and make loans.

- **Commercial banks**: Although they provide risk sharing and liquidity services, the most significant service provided by commercial banks is to reduce information costs. By gathering information about borrowers' default risk, they reduce adverse selection problems. Banks further reduce information costs by monitoring the borrower after the loan is made, thereby reducing moral hazard.

- **Saving institutions** specialize in mortgage lending.

- **Credit unions** specialize in consumer loans. Often, they are organized around a societal group, such as the employees of a particular company.

Besides private sector intermediaries, the U.S. government participates in financial markets directly through government-sponsored financial institutions and indirectly through loan guarantees.

Check List

When you finish this chapter, you should be able to:

✔ Distinguish among the five categories of financial institutions.

✔ Distinguish among investment bankers, dealers, and brokers.

- ✔ Distinguish among mutual funds, money market mutual funds, finance companies, insurance companies, pension funds, commercial banks, saving institutions, and credit unions.

- ✔ Identify the source of funds of each financial institution.

- ✔ Identify the use of funds of each financial institution.

- ✔ Identify the financial services provided by each financial institution.

Self-Test

True or False

1. Advertisements in *The Wall Street Journal* in which investment banks market new issues to institutional investors are called gravestones.

2. Buyers and sellers of securities are matched on the floor of the New York Stock Exchange by a broker-dealer known as a socialist.

3. The type of insurance company that sells protection to households and firms from risk of theft, fire, accident, or natural disasters is referred to as a property and casualty company.

4. Whole life policies pay off only at the death of the policyholder and have no cash value.

5. A university bases retirement benefits on the average income of the employee during his or her last five years of service multiplied by total years of service. This type of pension program is referred to as a defined benefit plan.

6. Today, the overlap in services provided by depository institutions is greater than it was 40 years ago.

7. One argument against government intervention in the financial system is that government-sponsored agencies compete against private sector lenders.

8. Money market deposit accounts have been in existence for a longer period of time than have many market mutual funds.

9. It is more difficult for an insurance company to protect against adverse selection in an individual plan than it would be in a group plan.

10. One reason pension funds are attractive is that they offer certain tax breaks that straight salary does not.

11. With the elimination of banks, the ratio of small to large businesses would most likely increase.

12. Depository institution's market share of financial services provided has been eroded since 1980 because of deregulation.

13. Expansion of investment banking should lead to an increase in capital formation in the United States.

14. The bid-asked spreads for corporate bonds are higher than those for U.S. government securities because they are less liquid

Fill in the Blank

1. A small issue is usually handled by a single underwriter. A large issue is often handled by a group of underwriters called a _____.

2. The _____ _____ _____ _____ regulates brokers and dealers to ensure disclosure of information and the prevention of fraud.

3. Mutual funds that charge management fees but no commissions are called _____ - _____ funds.

4. The practice by which business finance companies purchase accounts receivable of a small firm at a discount and hold them until maturity for a profit is called _____.

5. An auto insurance company that requires an owner to install an anti-theft device on his or her vehicle to receive anti-theft insurance is inserting a _____ _____ into their policy.

6. Insurance companies are regulated at the _____ level of government.

7. _____ refers to the length of service required before an employee is entitled to future pension benefits.

8. Government lending to _____ is the oldest U.S. government intervention in financial markets, whereas government intermediation for _____ is the largest of the government lending activities.

9. _____ life insurance pays off only at the death of the policy holder and has no accrued cash value.

10. Statisticians known as _____ compile probability tables to help predict event risk in the population.

11. Named after the Internal Revenue Code in which they are described, _____ plans give an employee the opportunity to make tax-deductible contributions through regular payroll deductions.

Multiple Choice

1. The author lists five broad groups of financial institutions. Finance companies would fall in the category of
    a. contractual saving institutions.
    b. investment institutions.
    c. depository institutions.
    d. security market institutions.

2. By placing their reputations on the line concerning the businesses they underwrite, investment bankers provide which financial service?
    a. risk-sharing services
    b. liquidity services
    c. information services
    d. transaction services

3. Secondary markets
    a. can be organized as exchanges.
    b. can be organized as over-the-counter markets.
    c. provide liquidity and risk sharing.
    d. all of the above.

4. Investment institutions that channel funds from small savers to various borrowers by selling shares in a portfolio of financial assets are called
    a. mutual funds.
    b. no-load funds.
    c. finance companies.
    d. commercial banks.

5. You want to buy a refrigerator at EZ Appliance. Because you do not have $1200 cash, you fill out a loan application with Blazer Financial that allows you to pay off the refrigerator in 24 monthly installments. Blazer is an example of a
    a. consumer bank.
    b. consumer finance company.
    c. dealer company.
    d. brokerage company.

6. Your friend Harry refuses to install a sprinkler system in his hotel. "I am covered by insurance, after all," he says. This is an example of
   a. normal hazard.
   b. risk aversion.
   c. adverse selection.
   d. moral hazard.

7. Insurance companies screen clients prior to selling insurance because they want to reduce the costs associated with
   a. normal hazard.
   b. risk aversion.
   c. adverse selection.
   d. moral hazard.

8. Monica's insurance policy requires her to pay 30 % of the cost of her medical care. This is an example of
   a. coinsurance.
   b. a deductible.
   c. a risk-based premium.
   d. moral hazard.

9. A defined benefit plan for which contributions together with projected future earnings are insufficient to pay the projected defined benefits is said to be
   a. zero funded.
   b. underfunded.
   c. fully funded.
   d. deductible.

10. Which depository institution specializes in real estate loans?
    a. money market mutual fund
    b. commercial banks
    c. savings and loan associations
    d. credit unions

11. Julie Seagall is the owner-operator of a small beauty salon. She told the bank that she would use her loan to finance the purchase of new equipment but she used the funds instead to build a pool in her backyard. This is an example of
    a. adverse selection.
    b. moral hazard.
    c. free-rider problems.
    d. lemon problems.

12. By screening potential borrowers, banks reduce
    a. adverse selection.
    b. moral hazard.
    c. free-rider problems.
    d. lemons problems.

13. By monitoring the operations of borrowers, banks reduce
    a. adverse selection.
    b. moral hazard.
    c. free-rider problems.
    d. lemons problems.

14. The U.S. government participates in financial intermediation
    a. through government sponsored financial institutions such as the Federal Home
       Loan Mortgage Company.
    b. through guaranteeing loans made by private financial institutions.
    c. by printing an endless supply of money.
    d. both (a.) and (b.).

15. Which of the following is NOT a government-sponsored agency involved in the
    mortgage market?
    a. Sally Mae
    b. Ginnie Mae
    c. Freddie Mac
    d. Fannie Mae

Essays

1. One service that an investment bank performs is underwriting. What is
   underwriting? In your answer, also discuss the spread.

2. Why are actuaries vital for the successful operation of insurance companies?

3. The volume of transactions in over-the-counter markets has grown rapidly in recent
   years compared to the volume on exchanges. What led to this development?

4. Recent developments in genetics raise the possibility of using genetic screening to
   determine individuals' susceptibility to many diseases.
   a. Why do such advances make adverse selection more of a problem in health
      insurance markets?
   b. What action might an insurance company take to protect itself from adverse
      selection?
   c. If the federal government prohibits the use of genetic screening by insurance
      companies, what is likely to happen?

5. Suppose that a state government required all drivers to carry insurance.
   a. Would such compulsory insurance eliminate adverse selection?
   b. Would insurance companies still charge risk-based premiums?
   c. Why might the state also require insurance companies to charge all policyholders the same premium?
   d. What might insurance companies do in response to the restriction in (c.)?

6. Why is health insurance that is purchased through an employer-based group plan less expensive than individual health insurance?

7. The text emphasizes the risk of moral hazard by policyholders toward insurance companies. But do policyholders also face moral hazard from insurance companies? Why or why not?

8. Explain how investment banking leads to an increase in capital formation.

9. How do term life and whole life policies differ?

10. The interest rate on a 30-year FHA home mortgage loan is usually below what it would be on a 30-year conventional home mortgage loan. Why?

ANSWERS TO SELF-TEST

True or False

1. False. The advertisements in *The Wall Street Journal* are called tombstones.
2. False. Buyers and sellers of securities are matched by specialists.
3. True.
4. False. This statement describes term life. A whole life policy does have a cash value, and that cash value can either be withdrawn at retirement or converted into annual payments.
5. True.
6. True.
7. True.
8. False. Money market deposit accounts became available in only 1982.
9. False. An insurance company is relatively helpless in protecting itself from adverse selection in a group plan. However, in the case of an individual, the company can gather information to prevent adverse selection from occurring.
10. True.
11. False. Small businesses rely far more on banks for financing than do large firms. Without banks, many small firms would disappear, causing the ratio to fall, not rise.
12. True.
13. True.
14. True.

Fill in the Blank

1. syndicate
2. Securities and Exchange Commission
3. no-load
4. factoring
5. restrictive covenant
6. state
7. Vesting
8. agriculture; housing
9. Term
10. actuaries
11. 401K

Multiple Choice

1. b   2. c
3. d   4. a
5. b   6. d

7. c   8. a
9. b   10. c
11. b   12. a
13. b   14. d
15. a

Essays

1. Underwriting is one way in which an investment bank earns income. The investment bank guarantees a price for the securities that the issuing firm is selling. The bank then tries to sell the issue at a higher price and keep the difference as profit. The spread is the difference between the price for which the investment bank sells the securities and the guaranteed price. The issuing firm is willing to allow a spread to pay for the informational value of the reputation that the investment bank puts behind the new issue.

2. To correctly set premiums, insurance companies use the law of large numbers to determine expected payouts. Actuaries have specialized skills in using the law of large numbers.

3. In the past, because agreeing on a single location to meet reduced transactions costs, exchanges had an advantage over the over-the-counter markets. Advances in telecommunications and computer technology, however, have made the over-the-counter market more competitive. In fact, some economists believe that exchanges will eventually cease to operate.

4. a. Individuals who learned that they were susceptible to a genetic disease would attempt to obtain health insurance. However, those who found that they were not susceptible to genetic diseases would be less likely to buy health insurance. Therefore adverse selection would be more of a problem. (Notice that the victim of the genetic disease who remained ignorant would be no more likely to obtain insurance than the average person, and there would not be a problem. It is the existence of asymmetric information that is the problem.)
    b. Insurance companies are likely to start screening for genetic diseases.
    c. The cost of health insurance would increase. This response would cause more low-risk individuals to drop out of the market. In the extreme, the health insurance market might completely break down.

5. a. No. Insurance companies could still *skim the cream* by charging lower premiums and then accepting only low-risk individuals. Of course, high-risk individuals also would try to obtain the low-cost insurance, creating an adverse selection problem. Therefore, insurance companies would have to continue to incur the cost of screening potential clients.
    b. Yes, if they wanted to *skim the cream*.

    c.   Because insurance companies would charge all clients the same and because they would be required to accept all risks, this restriction would eliminate cream skimming, greatly reducing the expense associated with adverse selection.

    d.   Because it is still profitable, insurance companies will still try to *skim the cream*. For example, they might open offices in areas of a city with fewer accidents, so as to get better clients on average.

6.   There are two reasons: (1.) Individuals who are well enough to work are less likely to have major health problems, and (2.) if all members of the group are covered, there is less chance of adverse selection.

7.   Yes. For example, an insurance company might attempt to avoid paying a legitimate claim.

8.   A small company or even larger companies might want to raise money for expansion. Investment bankers help them to do this.

9.   Whole life requires a constant premium over the life of the policy. The premium required by a term policy varies with the age of the insured. Whole life policyholders can borrow against the cash value, and individuals can either withdraw the total cash value at retirement or turn that value into an annuity. Term life pays off only at the death of the policyholder; the policy has no cash value. Hence premiums reflect only the probability of the policyholder dying during the insured interval.

10.   The FHA loan is guaranteed by the federal government and is therefore not subject to default risk.

13: THE BUSINESS OF BANKING

KEY CONCEPTS

The next several chapters focus on banking. In this chapter, we discuss the business of banking, that is, how banks manage their assets and liabilities to maintain liquidity, minimize risk, while at the same time exploiting profitable activities. Banking is an important industry, and in most developed countries, commercial banks are the leading financial intermediaries. As intermediaries, banks' primary profit-making activities entail acquiring funds from savers and lending those funds to borrowers while adding value by providing risk sharing, liquidity, and information services. Much of the focus in this chapter is on the bank's balance sheet, which lists its assets, liabilities, and net worth. Net worth is particularly important in banking, as it provides a buffer against the risk that depositors or other lenders will lose part of their investment should the bank suffer losses. However, banks have an incentive to reduce their net worth so as to increase their expected rate of return. Therefore, much of bank regulation focuses on banks' net worth. If a bank has inadequate equity, a **bank failure** could occur.

Banks earn profits by providing financial services to savers. They provide risk sharing by investing in a diversified loan portfolio. They provide liquidity services through deposits. And banks are actively involved in gathering and monitoring information about borrowers. The role of banks in reducing information costs is particularly important, as savers can obtain risk sharing and liquidity services from other types of intermediaries. Indeed, without banks, information costs would prevent many small borrowers from participating in the financial system. A potential problem that can arise in banking is moral hazard. There are two possible solutions to the problems of moral hazard:

- Depositors can use debt contracts to discipline banks. If a bank fails to meet stipulated payments, the bank's owners will lose their equity stake. The threat that depositors will withdraw their deposits also serves as a constraint on bankers' behavior.

- A second means of preventing moral hazard is to mandate the amount of capital invested by bankers and other shareholders. Bankers will act more responsibly when their own wealth is at risk.

Savers and banks must also be concerned with **liquidity risk**, which is the possibility that depositors may decide unexpectedly to withdraw more funds than the bank has on hand. Such a situation would force banks to sell illiquid loans, possibly taking a loss by receiving less than the loans' full value. Banks want to reduce their exposure to liquidity risk without sacrificing too much in forgone returns. To deal with liquidity risk, banks engage in asset management and liability management:

- Asset management involves structuring assets so that they are liquid but still earn interest.

- With liability management, the bank must weigh the increased liquidity risk that arises from borrowing short term against the increased interest rate risk from borrowing long term.

Two principal challenges are involved in the relationship between borrowers and banks. These are managing credit risk and managing interest rate risk. Credit risk arises from the possibility of default by the borrower. Banks attempt to minimize credit risk through diversification and by using **credit-risk analysis**. Indeed, expertise in credit-risk analysis is a major reason for using a bank. To limit adverse selection and moral hazard problems, banks may require collateral. Nevertheless, some borrowers may be subjected to **credit rationing**. That is, borrowers may not be able to borrow as much as they want at the going rate. To reduce moral hazard, banks monitor borrowers to make sure that they do not use the funds borrowed from the bank to pursue risky activities. A good way for the bank to gather information about a borrower or to monitor a borrower is for the bank to have a long-term relationship with the borrower. The borrower also gains from this long-term relationship by obtaining credit at a lower interest rate or with fewer restrictions.

Interest rate risk arises from changes in interest rates that affect the value of a bank's financial assets and liabilities. The **duration** of a bank's asset or liability is the responsiveness of the percentage change in the asset's or liability's market value to a percentage change in the market interest rate. The difference between the duration of assets and the duration of liabilities is the **duration gap**. It is a measure of the bank's exposure to interest rate risk. By reducing the size of the duration gap, the bank reduces its interest rate risk exposure. Banks can reduce interest rate risk by issuing **floating-rate debt** and through **interest rate swaps**.

Check List

When you finish this chapter, you should be able to:

✓ Describe the assets and liabilities that are found on a typical bank balance sheet.

✓ Understand why much of banking regulation focuses on net worth.

✓ Describe the role of reserves, marketable securities, and equity capital in limiting the risk of a bank failure.

✓ Explain how asset and liability management is used to mitigate liquidity risk.

✓ Discuss the significance of moral hazard and adverse selection and describe strategies for dealing with it.

✓ Describe the role of credit risk analysis, collateral, credit rationing, monitoring and restrictive covenants, and long-term relationships in limiting credit risk.

✔ Discuss the significance of interest rate risk and describe two strategies for dealing with it.

✔ Calculate duration gap and use it to evaluate interest rate risk.

✔ Discuss the significance of off-balance-sheet lending and credit card lending.

Self-Test

True or False

1. Checkable deposits that offer interest are called NOW accounts.

2. Time deposits in excess of $50,000 are negotiable CDs and can be bought and sold in the secondary market prior to maturity.

3. A bank with inadequate reserves can borrow from the Fed through the discount window.

4. The responsiveness of the percentage change in the asset's or liability's market value to a percentage change in the market interest rate is called the discount value of the bank.

5. Firms that issue commercial paper often get standby letters of credit, which promise that the bank will lend the firm funds to pay off their maturing commercial paper if necessary.

6. Credit cards typically charge interest rates that are two percentage points above prime.

7. Checkable deposits as a percentage are a larger source of funds to a bank today than they were in 1960.

8. Banks hold approximately the same amount of Treasury securities as corporate securities.

9. The interest rate on federal funds is usually below that on long-term U.S. government securities.

10. A bank cannot legally offer a long-time customer a lower rate on a loan than it offers a new customer.

Fill in the Blank

1. A _____ _____ is a statement showing an individual's or a firm's financial position at a particular time.

2. Bank holdings of U.S. government securities are sometimes called _____ _____.

3. Transaction and nontransaction accounts are insured by the government up to $_____.

4. Interbank loans occur in the _____ _____ market.

5. Assets minus liabilities equal _____ _____.

6. Assets that are pledged to a bank in the event that the borrower defaults are called _____.

7. A _____, which is a financial contract by which a bank agrees to sell the expected future returns from an underlying bank loan to a third party, is an example of an _____ - _____ - _____ transaction.

8. The banking industry in _____ faced problems in the mid-1990s that were similar to those of U.S. banks in the 1980s as a result of poor real estate lending decisions and poor management.

Multiple Choice

1. Which of the following is the most liquid bank asset?
   a. cash items in the process of collection
   b. reserves
   c. marketable securities
   d. loans

2. Which of the following is the least liquid bank asset?
   a. cash items in the process of collection
   b. reserves
   c. marketable securities
   d. loans

3. The largest source of bank funds is
   a. checkable deposits.
   b. Treasury securities.
   c. loans.
   d. nontransaction deposits.

4. The primary type of loans made by credit unions is
   a. mortgage loans.
   b. business loans.
   c. consumer loans.
   d. government loans.

5. What three important financial services do banks provide their customers?
   a. risk sharing, liquidity, and information
   b. risk sharing, information, and high return
   c. high return, information, and liquidity
   d. liquidity, high return, and risk sharing

6. Duration gap refers to
   a. the percentage change in the value of assets resulting from a change in interest rates.
   b. the percentage change in the value of liabilities resulting from a change in interest rates.
   c. the difference in the percentage change in the value of assets and liabilities resulting from a change in interest rates.
   d. the percentage change in the value of net worth resulting from a change in interest rates.

Use the following information to answer questions 7 through 9. Assume that the reserve requirement ratio is 10%.

Assets		Liabilities	
Reserves	20	Deposits	250
Marketable securities	50	Borrowing in the	
Loans	300	Fed funds market	50
		Net worth	70

7. Which of the following is NOT a means by which the bank could raise funds to meet its reserve requirement?
   a. Increase lending
   b. Sell marketable securities
   c. Borrow at the discount window
   d. Borrow in the Fed funds market

8. If the bank decided to borrow from the Fed, how much would the bank need to borrow?
   a. 10
   b 5
   c. 30
   d. 25

9. What is the capital asset ratio of this bank?
   a. 5.29
   b. 0.23
   c. 0.19
   d. 4.29

10. In managing credit risk, banks must be concerned about
    a. adverse selection.
    b. moral hazard.
    c. diversification.
    d. all of the above.

11. A *credit-scoring* system is a mechanism for
    a. calculating the duration gap.
    b. determining the overall riskiness of a loan portfolio.
    c. evaluating the productivity of loan officers.
    d. evaluating the likelihood of default.

12. Standby letters of credit make issuing commercial paper easier by
    a. reducing interest rate risk.
    b. ensuring that the commercial paper issuer will have funds to redeem the paper at maturity.
    c. ensuring that interest rate fluctuations are small relative to the overall value of the commercial paper.
    d. eliminating all illiquidity in the commercial paper market prior to issuing the commercial paper.

13. Bank net worth over the past three decades has remained relatively stable at about _____ of total funds raised.
    a. 3% to 5%
    b. 7% to 9%
    c. 12% to 14%
    d. 25%

14. Woodlands Bank is offering a 5% interest rate on its one-year CDs. It would be reasonable to expect that the prime rate will be
    a. above 5%.
    b. below 5%.
    c. 5%.
    d. above or below 5%, depending on what the inflation rate is.

15. Swaps are used to protect a bank against
    a. interest rate risk.
    b. liquidity risk.
    c. credit risk.
    d. default risk.

Essays

1. Why are savers willing to accept a lower interest rate on checkable deposits than on time deposits?

2. How does a time deposit differ from a saving deposit?

3. What are bank reserves, and why do banks hold them?

4. Savings and loan associations have moved away from making 30-year fixed-rate mortgages toward shorter-term loans. What effect should this shift have on the duration gap for S&Ls? In your answer, explain what a duration gap is.

5. Calculate the duration of a liability that requires payment of $1,000 at the end of each of the next three years if the initial interest rate is 8%. By how much will the market value of the liability change if the market interest rate falls from 8% to 5%?

6. What is the duration gap for a bank that has assets of $153 m. with a duration of 17 and liabilities of $105 m. with a duration of 14?

7. Suppose that you are the president of a bank. One of your managers has suggested to you that the bank more aggressively market variable rate mortgages.
   a. What would be the effect of such a strategy on the bank's duration gap?
   b. Would you expect mortgage default rates to rise or fall if the strategy were adopted? Why?
   c. Should the bank adopt your manager's idea? Why or why not?

8. Why are commercial bank deposits debts rather than equities?

9. The primary reason for regulating commercial banks is federal deposit insurance. Comment.

10. Bank regulators require banks to maintain a percentage of their assets as capital.
    a. Why do regulators impose capital requirements?
    b. Suppose that you are a banker. What strategies might you adopt to get around a capital requirement?
    c. Do the strategies you adopted in (b.) increase the risk that your bank faces?
    d. Now suppose that you are a government regulator. Is there a need for changes in regulations governing banking?

11. Compare and contrast a large- versus a small-denomination time deposit offered by a bank. Why might a risk-averse person prefer a small-denomination time deposit?

12. Because of the bank failures in the 1980s, the government decides that anyone opening a new bank has to contribute more of their own funds. How should this affect the moral hazard faced by the depositors of these banks? What effect would a reduction in the number of bank examiners have? Explain.

13. Match the following three off-balance-sheet bank lending innovations with their definition
    a.   standby letter of credit
    b.   loan commitments
    c.   loan sales

    (1) The bank agrees to provide a borrower with a stated amount of funds during some specified period of time.
    (2) The bank promises to lend a borrower funds to pay off the borrower's maturing commercial paper if necessary.
    (3) The bank agrees to sell the expected future returns from an underlying bank loan to a third party.

ANSWERS TO SELF-TEST

True or False

1. True.
2. False. Time deposits in excess of $100,000 are negotiable.
3. True.
4. False. It is called the duration.
5. True.
6. False. Credit card rates are usually far higher than 2% above prime.
7. False. Today, they are approximately 13%. In 1960, they were 60%.
8. False. Banks do not usually hold corporate securities.
9. True.
10. False. Banks can and do offer lower rates to long-time customers. With the long-time customer, there is probably less chance of default. In addition, the costs of information gathering and monitoring would be lower for such customers.

Fill in the Blank

1. balance sheet
2. secondary reserves
3. 100,000
4. federal funds
5. net worth (or equity capital)
6. collateral
7. swap; off-balance-sheet
8. Japan

Multiple Choice

1. b   2. d
3. d   4. c
5. a   6. c
7. a   8. b
9. c   10. d
11. d   12. b
13. b   14. a
15. a

Essays

1. Checkable deposits are highly liquid, and savers are willing to exchange some interest for greater liquidity.

2. Time deposits have a specified maturity date, have a significant penalty for early withdrawal, and are not as liquid as a savings deposit.

3. Bank reserves consist of vault cash, cash on hand in the banks, and deposits with the Federal Reserve System. The Fed requires banks to hold reserves, providing banks with liquidity to meet withdrawals from demandable deposits. Banks may also choose to hold excess reserves.

4. The duration gap is the difference between the average duration for the S&L assets and liabilities. By moving toward shorter-term loans, the S&Ls reduce their duration gap. Duration is the responsiveness of the percentage change in the asset's or liability's market value to a percentage change in the market interest rate.

5. $MV = 1000/1.08 + 1000/1.08^2 + 1000/1.08^3 = \$2,577.10$.
    $d = \{[(1000/1.08)/2577.10] + [2(1000/1.08^2)/2577.10] + [3(1000/1.08^3)/2577.10]\}$
    $= 1.95$. $\Delta MV/MV \cong -1.95(-0.03/1.08) = 5.42\%$.

6. Duration gap $= 17 - 14[105/153] = 7.39$.

7. a. The duration gap would be reduced because changes in interest rates would have less effect on the value of assets.
    b. Mortgage default rates would likely increase because, at times, high interest rates will cause mortgage payments to rise, which might cause some marginal borrowers to default.
    c. It depends. The bank must strike a balance between interest rate risk and default risk.

8. Banks specialize in gathering information on lesser-known individuals and companies. (After all, if the bank's customers were well-known, they would use financial markets directly instead of going through a bank.) Hence the performance of the bank's portfolio of investments (e.g., loans) is particularly costly to evaluate. By structuring deposits as debts, depositors need only audit the bank when it defaults. Thus, using debt reduces information costs.

9. Without deposit insurance, depositors and other lenders to the bank would screen potential banks to prevent adverse selection and monitor the bank to minimize moral hazard problems. Federal deposit insurance, however, removes the incentive for depositors to screen and monitor banks, increasing the scope for adverse selection and moral hazard. To counteract this potential, the government regulates banks more closely than other industries.

10. a. Since bank deposits are covered by federal deposit insurance, banks have an incentive to undertake undue risk. High capital levels reduce the incentive for management to engage in these excessively risky activities. That is, high capital requirements reduce moral hazard.

   b. Any off-balance-sheet activity, because it does not affect the value of the balance sheet, may be used to increase revenues while still meeting capital requirements.

   c. They certainly can. For example, an economic downturn could mean that the bank must honor standby letters of credit just as the bank is facing other difficulties.

   d. Possibly yes. Bank regulations are designed to overcome the moral hazard problems that arise from federal deposit insurance. Off-balance-sheet activities are another potential source of moral hazard problems that might require regulation.

11. A large-denomination time deposit is over $100,000 and negotiable. A small-denomination time deposit is under $100,000 and not negotiable, and there is a penalty for early withdrawal. A risk-averse individual might want to avoid a large-denomination time deposit, since deposits over $100,000 are not insured.

12. Having greater capital requirements would cause moral hazard to fall. Shareholders of the bank would have more of their own funds at risk. Having fewer bank examiners would increase moral hazard because banks would be aware that the chance of the government spotting high-risk loans would be diminished. Also, the chance of being fined would go down.

13. a. 2
   b. 1
   c. 3

14: THE BANKING INDUSTRY

KEY CONCEPTS

This chapter extends the discussion of banking from the management of individual banks to the banking industry as a whole. The emphasis is on the role of government regulation. Government is interested in regulating banks because of the need to ensure confidence in the banking system by maintaining liquidity. If depositors start to question the value of a bank's underlying assets, loss of confidence in the bank can occur. This loss of confidence by itself can trigger a **bank run**, in which depositors withdraw their funds because of fear of capital loss if the bank fails. Even if the bank's assets are sound, the need to liquidate assets to meet huge withdrawals can result in losses, causing the bank to be unable to meet all its obligations to depositors. The failure of one bank can result in a loss of confidence in other banks, a process known as **contagion**. Banks are subject to runs when other financial institutions typically are not because banks specialize in providing financial services to small, lesser-known businesses and individuals. Conveying information about a portfolio of loans held by the typical bank is very costly, so dispelling depositors' ignorance about the bank's true creditworthiness is difficult. In overcoming these problems, government regulation can be helpful.

Initially, U.S. banking regulation reflected the fears of rural populists concerning big city banking interests, particularly those in New York City. The National Banking Act of 1863 established the current **dual banking system** of state and federal regulation. Under the act, **national banks** are supervised by the Office of the Comptroller of the Currency, which is part of the U.S. Treasury Department. **State banks** are supervised by state authorities. There have been three major regulatory interventions in the banking industry since passage of the National Banking Act:

- the establishment of the Federal Reserve System as lender of last resort in 1913,

- the creation of **federal deposit insurance** during the Great Depression, and

- the implementation of restrictions on bank competition, especially **branching restrictions**.

The regulatory process starts when an application for a federal charter is filed with the Office of the Comptroller of the Currency or, for a state charter, with the appropriate state authority. After a bank receives a charter, it must file quarterly reports about earnings, assets and liabilities, and operations. Regulators also periodically examine the bank's financial conditions to ensure that the bank is in compliance with regulations. When examiners find problems with excessive risk taking or low net worth, they may classify the bank as a **problem bank**, subjecting the bank to more frequent examinations.

If the bank's net worth declines sufficiently, then regulators close it, and depositors are paid off by federal deposit insurance. Most commercial banks and savings institutions are insured by the **Federal Deposit Insurance Corporation** (FDIC). Credit unions are insured by the National Credit Union Insurance Fund. The federal deposit insurers generally use one of two methods to handle bank failures:

- **Payoff method**: The bank closes, and insured depositors are paid off.

- **Purchase and assumption method**: The bank is continued as a going concern by finding a financial institution that is willing to take over the bank.

Although the introduction of federal deposit insurance increased confidence in the banking system, it also weakened the incentive for savers to monitor banks, increasing the scope for moral hazard. Indeed, much of the regulation of the banking industry in the United States is an attempt to limit moral hazard on the part of banks arising as a by-product of deposit insurance. One way in which the FDIC and other regulators control moral hazard is by restricting the assets that banks can hold. A second way is to require banks to maintain a minimum net worth.

One important restriction imposed on banks has been on branching activity. Geographic restrictions may push banks toward local lending, lowering the cost of providing risk sharing, liquidity, and information services. However, because restrictions on branching protect inefficient banks by limiting competition, most economists believe that they are counterproductive. Restrictions reduce banks' ability to diversify assets. Also, because of fixed costs of funding individual banks, the large number of banks that result from branching restrictions may reduce banks' efficiency. Recent regulatory changes have, in effect, created a system of nationwide branching.

Check List

When you finish this chapter, you should be able to:

- Discuss the significance of the First and Second Banks of the United States, the Free Banking Era, the National Banking Act, the Federal Reserve Act, and federal deposit insurance

- Discuss the significance of information costs in bank runs and in the contagion effect.

- Understand that the major justification for regulation is the prevention of bank panics.

- Describe the regulatory process including the roles played by chartering, examination, and deposit insurance.

- Distinguish between the payoff method and the purchase and assumption method.

- Describe the role of lender of last resort, deposit insurance, and restrictions on competition.

- Discuss the impact of the Glass-Steagall Act on the banking industry.

- Recognize the major differences between banking in the United States, Japan, and Germany and discuss the significance of *keiretsu* and universal banking.

Self-Test

True or False

1. The United States has a dual banking system.

2. The FDIC was created in 1913.

3. As a consequence of deregulation, the number of bank failures increased during the 1980s.

4. The inflows from FDIC insurance premiums have always exceeded outflows.

5. More than 40 states provide some degree of interstate banking.

6. Universal banking is now permitted in both the United States and Germany.

7. Main banks in Japan usually charge a higher interest rate on loans than what is charged in the bond markets.

8. Europe is moving away from greater banking integration.

9. One reason why the banking industry in the United States is not highly concentrated is the McFadden Act.

10. The Bank of Japan is the central bank of that country.

11. The existence of deposit insurance encourages banks not to engage in risky activities.

12. The amount of bonuses paid on Wall Street would increase if banks were allowed to engage in activities that are currently limited to investment banking.

Fill in the Blank

1. National banks are supervised by the U.S. Treasury through the Office of the

    _____ _____ _____ _____.

2. The spread of bad news about one bank that raises concerns about the health of other banks is called _____.

3. The FDIC generally uses two methods to handle bank failures. They are the payoff method and the _____ _____ _____ method.

4. One large company that holds many different banks as subsidiaries is called a

    _____ _____ _____.

5. A _____ _____ affects an individual bank, whereas a _____ _____ is a generalized run against the banking system.

6. Many large Japanese firms are affiliated with one of the six major industrial groups called _____.

7. The central bank of Germany is called the _____.

8. The term "wildcat banking" describes the period of banking called the _____ _____ Period that began in 1836.

9. _____ machines and the creation of _____ _____ companies were two ways in which banks were able to get around branching restrictions.

10. Allowing banks to participate in nonfinancial activities is called _____ banking.

Multiple Choice

1. In 1992, seven of the ten largest banks in the world were located in
    a. the United States.
    b. Japan.
    c. France.
    d. Germany.

2. The U.S. Treasury Secretary who tried to establish a nationwide banking system in 1791 was
    a. Aaron Burr.
    b. James Adams.
    c. Andrew Jackson.
    d. Alexander Hamilton.

3. Congress created the Federal Reserve System in
    a. 1890.
    b. 1913.
    c. 1935.
    d. 1940.

4. The government agency that is responsible for supervising bank holding companies is the
    a. Federal Reserve System.
    b. Securities and Exchange Commission.
    c. FDIC.
    d. State Banking Commission.

5. The FDIC initially insured deposits up to _____ and now insures them up to _____
    a. $20,000; $50,000
    b. $5000; $50,000
    c. $10,000; $100,000
    d. $2500; $100,000

6. The Banking Act of 1933, which prohibited commercial banks from participating in underwriting corporate securities and brokerage activities, is also called the
    a. Glass-Steagall Act.
    b. McFadden Act.
    c. Morgan-Stanley Act.
    d. Kemp-Roth Act.

7. Banks are subject to runs because they
    a. specialize in lending to businesses that have high information costs.
    b. offer deposits that are liquid, allowing panic to be easily acted on.
    c. are overregulated, restricting their ability to offer stable contracts.
    d. face excessive competition from other intermediaries.

8. Bank runs impose costs on society by
    a. disrupting the ongoing relationship between banks and borrowers.
    b. increasing the cost of gathering information about small borrowers.
    c. leading to a contagion effect that can result in a bank panic.
    d. all of the above.

9. The monitoring of banks is necessary because
    a. bankers are often incompetent and need guidance.
    b. bankers are often more dishonest than other businesspeople.
    c. bankers have private information about their loan portfolio.
    d. federal law requires the FDIC to monitor banks closely.

10. Federal regulation of banking is necessary when federal deposit insurance is in force because
    a. federally chartered banks must be monitored by law.
    b. bank managers seek to obtain deposit insurance only when they know that their loan portfolio is subject to unusual risk (adverse selection).
    c. bank managers seek to obtain deposit insurance only when they plan on financing new loans that are subject to unusual risk (moral hazard).
    d. the presence of deposit insurance reduces the incentive for depositors to monitor banks.

11. Clackamas Cement Company has gone to the bank seeking a series of loans to finance the massive expansion of its business. If Clackamas's expansion proves successful, it will be able to repay its loans in full, earning a healthy profit for the bank. If its expansion fails, Clackamas will default, sticking the bank with large losses. The bank is MOST likely to finance Clackamas when the bank _____ covered by federal deposit insurance and has _____ capital.
    a. is not; adequate
    b. is; adequate
    c. is not; inadequate
    d. is; inadequate

12. Universal banking refers to the practice of allowing
    a. anyone to deposit funds, regardless of social or economic circumstances.
    b. lending to any borrower, regardless of social or economic circumstances.
    c. banks and other types of businesses to be combined in one firm, with no geographic restriction.
    d. international borrowing and lending by banks, without regard to national origin.

13. Which of the following countries allows universal banking?
    a. United States
    b. Japan
    c. Germany
    d. All three countries allow universal banking.

14. There are _____ Federal Home Loan Bank districts.
    a. 7
    b. 11
    c. 12
    d. 20

15. The insurance premiums that are paid on deposits by the savings and loans and commercial banks to the FDIC are
    a. the same.
    b. higher for savings and loans.
    c. higher for commercial banks.
    d. premiums that used to be paid but are no longer.

Essays

1. What did the McFadden Act of 1927 do?

2. Ironically, the large number of banks in the United States indicates a lack of competition. Explain.

3. Complete the following table.

Type of Institution	Primary Regulator	Insurer
National Bank		
State bank that is a member of the Fed		
State bank that is not a member of the Fed		
Savings and loan association		
Credit union		
Bank holding company		

4. In an attempt to prevent bank failures, Congress created the Federal Reserve System as a lender of last resort. Explain how that works.

5. If there were no information costs, then there would be no need for deposit insurance. But, there would also be no need for banks. Comment.

6. Adjustable-rate mortgages (ARMs) reduce interest rate risk but they also increase default risk. Explain.

7. What is a *keiretsu*? Give some arguments for and against *keiretsus*.

8. What is universal banking? Give some arguments for and against universal banking.

9. Banks are among the most highly regulated industries in the United States. What is the purpose of this government regulation? What might be a drawback of having banks be highly regulated?

10. Banking in the United States is more concentrated today than it was 10 years ago and should become even more concentrated in the near future.
    a. What changes in the regulatory environment have led to this?
    b. How could the increased concentration benefit consumers?

ANSWERS TO SELF-TEST

True or False

1. True.
2. False. The FDIC was created in 1934. It was the Federal Reserve System that was created in 1913.
3. True.
4. False. The FDIC experienced several years of deficits starting in 1988.
5. True.
6. False. Universal banking is still not permitted in the United States.
7. True.
8. False. The European Community has proposed removing national barriers to financial markets. The Second Banking Directive would go a long way toward moving banking in that direction.
9. True.
10. True.
11. False. Since bank deposits are insured, banks have an incentive to engage in risky activities because they do not bear the full cost of failures.
12. False. The amount of competition will increase, and instead of profits rising, Wall Street firms will suffer a decrease in profits.

Fill in the Blank

1. Comptroller of the Currency
2. contagion
3. purchase and assumption
4. bank holding company
5. bank run; bank panic
6. *keiretsu*
7. Bundesbank
8. Free Banking
9. ATM; bank holding
10. universal

Multiple Choice

1.	b	2.	d
3.	b	4.	a
5.	d	6.	a
7.	b	8.	d
9.	c	10.	d
11.	d	12.	c

13. c   14. c

15. b

Essays

1. The McFadden Act prohibited national banks from operating branches outside their home states and required them to abide by the branching restrictions imposed by their home state.

2. Small banks are able to survive because they are protected from competition from other banks. Consequently, the U.S. banking system is less efficient than it would be without restrictions on competition.

3.

Type of Institution	Primary Regulator	Insurer
National Bank	Office of the Comptroller of the Currency	FDIC
State bank that is a member of the Fed	State authorities and the Fed	FDIC
State bank that is not a member of the Fed	State authorities and, if federally insured, the FDIC	FDIC (typically)
Savings and loan association	Office of Thrift Supervision	FDIC
Credit union	National Credit Union Administration	NCUIF
Bank holding company	Federal Reserve System	Not applicable (Individual banks are insured)

4. To prevent bank panics and failures, the Fed stands ready to serve as an ultimate source of credit to which banks can turn.

5. Federal deposit insurance exists to maintain confidence in the banking system. Without information costs, confidence would have to be maintained through direct evaluation of banks' portfolios. Therefore if there were no information costs, there would be no need for deposit insurance. Of course, the distinguishing characteristic of banks is that they specialize in gathering and monitoring information. If there were no information costs, there would be no banks.

6. Because the interest that is charged on ARMs varies with the market interest rate, the market value of the underlying mortgage is not subject to capital gains and losses arising from changes in interest rates (i.e., not subject to interest rate risk). However, interest rates often rise just as the economy takes a downturn. Therefore, just as households are facing financial distress, they must meet a higher mortgage payment, increasing the chance that they will default.

7. In Japan, large firms are associated with industrial groups called *keiretsu*. The firms within the group are diversified and tend to trade among themselves. Each group has a main bank that owns some equity in the member firms and is also a primary source of credit for group firms.
    Arguments for: Because of the close linkage among firms in the *keiretsu*, information costs are less.
    Arguments against: Conflicts of interest can arise.

8. Universal banking allows banks to carry out banking and many nonbanking activities within a single firm and with no geographic restrictions. Banks often have an ownership interest in corporations. For example, Deutsche Bank owns stock in Daimler-Benz, a car manufacturer.
    Arguments for: Close alliances between banking and industry reduce information costs and makes monitoring easier. The cost of adverse selection and moral hazard is less.
    Arguments against: Universal banking would expose the FDIC to additional risk. For example, if a nonbank business failed, it might result in the failure of the bank. Also, conflict of interest problems might arise.

9. Government regulation is intended to maintain the financial health of the lender. One drawback of bank regulation is that incentives are created for unregulated financial institutions and markets to compete with banks by offering close substitutes for bank deposits and loans.

10. a. Regulatory changes that began with Maine in 1975 have removed restrictions on interstate banking. Beginning in July 1997, interstate branching will be allowed.
    b . Relaxing these restrictions will allow banks to operate more efficiently. Increased competition might force banks to pass these savings on to consumers.

15: BANKING REGULATION: CRISIS AND RESPONSE

KEY CONCEPTS

The previous two chapters have dealt with bank management and with the banking industry. This chapter focuses on the interaction between government regulation and the structure of the banking industry. The regulatory process usually follows the following sequence of events:

- A crisis occurs in the financial system;

- government regulation is enacted in response to the crisis;

- the financial system responds to government regulation through financial innovation;

- a new crisis arises from the financial innovation and regulation;

- and so on.

This cycle has been repeated often. We look at three examples in detail.

- Congress created the Fed as a **lender of last resort** in response to the wave of bank failures and contractions in bank lending during the late nineteenth and early twentieth centuries. The first test of the Fed was the stock market crash of October 1929. Initially, the Fed performed its function well by quickly and decisively extending credit. The Fed was less successful in dealing with the bank panics that followed the stock market crash. Ultimately, the Congress responded by passing legislation that broadened the definition of permissible collateral for discount loans and decentralized the Fed's decision making.

- To promote banking stability, Congress limited competition among banks and between banks and other financial institutions. Such intervention was intended to reduce the likelihood of bank runs and to reduce the chance of moral hazard in banks' behavior. Anticompetitive regulations did not promote banking stability in the long run, however. Instead, they created an incentive for unregulated financial institutions and markets to compete with banks by offering close substitutes for bank deposits and loans. For example, **Regulation Q** imposed a ceiling on interest rates that banks could pay depositors. But when market interest rates rose above the ceiling, savers switched to alternative assets, a process known as **disintermediation**. Banks responded to disintermediation with financial innovation, offering standby letters of credit, and **negotiable certificates of deposits**, for example. Eventually, Congress deregulated banking by enacting two pieces of legislation: the **Depository Institution Deregulation and Monetary Control Act (DIDMCA) of 1980** and the **Garn-St. Germain Act of 1982**.

- Introduced as a response to the banking crises of the 1930s, federal deposit insurance functioned smoothly from its inception in 1934 until the early 1980s. Unnoticed, however, problems were developing. The S&Ls were the first depository institutions to show signs of trouble. These institutions held long-term, fixed-rate mortgages and financed them with short-term time deposits. The mismatch between the maturities of assets and liabilities created the potential for interest rate risk. As it turned out, the rise in interest rates in late 1979 caused the balance sheets of S&Ls to deteriorate. This was followed by the 1981–1982 recession, which raised default rates, especially in farm and energy-producing states. Congress tried to help the thrifts by relaxing the restrictions on their asset holdings. This action enabled thrifts to diversify, but it also increased the potential for moral hazard. By the end of 1982, more than half the S&Ls had a negative net worth. Congress passed the **Financial Institution Reform, Recovery, and Enforcement Act of 1989** (FIRREA), the so-called S&L bailout bill.

FIRREA provided substantial resources to help dissolve failed savings and loan associations. However, many analysts believe that the act imposed unnecessary restrictions on the activities of depository institutions without addressing the fundamental problems of adverse selection and moral hazard. Currently, there are numerous proposals for further regulatory reform. Among these are reducing insurance coverage, narrow banking, replacing federal deposit insurance with private insurance, risk-based premiums, stepped-up supervision, and more strictly enforced capital requirements.

Check List

When you finish this chapter, you should be able to:

✔ Describe the sequence of events in the regulatory process.

✔ Explain how financial crisis induces new regulation.

✔ Explain how regulation interacts with market forces leading to financial innovation.

✔ Explain how financial innovation can lead to new financial crisis.

✔ Illustrate the regulatory process using the examples of the Federal Reserve as lender of last resort, competitive restrictions, and deposit insurance.

✔ Discuss proposals for further regulatory reforms and give the rationale underlying each.

Self-Test

True or False

1. During the 1931 banking panic, the Fed lowered the interest rate that it charged member banks (i.e., the discount rate).

2. Negotiable CDs have penalties for early withdrawal.

3. The major distinction between NOW accounts and demand deposits is that NOW accounts have a penalty for early withdrawal.

4. The Depository Institutions Deregulation and Monetary Control Act of 1980 increased competition among depository institutions.

5. Interest rate ceilings on deposits still exist.

6. The FSLIC still exists.

7. Since the passage of FIRREA, savings and loan associations are more tightly regulated.

8. By insuring deposits beyond $100,000, the too-big-to-fail doctrine weakens the desire of large depositors to incur costs of monitoring a bank.

9. The need for the federal government to establish a government fund for insurance companies is reduced if insurance plans are fully funded.

10. Risk-based pricing of bank deposit insurance began in January 1993.

Fill in the Blank

1. _____ _____ placed ceilings on allowable interest rates for time and savings deposits and prohibited interest payments on demand deposits.

2. The exit of savers and borrowers from banks to financial markets is known as _____.

3. The _____-_____ _____ _____ allowed saving institutions to invest in areas other than mortgages.

4. The federal deposit insurance ceiling was raised from _____ to _____ in 1980.

5. Basing deposit insurance premiums on how well a bank is capitalized is called
   _____ - _____ _____.

6. The Pension Benefit Guaranty Cooperation was created to ensure payment of
   _____ _____ pensions when companies go bankrupt.

7. Savings and loan associations ran into the problem of _____
   _____ risk resulting from the mismatch between the maturities of their
   assets and liabilities.

8. The Congressional Budget Office has estimated that the present value of the
   cumulative cost of the savings and loan debacle through the year 2000 could be as
   much as _____ billion in 1992 dollars.

9. The _____ _____ was a Bush administration proposal for
   reform of the banking system.

10. Falling stock market and real estate prices in _____ have plagued the
    banking industry in this country in the 1990s.

11. The PBGC is to the _____ _____ industry as the FDIC is to
    the banking industry.

Multiple Choice

1. The cycle of crisis and response follows a sequence of
   a. financial innovation, regulatory response, financial crisis, and regulation.
   b. financial crisis, financial innovation, regulation, and regulatory response.
   c. financial crisis, regulation, financial innovation, and regulatory response.
   d. financial innovation, financial crisis, regulation, and regulatory response.

2. Which of the following was NOT a financial innovation in response to restrictions
   on bank competition?
   a. the expansion of finance companies
   b. the expansion of money market mutual funds
   c. the expansion of the commercial paper market
   d. the expansion of the U.S. government bond market

3. The failure of Penn Central was significant because it undermined investors'
   confidence in
   a. other issuers of commercial paper.
   b. the Fed's willingness to lend to prevent bank failures.
   c. other issuers of negotiable certificates of deposit.
   d. the financial health of broker-dealers.

4. Fearing that the failure of Franklin National Bank would undermine investors' confidence in negotiable certificates of deposit, the Fed responded to the crisis by
   a. extending discount loans to good banks.
   b. extending discount loans to the large depositors.
   c. imposing regulations forbidding withdrawals from negotiable certificates of deposit.
   d. reopening the failed bank as rapidly as possible.

5. The significance of the failure of the Hunt brothers' scheme to corner the silver market was that it undermined confidence in
   a. commercial paper.
   b. the Fed's willingness to lend to prevent bank failures.
   c. negotiable certificates of deposit.
   d. the financial health of broker-dealers.

6. What was the consequence of the FDIC's decision to guarantee both insured and uninsured deposits of Continental Illinois when it failed in 1984?
   a. fear that large banks would be allowed to fail
   b. foreign depositors became less confident
   c. increased risk taking by other large banks
   d. bank panic similar to the Great Depression

7. Suppose that a large commercial bank has failed. As a consequence, many large foreign depositors are panicking and withdrawing funds from U.S. banks. Which of the following would be the best response by the Fed to this event?
   a. extend discount loans to banks suffering deposit losses
   b. extend discount loans to the large foreign depositors
   c. impose regulations forbidding withdrawals by foreigners
   d. reopen the failed bank as rapidly as possible

8. Which of the following was NOT a contributing factor to the savings and loan crisis?
   a. political pressure from members of Congress placed on regulators to laxly enforce regulations
   b. S&Ls having low net worth, which caused them to take unwarranted risks
   c. a large duration gap between mortgage assets and deposit liabilities
   d. regulatory accounting practices that were stricter than generally accepted accounting practices

9. Which of the following agencies was created by FIRREA?
   a. FDIC
   b. RTC
   c. FSLIC
   d. FBLBB

10. Citibank created negotiable CDs to compete with
    a.   Treasury bills.
    b.   Treasury bonds.
    c.   mutual funds.
    d.   commercial paper.

11. The federal government, in an attempt to prevent a repeat of the 1980 S&L crisis, took a number of actions. Which of the following actions was NOT taken?
    a.   raising insurance premiums
    b.   tightening lending rules
    c.   raising capital requirements
    d.   reducing the amount of housing-related loans an S&L can make

12. Nine of the ten largest banks in this state in 1980 had gone out of business or had been acquired by 1990. The state is
    a.   Texas.
    b.   New York.
    c.   California.
    d.   Pennsylvania.

13. The too-big-to-fail policy was applied to which of the following banks?
    a.   First Boston
    b.   Chase Manhattan
    c.   Continental Illinois
    d.   Penn Square

14. According to the author, which of the following is NOT a reform that is currently under active discussion among policymakers?
    a.   changes in insurance coverage
    b.   restricting bank branching
    c.   narrow banking
    d.   private deposit insurance

Essays

1. The author discusses three ways in which the government intervened to promote the stability of financial institutions. What are they? Discuss each briefly.

2. How could the limiting of competition among banks cause banking instability in the long run?

3. Suppose that you are a bank president. You notice that customers desire both the liquidity of commercial paper, which can be traded in the marketplace, and the safety of federal deposit insurance.
    a. What innovation might you implement to satisfy both these desires?
    b. What motivates you to offer such a product?

4. The savings and loan industry ran into real trouble in late 1979. Briefly discuss the causes of its problems.

5. What is the Resolution Trust Corporation (RTC)?

6. How would narrow banking reduce moral hazard?

7. In February 1991, the U.S. Treasury Department suggested several regulatory reforms for the banking system. What were some of the reforms that were suggested?

8. First National Bank of Midland has much of its assets tied up in real estate. If real estate prices fall, why might this situation encourage the bank to take more risks?

9. FDICIA requires regulators to close problem banks promptly. Is this a good idea? Why or why not?

10. Suppose that you are chairman of the Federal Reserve System. Devise a response to each of the following events.
    a. A rapid drop in stock prices threatens the financial health of specialists, undermining market liquidity.
    b. A bank that is deemed too big to fail faces financial distress.
    c. The largest bank in the United States fails before settling its outstanding checks, threatening the stability of the CHIPS system.

11. The Federal Reserve did all it could in the early 1930s to try to prevent the Great Depression. Comment.

12. High interest rates in the late 1970s contributed to disintermediation and the rapid growth of money market mutual funds. Explain.

ANSWERS TO SELF-TEST

True or False

1. False. The Fed raised the discount rate.
2. True.
3. False. NOW accounts are basically checking accounts that offer interest.
4. True.
5. False. Interest rate ceiling were phased out between 1980 and 1986.
6. False. It was eliminated in 1989 along with the Federal Home Loan Bank Board.
7. True.
8. True.
9. True.
10. True.

Fill in the Blank

1. Regulation Q.
2. disintermediation
3. Garn-St.Germain Act
4. $40,000; $100,000
5. risk-based pricing
6. defined benefit
7. interest rate
8. $200
9. Treasury Plan
10. Japan
11. pension fund

Multiple Choice

1.	c	2.	d
3.	a	4.	a
5.	d	6.	c
7.	a	8.	d
9.	b	10.	d
11.	d	12.	a
13.	c	14.	b

Essays

1. The three ways listed are the following:
   a. *Creation of a lender of last resort*: The Federal Reserve System was created in response to the wave of bank failures and contractions in bank lending during the late nineteenth and early twentieth centuries.
   b. *Restriction of competition*: The intent was to (1.) reduce the likelihood of bank runs and (2.) reduce the chance of moral hazard in banks' behavior.
   c. *Reduction of risks*: By providing deposit insurance, the government reduced the risk incurred by savers.

2. Incentives would be created for unregulated financial institutions and markets to compete with banks by offering close substitutes for bank deposits and loans. For example, interest rate ceilings on deposits led to a decline in bank deposits and people withdrew their money from banks and placed them in unregulated money market mutual funds.

3. a. Negotiable CDs: They are both liquid (because their titles are transferable) and covered by federal deposit insurance, at least up to $100,000. In fact, negotiable CDs were created by Citibank in the early 1960s. There is a penalty for early withdrawal, but they are negotiable, meaning that they can be sold to someone else prior to maturity without penalty. They come in a minimum denomination of $100,000 and typically have a maturity of six months.
   b. Profit: By issuing negotiable CDs, the bank can raise funds at a lower cost than otherwise.

4. Interest rates rose dramatically in late 1979. As a result, the cost of funds to thrifts escalated, the present value of their existing mortgage assets plummeted, and their net worth declined precipitously. At the same time, the recession raised default rates on mortgages, particularly for thrifts in farm and energy-producing states.

5. The Financial Institution Reform, Recovery, and Enforcement Act of 1989 (FIRREA) created the RTC to handle thrift insolvencies and sell off the more than $300 billion of real estate owned by failed thrifts.

6. The management of narrow banks would have far less latitude in choosing investments. The reason is that with narrow banks, only deposits that are backed by safe assets such as T-bills or high-quality commercial paper are insured.

7. a. *Removal of anticompetitive restrictions*: Full nationwide branching would be authorized by 1994; banks would be allowed to participate in the securities and insurance business.
   b. *Insurance coverage*: Deposit insurance coverage would be reduced to $100,000 per depositor per institution, with an additional $100,000 coverage for an IRA.

    c.   *Supervision by regulatory agencies*: The Fed would regulate all state-chartered banks; a new Federal Banking Agency would regulate nationally chartered banks and savings institutions.

8.   Lower net worth increases the potential for moral hazard. Taking no action may result in Midland eventually being shut down by regulators. On the other hand, by under-taking higher risk, the bank might be able to earn enough to eventually return to health, although exposing the FDIC to potentially greater losses in the meantime.

9.   Yes. The incentive for moral hazard is greatest when net worth is low, and problem banks usually have low net worth.

10.   a.   You could make discount loans to banks that extend bridge loans to specialists. In the extreme, you could extend credit directly to the specialists.
       b.   You could extend a discount loan to the troubled bank.
       c.   You could offer to make good the unsettled transactions. Later you might try to collect from the failed bank.

11.   The Federal Reserve did little to help banks and in fact may have made things worse. Rather than lowering the discount rate, the Fed raised it. Furthermore, the Fed would lend only to banks that pledged good quality commercial loans as collateral.

12.   Regulation Q placed ceilings on the allowable interest rate that banks could offer on time and saving deposits and prohibited the payment of interest on demand deposits. Money market mutual funds were not subject to these ceilings. With the high interest rates, banks could not offer market interest rates on their deposits, so savers switched to money market mutual funds.

KEY CONCEPTS

The previous chapters dealt with the role of banking in the domestic economy with a primary emphasis on the United States (although other countries were discussed). In this chapter, we turn to a discussion of the role of **international banking**. International banks, like domestic banks, earn profits by providing risk-sharing, liquidity, and information services at low cost. There are three key similarities between the activities of domestic and international banks:

- Both accept deposits from savers and lend to borrowers.

- Both domestic and international banks lower transactions and information costs.

- Financial regulation can lead to financial innovation in international banking just as in domestic banking.

The foreign activities of domestic U.S. banks are regulated by the Federal Reserve System. U.S. banks use one of four structures:

- U.S. banks operate wholly owned branches in foreign countries, which accept deposits and make loans.

- Special subsidiaries of U.S. banks, **Edge Act corporations**, offer only international banking services, which are exempt from certain domestic regulations.

- Domestic banks are allowed to own controlling interests in foreign financial services companies.

- **International banking facilities** (IBFs) are special banks that are created to serve foreign customers and are exempt from many domestic regulations but are also restricted from doing business with domestic customers.

Foreign bank operations in the United States are regulated by the Fed. Since passage of the International Banking Act of 1978, foreign bank branches have faced essentially the same regulations as domestic bank branches. In response to the Bank of Credit and Commerce International (BCCI) scandal, Congress passed the Foreign Bank Supervision Enhancement Act of 1991. This act requires that, before giving permission to operate, the Fed must certify that a foreign bank's worldwide operations are adequately supervised by the bank's home country. When operating in the United States, a foreign bank can organize its operation in one of three ways:

- An **agency office** cannot accept deposits from U.S. residents, although it can transfer funds and make loans.

- **Foreign bank branches** are full-service institutions that accept deposits and make loans. They operate just like branches of domestic banks, but foreign banks own them.

- Foreign banks can operate **U.S. subsidiaries**, which are subject to the same regulations as domestic banks.

International banks often have assets that are denominated in different currencies. This condition exposes them to **exchange rate risk**—fluctuations in net worth because of changes in exchange rates. Approaches that can be used to hedge against exchange rate risk include the following:

- issuance of deposits denominated in the same currency that is used for lending (for example, a bank lending to a French company using francs could issue franc deposits),

- use of futures and options contracts, and

- arrangement between two banks of a currency swap, which is an exchange of the expected future return on debt instruments denominated in different currencies.

One important service offered by international banks that is aimed at reducing credit risk is the use of **banker's acceptances**, which are orders to pay specified amounts of money to holders of the acceptances on specified dates. Because the bank promises to honor acceptances, foreigners are willing to accept them in payment even if the U.S. buyer is not well known. International banks are also active in the **Eurocurrency** market. **Eurocurrency deposits** are essentially time deposits denominated in a currency other than that of the issuing domestic financial center. For instance, a **Eurodollar** is a dollar-denominated deposit held outside the United States. Eurodollars are popular because the dollar is the **international transaction currency** and because they are not subject to the same regulations as domestic U.S. dollar accounts. In fact, much of international banking is conducted in the relatively unregulated **Euromarkets**.

As in domestic markets, government regulation of international banking often sets into motion a cycle in which banks create new services, which then result in new regulations. Recently, attempts have been made to coordinate international banking regulation of capital requirements, deposit insurance, central bank intervention, and international coordination. For example, the **Basel agreement** is a treaty between 12 major industrialized countries, including the United States. It established uniform capital requirements for signatory countries' banks. Implementing this agreement has not been easy, however. International differences in accounting requirements and in the definition of capital have caused problems.

Check List

When you finish this chapter, you should be able to:

✔ Describe the similarities between domestic and international banking.

✔ Distinguish among Edge Act corporations, controlling interest in foreign financial services companies, and international banking facilities.

✔ Distinguish among agency offices, foreign branches, and U.S. subsidiaries.

✔ Discuss how to limit exchange rate risk.

✔ Explain the role played by banker's acceptances in international trade.

✔ Explain the role played by Eurocurrency markets.

✔ Discuss the Basel agreement.

✔ Discuss how authorities might better coordinate regulation of international banks.

Self-Test

True or False

1. Foreign banks hold about 50% of total bank assets in the United States.

2. Foreign banks operating in the United States are under greater scrutiny today than they were in 1990.

3. If the exchange rate of dollars against yen changed from $1 = ¥150 to $1 = ¥200, a U.S. bank that had a large number of loans denominated in yen would benefit from increased net worth.

4. The Eurodollar market encompasses more than just Europe.

5. Improved technology has allowed greater global integration.

6. The United States has the least generous deposit insurance program when compared to other large industrial countries.

7. The international financial community is moving toward greater coordination of bank regulation and supervision.

8.   International banking has always been important for U.S. banks, savers, and borrowers.

9.   Before 1978, foreign banks operating in the United States enjoyed cost advantages over U.S. banks because they were exempt from limits on branching across state lines and from reserve requirements.

10. The more volatile exchange rates tend to be, the greater is the incentive to engage in currency swaps.

Fill in the Blank

1.   The two countries that have the longest history in international banking are _____ and the _____ _____.

2.   The large foreign bank that failed in 1991 and had Clark Clifford as an officer was the Bank of _____ _____ _____ _____.

3.   Before World War II, the preeminent global financial and commercial center was located in _____.

4.   The dominant currency in the Eurocurrency market is the _____ _____.

5.   _____ is the interest rate at which Eurodollar banks lend to one another.

6.   The typical Eurodollar loan is a _____-rate obligation with a maturity of between _____ _____ and _____ _____.

7.   An international bank in its foreign transactions might hedge against _____ _____ risk by using financial futures and options.

8.   Euroloans are made at an interest rate that is based on _____.

Multiple Choice

1.   An important offshore international financial center is
     a.   Hawaii.
     b.   the Caribbean.
     c.   Malaysia.
     d.   Korea.

2. The expansion of international banking based in Japan can be explained by the
   a. liberalization of Japanese banking regulation.
   b. increasing volume of Japanese exports.
   c. decline of the United States as a world power.
   d. expansion of China, with which the Japanese do much business.

3. International banking facilities are
   a. foreign institutions that are allowed to compete in domestic markets against U.S. banks.
   b. U.S. institutions that cannot conduct domestic banking activities.
   c. foreign institutions that do not operate in foreign markets but may conduct business in the United States.
   d. foreign institutions that are not subject to U.S. regulations.

4. International Banking Facilities allow
   a. time deposits to be accepted from foreign firms and households.
   b. U.S. banks to operate overseas as if they were domestic banks.
   c. foreign banks to operate domestically as if they were domestic banks.
   d. foreign banks to operate overseas as if they were domestic banks.

5. Federal Reserve Regulation K
   a. prohibits interstate branching of foreign banks.
   b. regulates the international activities of member banks.
   c. sets the maximum allowable interest rate payable on time deposits.
   d. prohibits foreign banks from accepting deposits from domestic residents.

6. Which of the following statements is true about an agency office?
   a. An agency office can accept funds from foreign depositors.
   b. An agency office cannot make loans in the United States.
   c. An agency office can accept deposits from U.S. citizens.
   d. An agency office cannot transfer funds from abroad into the United States.

7. Banker's acceptances reduce _____ risk to the exporter.
   a. interest rate
   b. exchange rate
   c. default
   d. credit.

8. The market niche that is served by most international banks is that of
   a. wholesale banking.
   b. retail banking.
   c. commercial banking.
   d. residential mortgage lending.

9. Which currency is currently considered the international transaction currency?
    a. The British pound.
    b. The U.S. dollar.
    c. The Japanese yen.
    d. The Euro.

10. The likely direction of international financial regulation
    a. is regulation by function.
    b. is regulation by institution.
    c. is to have no regulation.
    d. is to create a world Federal Reserve System.

11. In which of the following areas have international financial regulators met to achieve a consensus?
    a. deposit insurance.
    b. minimum capital requirements
    c. central bank intervention in an international banking crisis.
    d. all of the above.

12. By agreeing to honor a banker's acceptance, a bank reduces
    a. transactions costs.
    b. transportation costs.
    c. information costs.
    d. liquidity costs.

13. _____ and _____ are the largest source of Eurodollar deposits today.
    a. Japan; South Korea
    b. Japan; United States
    c. Germany; China
    d. United States; Saudi Arabia

14. Some large banks in the United States and other countries suffered substantial losses when a number of developing countries failed to meet their debt obligations. This debt crisis in international banking began in the
    a. early 1990s.
    b. late 1980s.
    c. early 1980s.
    d. late 1970s.

15. Which of the following statements is true about international regulation of banking?
    a. The Basel agreement requires all countries to treat off-balance sheet liabilities the same.
    b. International standards in regard to deposit insurance have been established.
    c. Dollar-denominated Euromarkets are regulated by U.S. authorities.
    d. Home country authorities have primary responsibility for regulating banks.

Essays

1. What developments have led to the significant expansion of international banking since World War II?

2. In December 1987, representatives of 12 countries met in Basel. What was the purpose of this meeting?

3. The reserve requirements on large U.S. banks were higher in the 1970s than they are today.
    a. Did high reserve requirements promote or retard the growth of the Eurodollar market? Why?
    b. What advantage did these requirements give foreign banks located in the United States?
    c. Why would this advantage not be as important today?

4. What is exchange rate risk, and how can banks reduce it?

5. Banker's acceptances are more likely to be issued by large banks than by small banks. Why? In your answer, explain what a banker's acceptance is.

6. Under the new FDIC rules that base insurance premiums on risk, why would a commercial bank be more likely to become involved in a Eurodollar syndication than in the past?

7. DIDMCA and the Garn-St. Germain Act, which deregulated banking, were passed to make it easier for banks to compete with money market mutual funds. An alternative would have been not to deregulate banking, but to regulate money market mutual funds. On the basis of the discussion in this chapter, why would the latter approach not have worked?

8. Suppose that you are the president of a small electronics manufacturing company. To save labor costs, you decide to buy components from a company in Mexico. The contract between your company and the Mexican subcontractor calls for delivery in 90 days, at which time payment will be made in dollars.
    a. Does your company face exchange rate risk? Does the Mexican subcontractor?
    b. Would your answer to (a.) change if you knew that the Mexican subcontractor buys microchips from a U.S. manufacturer?
    c. What strategies could you use to hedge against exchange rate risk?

9. The substantial growth in the Eurodollar market can be explained in part by interest rate ceilings on deposits imposed by the Federal Reserve. Explain.

ANSWERS TO SELF-TEST

True or False

1. False. The percentage is closer to 16%.
2. True.
3. False. For example, a bank that initially had loans totaling ¥600 million would have a decrease in the dollar value of its loans from $4 million to $3 million. This decrease would lower the bank's net worth by $1 million.
4. True.
5. True.
6. False. The United States has the most generous deposit insurance program.
7. True.
8. False. Before World War II, the U.S. economy was basically a closed economy.
9. True.
10. True.

Fill in the Blank

1. Switzerland; United Kingdom
2. Credit and Commerce International
3. London
4. U.S. dollar
5. LIBOR (London Interbank Offered Rate)
6. floating; five years; ten years
7. exchange rate
8. LIBOR

Multiple Choice

1.	b	2.	a
3.	b	4.	a
5.	b	6.	a
7.	d	8.	a
9.	b	10.	a
11.	d	12.	c
13.	a	14.	c
15.	d		

Essays

1. Expansion in international trade and capital mobility and advances in data processing and telecommunications that reduced the costs of providing transactions and information services have led to the growth of international banking.

2. They met to try to coordinate capital standards for commercial banks in the hope that this would reduce the exposure of central banks to the risk of an international banking crisis.

3. a. Stricter regulation reduces the return on regulated accounts, making Eurodollar accounts, which are not regulated, relatively more attractive. Therefore, higher reserve requirements promoted development of the Eurodollar market.
   b. Before the passage of the International Banking Act of 1978, foreign banks operating in the United States were exempt from reserve requirements.
   c. Foreign banks are no longer exempt from U.S. banking regulations.

4. Exchange rate risk occurs when a bank's net worth fluctuates with increases or decreases in exchange rates. A bank can reduce the risk by matching the currency denomination of assets and liabilities, by using options and futures, or by using currency swaps.

5. A banker's acceptance is a time draft that is an order to pay a specified amount to the holder of the acceptance on a specified date. For a banker's acceptance to be useful, a bank's creditworthiness must be easily ascertained. Large banks are better known than small banks. Also banks need to have a staff that is knowledgeable about the creditworthiness of firms that are involved in international trade. A large bank is more likely to have the necessary staff.

6. In a Eurodollar syndication, individual banks hold a fraction of a Eurodollar loan, which is usually very large. This approach allows a bank to diversify and reduce its risk through risk sharing.

7. Because of the increasing globalization of financial markets that was occurring in the early 1980s, regulating money market mutual funds would have caused these funds to move overseas. Hence in designing regulation, authorities must be careful about the effect of regulation on international competitiveness.

8. a. Because the contract is denominated in dollars, your company does not face exchange rate risk, but the Mexican subcontractor does.
   b. Because there is no need to obtain pesos, the Mexican subcontractor's exposure to exchange rate risk is less to the extent that it can use the dollars you pay it to buy the microchips. However, unless there is a perfect match between the value of your contract with the Mexican subcontractor and the value of the subcontractor's purchase of microchips, the Mexican firm still faces some exchange rate risk.

c.   Futures, options, or a currency swap could be used as a hedge against exchange rate risk.

9.   Eurodollars are the dollar-denominated accounts in the foreign branches of U.S. banks. Regulation Q ceilings on domestic deposits led to the loss of deposits in U.S. banks. Deposits held in European branches of U.S. banks were not subject to these interest rate ceilings. To make domestic loans, the U.S. parent bank would have the branch bank transfer deposits to the parent bank in the U.S.

17: THE MONEY SUPPLY PROCESS

KEY CONCEPTS

This chapter begins Part IV of the book, which deals with the money supply process and monetary policy. These are important issues because the money supply is an important determinant of economic variables such as interest and inflation rates. This chapter deals specifically with the money supply process. This process describes how the money supply is determined through the interaction of the Fed, the nonbank public, and banks. There are two essential elements in the process:

- The first is the **monetary base**, which is the total of reserves held by banks and currency in the hands of the general public.

- The second element is **deposit expansion**, which involves the depositing and redepositing of funds in banks. Both banks and depositors play crucial roles in deposit expansion, as do decisions by the Fed.

Because the monetary base is deposited, reloaned, and deposited again, deposit expansion results in a multiple expansion of the money supply. This multiple expansion is expressed by the **money multiplier**. Specifically, the relationship between the money supply, the monetary base, and the money multiplier is

$$\text{Money supply} = \text{Money multiplier} \times \text{Monetary base.}$$

The Fed is able to influence the money supply through its control of the monetary base, which it can change through its ability to manipulate the asset side of its own balance sheet. The Fed uses two primary mechanisms for changing its asset holdings:

- **Open market operations** involve the purchase or sale of government securities. **Open market purchases** raise the monetary base, while **open market sales** reduce the monetary base.

- **Discount loans** are from the Fed to banks. An increase in discount lending raises the monetary base. A reduction in discount lending reduces the monetary base.

To fully understand the money supply process, one needs to understand how reserves work. **Reserves** consist of vault cash and deposits at the Fed. **Required reserves** are reserves that the Fed requires banks to hold. For example, suppose that the **required reserve ratio** is 0.10 and that checkable deposits are $10 million. The bank would then be required to hold $1 million. Reserves held by banks in excess of required reserves are referred to as **excess reserves**. Excess reserves are available for the bank to lend if desired.

By expanding the monetary base, the Fed is able to channel reserves to banks. Banks then lend these reserves, creating money. This process is referred to as multiple deposit expansion. The steps in the multiple deposit expansion process are as follows:

- Banks lend excess reserves, creating deposits, and because deposits are a component of *M1*, money is created.

- Borrowers spend the proceeds of the loans.

- Some of the proceeds of the loans are deposited in banks, becoming excess reserves available for lending.

- The process repeats.

Multiple deposit contraction occurs when the Fed reduces the monetary base. The steps for a multiple deposit contraction are essentially the opposite of those for multiple deposit expansion. The crucial step in money creation is lending by banks. Therefore anything that affects lending by the banks, given the monetary base, affects the money supply.

- By changing reserve requirements, the Fed changes the amount of reserves available for lending. Therefore, an increase in reserve requirements reduces money supply.

- The nonbank public's decision about the portion of its portfolio that is held as currency rather than as checkable deposits is one factor that can affect funds available to banks. If the nonbank public holds more currency, fewer reserves are available to banks, so deposit expansion is less. Thus, an increase in the **currency-deposit ratio** will cause the money supply to fall.

- Banks influence the money supply process through their decisions about holding excess reserves and borrowing at the discount window. If banks decide to hold more excess reserves, they lend less, and less money is created. If banks borrow more from the Fed at the discount window, the reserves available increase and banks can lend more. Thus, the money supply increases.

Check List

When you finish this chapter, you should be able to:

✔ Explain how the money multiplier and the monetary base interact to determine the money supply.

✔ Understand the relationship between the Fed's balance sheet and the monetary base.

✔ Explain how the Fed can use discount lending and open market operations to change the monetary base.

✔ Distinguish between required and excess reserves and be able to calculate required reserves.

✔ Use T-accounts to show the difference between an open market operation involving banks and the nonbanking public and discounting lending.

✔ Distinguish between the nonborrowed base and borrowed reserves and explain their significance.

✔ Use T-accounts to illustrate multiple expansion and contraction of the money supply.

✔ Use the simple money multiplier to calculate the money supply and determine the effect of a change in base on the money supply.

✔ Explain how changes in reserve requirements affect the money supply.

✔ Explain how changes in the currency-deposit ratio, excess reserves voluntarily held by banks, and the willingness of banks to borrow at the discount window affect the money supply.

✔ Describe the factors that determine the currency-deposit ratio and explain the effect of each.

✔ Describe the factors that determine the excess reserve-deposit ratio and explain the effect of each and describe the factors that determine banks' willingness to borrow discount loans.

✔ Use the money multiplier to calculate the money supply and to determine the effect of a change in the monetary base on the money supply.

Self-Test

True or False

1. Excess reserves are the difference between total bank reserves and required reserves.

2. A decrease in the amount of government securities held by the Fed would increase the money supply, everything else being equal.

3. Banks borrow less often from the Fed than from other banks.

4. The Fed has greater control over discount lending than over open market operations.

5. A rash of bank failures would tend to increase the money supply.

6. Currency has an anonymity premium.

7. Over the short run, the Fed has been quite successful in predicting changes in the money supply resulting from changes in the monetary base.

8. The Fed generally encourages banks to borrow through the discount window.

9. If banks decide to hold more excess reserves as a result of an increase in the discount rate, this action should decrease the money multiplier.

10. The amount of Treasury securities held by the Fed is about $100 billion.

11. The Fed sets the value of both the discount rate and the money multiplier.

12. The most important determinant of changes in the monetary base is the Fed's actions to change the nonborrowed base through open market operations.

Fill in the Blank

1. A(n) _____ in the discount rate would increase the money supply.

2. A single bank cannot lend an amount greater than its _____ _____.

3. The simple deposit multiplier, by which checkable deposits expand as a result of an open market operation, is equal to the reciprocal of the _____ _____ _____.

4. Illegal economic activities such as drug trafficking are usually not reported to the government and therefore are not included in the formal government statistics. Such unreported activities are considered part of the _____ economy.

5. Acceleration of income growth in the U.S. economy would cause the money multiplier to _____ because the currency-deposit ratio would _____.

6. Analysis of changes in the money supply during the 1980s and late 1990s shows that changes in the _____ _____ may lead to significant changes in the money supply in the short run, but in the long run, changes in the money supply can be explained by changes in the _____ _____.

7. An open market purchase of securities of $2 million will always lead to an increase of $2 million in the _____ _____.

8. Another name for borrowed reserves is _____ loans.

9. During a period of strong economic growth, we would expect the currency-deposit ratio to _____.

10. In a black-market economy, we would expect the _____ premium to be quite high.

Multiple Choice

1. The *M1* definition of the money supply includes
    a. checkable deposits.
    b. savings deposits.
    c. time deposits.
    d. money market mutual funds.

2. Which of the following is NOT an asset or liability of the Federal Reserve?
    a. U.S. government securities
    b. currency in circulation
    c. reserves
    d. demand deposits

3. Any income that the Fed earns above and beyond the amount needed to cover its operating expenses
    a. goes as profit to shareholders.
    b. goes as bonuses to management.
    c. is paid out as interest on deposits at the Fed.
    d. is returned to the Treasury.

4. The interest rate that the Fed charges depository institutions for loans is called the
    a. federal funds rate.
    b. discount rate.
    c. prime rate.
    d. base rate.

5. The Fed engages in an open market sale of securities of $100,000. If the reserve requirement ratio is 12%, the maximum expansion of checkable deposits would be
    a. $100,000.
    b. $1 million.
    c. $10,000.
    d. None of the above. Checkable deposits would contract.

6. The Fed engages in an open market purchase of securities of $800,000 from First
    National Bank of America. If the required reserve ratio on checkable deposits is 6%,
    the change in First National's excess reserve position resulting from the open market
    operation is a(n)
    a.   increase of $800,000.
    b.   decrease of $800,000.
    c.   increase of $752,000.
    d.   decrease of $752,000.

7. What would be the rate of growth of the money supply if the money multiplier grew
    at a 3% rate and the monetary base grew at an average annual rate of 4%?
    a.   12%
    b.   7%
    c.   4%
    d.   3½%

8. Open market operations have their greatest immediate impact on
    a.   the money multiplier.
    b.   borrowed reserves.
    c.   nonborrowed reserves.
    d.   required reserves.

9. The opportunity cost of holding excess reserves equals
    a.   the interest income that the banks could have received by lending out the excess
         reserves.
    b.   the dollar value of the excess reserves held.
    c.   the dollar value of the required reserves held.
    d.   the discount rate.

10. Assume that individuals want to hold $2 of currency for every $5 of checkable
    deposits and banks want to hold $2 of excess reserves for every $100 of checkable
    deposits. If the reserve requirement ratio on checkable deposits is 8%, the money
    multiplier would be
    a.   2.8.
    b.   2.0.
    c.   12.5.
    d.   0.36.

11. The narrowest definition of the money supply in the United States is
    a.   the monetary base.
    b.   *M1*.
    c.   *M2*.
    d.   *M3*.

12. Excess reserves as a percentage of total reserves are
    a. over 50%.
    b. under 5%.
    c. between 10% and 20%.
    d. 100%.

13. The Fed makes a $2 million discount loan to First City Bank. The monetary base and the Fed's balance sheet will change as follows:
    a. The monetary base increases by $2 million, and the assets and liabilities of the Fed increase by $2 million.
    b. The monetary base increases by $2 million, and the assets and liabilities of the Fed remain unchanged.
    c. The monetary base remains unchanged, and the assets and liabilities of the Fed increase by $2 million.
    d. The monetary base decreases by $2 million, and the assets and liabilities of the Fed remain unchanged.

14. In the simple deposit multiplier model, if the required reserve ratio on checkable deposits is 10%, then a deposit of $10,000 into a savings account at First National Bank will allow that bank to make a loan equal to a maximum of
    a. $10,000.
    b. its newly created required reserves.
    c. $9,000.
    d. zero.

15. The currency held by the nonbank public is _____ the amount of checkable deposit held.
    a. less than half
    b. approximately equal to
    c. twice as large as
    d. four times as large as

Under the following conditions, answer questions 16, 17, and 18. Assume that the reserve requirement on checkable deposits is 0.20 and banks want to hold 2% of their demand deposits as excess reserves. Further assume that the general public wants to hold $0.10 of currency and $2 of time deposits for every $1 of checkable deposits.

16. The *M1* money multiplier is approximately
    a. 3.1575.
    b. 3.3125.
    c. 3.4375.
    d. 4.0525.

17. If the reserves of the banking system increase by $500,000 as a result of an open market operation, by how much will the *M1* money supply increase?
    a. $1,560,000
    b. $1,718,750
    c. $1,925,243
    d. $2,210,000

18. As a result of this action, the level of excess reserves in the economy will increase by
    a. $18,600.
    b. $28,575.
    c. $31,250.
    d. $36,275.

Essays

1. Numerically, would you expect the monetary base or *M1* to be larger? Explain.

2. What are the three general functions of the Fed?

3. If the Fed imposed reserve requirements on time deposits, the money supply would rise. Comment.

4. Interest rates during the early part of 1993 were quite low. What impact should this condition have on bank excess reserves?

5. The Fed decides to increase the money supply.
    a. What would be the appropriate open market operation?
    b. What immediate effect would this action have on the monetary base and the interest rate? Explain.

6. a. The Fed engages in an open market purchase of securities of $500,000. Assuming that the reserve requirement ratio on demand deposits is 8%, what would be the total change in checkable deposits in the simple deposit multiplier model? Show your work.
    b. If the reserve requirement was lowered to 6%, how would this change the result in (a.)? Show your work.
    c. Again suppose that the reserve requirement is 6%, but now the general public holds some currency. Explain in words what would happen. (*Hint*: Use the three steps of the money supply process.)

7. The author argues that currency should have a lower explicit return than checkable deposits because of its anonymity premium. What does he mean?

8. The administration and Congress are raising marginal tax rates. What impact should this action have on the money multiplier?

9. Large banks have a higher percentage of large deposits than small banks do. Also, large depositors' deposits are more volatile than those of small depositors. On the basis of this information, would a small or large bank hold a higher percentage of excess reserves?

10. The reserve requirement ratio on checkable deposits is 0.10. Banks want to hold $0.10 of excess reserves for every $2 of checkable deposits, and the public wants to maintain a ratio of checkable deposits to currency of 4 to 1. Using this information and assuming a monetary base of $200 billion, determine values for each of the following. Show how you obtained your answer.
   a. checkable deposits
   b. *M1*
   c. currency held by the nonbank public
   d. bank reserves

11. Fill in the following table:

Table 1: Deposit Expansion

Assumptions: (1) The initial open market operation increases reserves by $100; (2) the required reserve ratio is 0.20; (3) no currency is held by the nonbank public; (4) no excess reserves are held by banks.

Step	Total Money Created	Money Created	Excess Reserves	Required Reserves
1	_____	_____	_____	_____
2	_____	_____	_____	_____
3	_____	_____	_____	_____
4	_____	_____	_____	_____
.	.	.	.	.
.	.	.	.	.
.	.	.	.	.
∞	500	0	0	100

12. The Fed engages in an open market operation that leads to a decrease in interest rates, particularly the yield on government securities. What impact should this have on the amount of excess reserves held by banks?

13. If the reserve requirement ratio on checkable deposits is 100%, then there would be no deposit expansion. Do you agree or disagree? Explain.

14. Assume that banks want to hold a lower level of excess reserves against time deposits than checkable deposits. How would the money multiplier equation change?

ANSWERS TO SELF-TEST

True or False

1. True.
2. False. The money supply would fall.
3. True.
4. False. The Fed decides on the amount of the open market operation whereas the bank decides whether it wants to borrow from the Fed.
5. False. The money supply would fall because the currency-deposit ratio would rise.
6. True.
7. False. The correlation between the Fed's reaction to changes in the monetary base and actual changes in the money supply have not been that precise.
8. False. The Fed generally discourages banks from borrowing through the discount window.
9. True.
10. False. The amount was $458 billion as of September 1998.
11. False. The Fed sets the discount rate, but the money multiplier is determined by the Fed, the nonbank public, and banks in the banking system.
12. True.

Fill in the Blank

1. decrease
2. excess reserves
3. reserve requirement ratio
4. underground
5. increase; decrease
6. money multiplier; monetary base
7. monetary base
8. discount
9. decrease
10. anonymity

Multiple Choice

1.	a	2.	d
3.	d	4.	b
5.	d	6.	a
7.	b	8.	c
9.	a	10.	a
11.	b	12.	b
13.	a	14.	a

15. a   16. c
17. b   18. c

Essays

1. *M1* is larger than the monetary base. *M1* = multiplier × monetary base. Because the multiplier is greater than 1, *M1* is greater than the monetary base.

2. The first general function is the Fed's role as a banker's bank. It clears checks by settling claims among banks. The second is that it regulates the operation of banks under federal law. The third is to guide monetary policy by managing the nation's money supply.

3. The money supply would fall, all other things equal. Since banks must hold required reserves on time deposits, these reserves will not be available for deposit expansion.

4. Bank excess reserves probably would increase because the cost of holding these excess reserves, forgone interest, would be low.

5. a. The Fed should buy government securities.
    b. This action would increase bank reserves and the monetary base. Interest rates would fall because more funds would be available to lend.

6. a. Δ in checkable deposits $= \left[\dfrac{1}{0.08}\right]$ ($\$500,000$) $= \$6,250,000$.

    b. Δ in checkable deposits $= \left[\dfrac{1}{0.06}\right]$ ($\$500,000$) $= \$8,333,333$.

    c. Less is deposited, so banks have fewer funds to lend and less money is created. Therefore, the change in checkable deposits would be less.

7. Currency leaves no paper trail, unlike checkable deposits. Therefore, currency is valued more highly than checkable deposits for its usefulness in illegal activities, particularly tax evasion and drug transactions.

8. Higher tax rates will cause the currency-deposit ratio to rise as tax evaders hold more cash. The greater is the currency-deposit ratio, the smaller is the money multiplier.

9. A large bank will hold more excess reserves. The theory of portfolio selection predicts that an increase in the expected level of variability of deposit outflows increases excess reserves.

10.

$$ER/D = \frac{\$0.10}{\$2.00} = 0.05; \quad R/D = 0.10; \quad C/D = \frac{\$1}{\$4} = 0.25; \quad B = \$200 \text{ billion}.$$

a. $D = \dfrac{1}{C/D + R/D + ER/D}(B) = \dfrac{1}{0.25 + 0.10 + 0.05}(\$200 \text{ billion})$

$= \dfrac{1}{0.40}(\$200 \text{ billion}) = \$500 \text{ billion}.$

b. $M1 = \dfrac{1 + C/D}{C/D + R/D + ER/D}(B) = \dfrac{1 + 0.25}{0.40}(\$200 \text{ billion}) = \$625 \text{ billion}.$

c. $C = (M1 - D) = (\$625 \text{ billion} - \$500 \text{ billion}) = \$125 \text{ billion}$, or:

$C = 0.25D = 0.25(\$500 \text{ billion}) = \$125 \text{ billion}.$

d. $R = (B - C) = (\$200 \text{ billion} - \$125 \text{ billion}) = \$75 \text{ billion}.$

11.

Table 1: Deposit Expansion				
Assumptions: (1) The initial open market operation increases reserves by $100; (2) the required reserve ratio is 0.20; (3) no currency is held by the nonbank public; (4) no excess reserves are held by banks.				
Step	Total Money Created	Money Created	Excess Reserves	Required Reserves
1	0	0	100	0
2	100	100	80	20
3	180	80	64	36
4	244	64	51.20	48.80
.	.	.	.	.
.	.	.	.	.
.	.	.	.	.
∞	500	0	0	100

12. The amount of excess reserves held would probably increase. The interest rate that banks receive on their loans would fall, that would decrease the cost of holding excess reserves. Furthermore, bank holdings of government securities would fall because of their lower return. Also, since the open market operation would be a purchase of securities by the Fed, that too should lead to more excess reserves.

13. Agree. Anytime you deposit money into your checking account, banks would have to hold 100 percent of the deposit as required reserves. Since there are no excess reserves, and banks can only loan out excess reserves, there would be no multiple deposit creation.

14. Before:

(1) $B = (C/D)(D) + (R/D)(D) + (ER/D)(D)$

where (2) $ER = (ER/D)(D)$

But now:

(3) $ER = (ER/D)(D) + (ER/T)(T)$ where "T" represents time deposits

Therefore:

(4) $B = (C/D)(D) + (R/D)(D) + (ER/D)(D) + (ER/T)T$

Assuming that time deposits are a constant percentage of checkable deposits, we get:

(5) $T = (T/D)(D)$

Substituting equation (5) into equation (4), we get:

(6) $B = (C/D)(D) + (R/D)(D) + (ER/D)(D) + (ER/T)(T/D)(D)$

$= [(C/D) + (R/D) + (ER/D) + (ER/T)(T/D)](D)$

Dividing both sides by the term in brackets, we get:

(7) $D = \dfrac{B}{(C/D) + (R/D) + (ER/D) + (ER/T)(T/D)}$

since

(8) $M1 = C + D = D[1 + (C/D)]$

(9) $M1 = \left[\dfrac{(1 + C/D)}{(C/D) + (R/D) + (ER/D) + (ER/T)(T/D)} \right] B$

The expression in the brackets in equation (9) is the money multiplier. *Ceteris paribus*, the new money multiplier will be smaller than the old money multiplier.

18: Changes in the Monetary Base

KEY CONCEPTS

You have seen that the monetary base is an important element in the money supply process. In Chapter 17, we showed that the Fed could manipulate the monetary base by changing the value of its total assets. In this chapter, we examine the Fed's influence over the monetary base in more detail. We do so by looking more closely at the Fed's balance sheet. Recall that the Fed can influence the monetary base through open market operations and discount lending. Here, we examine other sources of change in the monetary base, again by focusing on the Fed's balance sheet.

The monetary base is the total of currency in the hands of the public plus reserves. Both currency and reserves are liabilities of the Fed; their value can be derived from the Fed's balance sheet by subtracting from total assets all liabilities except currency in the hands of the public and reserves. Hence:

$B = C + R$ = Securities + Discount loans + Federal Reserve float + Other Federal Reserve assets + Gold and SDR certificates + Treasury currency outstanding – U.S. Treasury deposits – Foreign and other deposits – Other Federal Reserve liabilities.

Changes in the monetary base arise from changes in any of the items on the right-hand side of the preceding equation. The two most important items are securities and discount loans, which can be influenced directly by the Fed's use of open market operations and discount lending, respectively. The other items on the right-hand side also influence the monetary base, and the Fed must allow for them in conducting monetary policy.

The following items from the Fed balance sheet are directly related to the monetary base:

- **Securities and discount loans**: The Fed increases its securities holdings through open market purchases and decreases them through open market sales. The Fed influences discount lending through the discount rate.

- **Federal Reserve float**: Federal Reserve float arises from the check-clearing process. It occurs when the Fed does not credit a bank with payment at the same time that it debits another bank on which the check is drawn. Because checks continually flow through the Fed's clearing system, cash items that are in the process of collection typically exceed deferred availability cash items. Therefore, the float is usually positive.

- **Gold and SDR certificate accounts and other Federal Reserve assets**: An increase in the Fed's holdings of any of these assets will result in an increase in the monetary base. A decrease in these assets will cause a decline in the monetary base.

- **Treasury currency outstanding**: An increase in the amount of Treasury currency held in banks or by the nonbank public leads to an increase in the monetary base. A decrease in this item leads to a decrease in the monetary base.

The following items have an inverse relationship with the monetary base:

- **Foreign and other deposits and other Federal Reserve liabilities**: Increases in any of these items cause the monetary base to fall. The reverse is also true: A decrease in these items causes the monetary base to rise.

- **U.S. Treasury deposits at the Fed**: The U.S. Treasury's account at the Fed is known as the **General Account**. An increase in the General Account decreases the monetary base, and a decrease in the General Account increases the monetary base.

The Treasury uses the General Account for transaction purposes, and day-to-day variation in the Treasury's expenditures and receipts can cause fluctuations in the monetary base. Recognizing this, the Treasury has agreed to a procedure that is designed to minimize changes in the General Account to reduce the impact on the monetary base by timing deposits and withdrawals to closely approximate each other. That is, its deposits into and withdrawals out of the General Account are timed so that, on net, the General Account changes little.

To finance the budget deficit, the Treasury sells securities and uses the proceeds to finance government activities. These securities may ultimately be held either by the general public or by the Fed. A sale of securities by the Treasury to finance the deficit does not necessarily increase the monetary base. However, if the Fed ultimately purchases the securities, the monetary base does expand, a process that is referred to as **monetizing the debt**. Often, the media refer to monetizing the debt as **printing money**, although in the United States, the process involves no physical printing of money, but rather is accomplished through accounting entries. People are concerned about monetization of the debt because monetization would result in a rapid expansion of the monetary base and ultimately inflation.

Check List

When you finish this chapter, you should be able to:

✔ Understand the relationship between the Fed's balance sheet and the monetary base.

✔ Understand how an increase in each of the following causes an increase in the monetary base: securities, discount loans, Federal Reserve float, other Federal Reserve assets, gold and SDR certificates, or Treasury currency outstanding.

✔ Understand how an increase in each of the following causes a decrease in the monetary base: U.S. Treasury deposits, foreign and other deposits, and other Federal Reserve liabilities and capital accounts.

✔ Describe the government budget constraint.

✔ Understand how monetizing the debt can lead to inflation.

Self-Test

True or False

1. An open market purchase of Treasury securities by the Fed will increase the money supply.

2. An increase in Federal Reserve float reduces the monetary base and causes the money supply to expand.

3. Using the General Account for day-to-day transactions can cause fluctuations in the monetary base.

4. Budget deficits always cause the monetary base to expand.

5. The less independent the central bank is, the more likely the central bank is to monetize government debt.

6. Government budget deficits increase the monetary base only when the Fed purchases Treasury bonds that are issued to finance the deficit.

7. Selling bonds to the public to finance government spending would have the same effect as selling the bonds to the Fed.

8. There is no direct relationship between government deficits and the monetary base.

Fill in the Blank

1. Most changes in the monetary base arise from _____ _____ _____ or from _____ _____.

2. An increase in the General Account _____ the monetary base.

3. To reduce the impact of its transactions on the monetary base, the Treasury first deposits most of its receipts in the Treasury _____ _____ _____ accounts kept at _____ _____.

4. Check clearing is an important element of the _____ _____.

5. The _____ _____ _____ depicts the relationships among federal spending, tax decisions, sales of securities, and changes in the monetary base.

6. When the Fed purchases Treasury securities sold to finance budget deficits, it is _____ the debt.

7. Alberto Alesina of Harvard University analyzed the independence of central banks and found that countries with relatively independent central banks had _____ rates of growth of the money supply.

Multiple Choice

1. An expansion of the monetary base causes multiple
   a. contraction of economic activity.
   b. expansion of the money supply.
   c. expansion of interest rates.
   d. contraction of the financial system.

2. To reduce the impact of its transactions on the monetary base, the U.S. Treasury
   a. keeps its actions secret from the Fed and from commercial banks.
   b. communicates its planned transactions to the Fed so that the Fed can plan defensive open market operations.
   c. communicates its planned transactions to commercial banks so that banks can adjust their excess reserves.
   d. communicates its planned transactions to the general public, figuring that the Fed reads the newspaper.

3. Which of the following is NOT an asset of the Federal Reserve system?
   a. discount loans
   b. cash items in the process of collection
   c. other Federal Reserve assets
   d. U.S. Treasury deposits

4. As the U.S. Treasury shifts funds from tax and loan accounts into the General Account, the monetary base will fall because
   a. banks lose reserves as the Treasury withdraws funds.
   b. deposits at the Fed count as reserves in meeting reserve requirements.
   c. the Fed loses reserves to the Treasury.
   d. the general public pays money to satisfy tax bills.

5. Federal Reserve float arises because
   a. individuals, counting on the time it takes for checks to clear, will write checks for which they have no funds.
   b. banks count checks as cleared before they actually are, which is a problem with any payments system.
   c. the Fed clears deferred availability cash items before clearing the corresponding cash item in the process of collection.
   d. it is a by-product of the Fed's discount lending process during periods of illiquidity.

6. Monetizing the debt involves the
   a. purchase of securities by the public.
   b. purchase of Treasury securities by the Fed.
   c. creation of money through discount lending.
   d. creation of public debt rather than private debt.

7. The phrase *printing money* refers to the
   a. physical printing of Federal Reserve Notes and other currency.
   b. physical creation of notes, coins, and bills by the U.S. Mint.
   c. creation of money as a by-product of monetizing the debt.
   d. physical printing of U.S. $1 bills and other notes.

8. A government budget deficit will
   a. inevitably result in expansion of the monetary base if the Treasury sells securities to either the general public or the Fed.
   b. result in expansion of the monetary base only if the Treasury sells securities to the general public.
   c. typically not result in expansion of the monetary base even if the Treasury sells securities to the Fed.
   d. result in expansion of the monetary base only if the Treasury sells securities to the Fed.

9. Which of the following is NOT a liability of the Fed?
   a. discount loans
   b. currency in circulation
   c. U.S. Treasury deposits
   d. foreign and other deposits

10. An increase in the monetary base will most likely result in
   a. a drop in the money supply.
   b. slower inflation.
   c. slower employment growth.
   d. more rapid inflation.

11. The principal liability of the Federal Reserve is
    a. Treasury securities.
    b. deposits by depository institutions.
    c. currency outstanding.
    d. none of the above. The Fed has no liabilities.

12. After the Fed obtains a check for clearing, it has _____ business days to credit the payee's bank account.
    a. one
    b. two
    c. seven
    d. none of the above

13. Financing government spending by raising taxes will ultimately cause the monetary base to
    a. increase by the amount of the tax.
    b. decrease by the amount of the tax.
    c. increase by an amount that is less than the tax.
    d. remain unchanged.

Essays

1. Suppose that Federal Reserve float increases by $142 million. If the money multiplier is 2.54, by how much will the money supply change?

2. If the Fed's assets increase, the monetary base will expand. Explain.

3. This question deals with Federal Reserve float.
    a. A more efficient check-clearing system will help to stabilize the money supply. Explain.
    b. The greater the reliance of the payments system on checks, the less stable *M1* will be. Why?

4. Why is monetization of the debt a concern?

5. Although government budget deficits in the United States do not necessarily lead to monetization of the debt, government budget deficits in Serbia probably would be monetized. Why?

6. If the Fed decides to stabilize the dollar in foreign-exchange markets by buying Japanese yen, what is the effect on the monetary base?

7. Why does a more independent central bank lead to less rapid growth in the monetary base?

8. Identify with a ↑ the items that are positively related to the money base, and identify with a ↓ the items that are negatively related to the money base

___ Foreign and other deposits   ___ Deferred available cash items

___ Securities   ___ Cash items in the process of collection

___ Treasury currency outstanding   ___ Other Federal Reserve liabilities

___ Discount loans   ___ Other Federal Reserve assets

___ Gold and SDR certificates   ___ U.S. Treasury deposits

9. Suppose that you are the Fed official responsible for the operation of the Trading Desk at the New York Federal Reserve Bank. The FOMC's directive is to maintain steady money growth. Develop a strategy to deal with each of the following events.
    a. The Treasury informs you that it will be making a $116 million expenditure tomorrow at 12:36 p.m. from its General Account.
    b. The Board of Governors makes a $2 billion extended credit loan to a large bank that is suffering from liquidity problems.
    c. The Federal Reserve Bank of San Francisco pays out $30 million for a site for a new building.
    d. You notice that the float is larger than usual by $100 million.
    e. Kuwait transfers to the U.S. government $1.5 billion of SDRs to help pay the cost of U.S. troops stationed along the Iraqi border.

10. What impact should bad weather in Chicago have on the monetary base and Federal Reserve float?

11. Would you expect Federal Reserve float to increase or decrease during Christmas time?

ANSWERS TO SELF-TEST

True or False

1. True.
2. False. An increase in FR float increases reserves and the monetary base.
3. True.
4. False. Budget deficits cause the monetary base to expand only when the Fed monetizes the debt.
5. True.
6. True.
7. False. Selling the bonds to the public would leave the monetary base unchanged. Selling the bonds to the Fed would increase the monetary base.
8. True.

Fill in the Blank

1. open market operations; discount loans
2. decreases
3. tax and loan; local banks
4. payments system
5. government budget constraint
6. monetizing
7. slower

Multiple Choice

1.	b	2.	b
3.	d	4.	a
5.	c	6.	b
7.	c	8.	d
9.	a	10.	d
11.	c	12.	b
13.	d		

Essays

1. Δ Money supply = multiplier $\times$ Δ monetary base = $2.54 \times \$142$ million $\approx \$361$ million.

2. When the Fed acquires assets, it pays for them by increasing the monetary base. For example, when the Fed purchases office furniture, it does so with a check. If the check is deposited, the reserves of the bank at which the check is deposited increase. Because reserves are part of the monetary base, the increase in reserves increases the monetary base. But if the Fed's check is cashed, currency expands, again increasing the monetary base. Either way, an increase in the Fed's assets expands the monetary base. Note that the acquisition of office furniture works exactly the same as an open market purchase of U.S. securities.

3. a. Federal Reserve float, a by-product of the check-clearing process, is a source of fluctuations in the monetary base and hence the money supply. Everything else being held constant, a more efficient check clearing system would result in a smaller float, reducing fluctuations in the money supply.

   b. Greater reliance on checking in the payments system increases the float relative to *M1* and reduces the stability of the money supply.

4. Monetizing the debt increases the monetary base and thus the money supply. The money supply, in turn, influences other economic variables such as interest rates and employment. A special concern is that monetization of the debt will lead to inflation.

5. The U.S. government has the option of selling securities to the general public. Such an option is not available to the Serbian government. (Would you hold Serbian bonds in your personal portfolio?) Therefore, Serbia would have to rely on security sales to the central bank to finance its debt.

6. Acquiring foreign currencies causes the monetary base to expand.

7. Faced with financing government spending, politicians can raise taxes, sell securities, or monetize the debt. Often, the third way is the most popular choice in the short run. Therefore politicians who are interested in being reelected will pressure the central bank to monetize the debt. The cost of this policy, however, is expansion of the monetary base and inflation. A politically independent central bank can better resist political pressure and will be less likely to monetize the debt.

8.

↓ Foreign and other deposits   ↓ Deferred available cash items

↑ Securities   ↑ Cash items in the process of collection

↑ Treasury currency outstanding   ↓ Other Federal Reserve liabilities

↑ Discount loans   ↑ Other Federal Reserve assets

↑ Gold and SDR certificates   ↓ U.S. Treasury deposits

9. In each case, a defensive open market operation is the appropriate response.
    a. U.S. Treasury deposits are inversely related to the monetary base, so the expenditure by the Treasury will increase the monetary base. The $116 million open market sale will restore the monetary base.
    b. The extended credit discount loan increases the monetary base by $2 billion, so an open market sale of $2 billion is the appropriate response.
    c. The purchase of the new building site increases other assets of the Fed and hence the monetary base. An open market sale of $30 million would offset the increase in other assets.
    d. The larger the float is, the greater the monetary base is; an open market sale of $100 million would reduce the monetary base to the desired level.
    e. An increase in SDR holdings increases the monetary base. An open market sale of $1.5 billion is needed to return the base to its previous level.

10. Bad weather would cause a delay in check clearing, and this would lead to an increase in Federal Reserve float and the monetary base.

11. At Christmas time, people are going on trips and writing out-of-town checks. Also, checks are sent in the mail as gifts. The Fed has more checks to clear, which causes the float to increase.

19: Organization of Central Banks

KEY CONCEPTS

This chapter turns to a discussion of the central bank of the United States, which is the **Federal Reserve System**. This is an important topic, since it is the Fed that determines the U.S. money supply. That the Fed is a complicated institution arises from the historical circumstances surrounding its founding. The United States had two previous central banks, called the First and Second Banks of the United States. Because of distrust of "financial interests," these banks were politically unpopular, and Congress had allowed the charters of both to expire. To generate public support for the new central bank, Congress, in passing the Federal Reserve Act, created a system with checks and balances that were designed to diffuse economic power between bankers and businesses, between states and regions, and between the government and the private sector.

The Federal Reserve System has four primary components: the Federal Reserve banks, member banks, the Board of Governors, and the Federal Open Market Committee.

- The United States is divided into 12 geographically and economically diverse Federal Reserve districts, each served by a **Federal Reserve bank**. This structure, which combines diverse groups, was intentional. Congress wanted to prevent one state, region, or special interest group from gaining special treatment from a district Federal Reserve bank. As things stand, competing groups balance each other.

- **Member banks** are the commercial banks that belong to the Federal Reserve System. In principle, the member banks in each district are the owners of the Federal Reserve banks.

- The **Board of Governors** consists of seven members who are appointed by the President and confirmed by the Senate. To ensure the independence of the Fed, members of the board serve nonrenewable 14-year terms. They cannot be fired by a President. Geographical restrictions ensure that no one region dominates the board. One member of the board, who is appointed by the President and confirmed by the Senate, serves as chairman for a four-year term.

- The **Federal Open Market Committee** (FOMC) directs open market operations. The members of the FOMC are the chairman of the Board of Governors (who is also chairman of the FOMC), the other six governors, the president of the Federal Reserve Bank of New York, and four of the remaining eleven Federal Reserve bank presidents on a rotating basis. Because the Fed influences the monetary base primarily through open market operations, the FOMC is, in practice, the centerpiece of Fed policymaking. As a consequence, considerable media attention accompanies the periodic meetings of the FOMC.

Politicians might be tempted to pressure the Fed to adopt inflationary policies. To limit the possibility of this happening, checks and balances were incorporated into the Fed to insulate it from external pressures:

- Members of the board are appointed to long, nonrenewable terms, limiting the ability of a President to influence the board through appointments.

- The Fed, unlike other government agencies, is exempt from the congressional appropriation process. Instead, the Fed finances its own operations with earnings from its portfolio of government securities.

Despite attempts to protect the Fed's independence, it is not completely insulated from external pressures:

- Because most members serve less than 14 years, the President can usually influence the board through appointments. Also, every four years, the President can appoint a new board chairman. Traditionally the incumbent chairman resigns when his term ends, freeing a position for the President to fill.

- The Fed is a creature of Congress, which can amend the Federal Reserve Act to change the Fed's power or even abolish it. (Remember that the United States had two central banks prior to the Fed, the charters of which were allowed to expire.)

A contemporary theme in modern central banking is the push for more independent central banks in order to pursue more successfully the goal of price level stability. Studies have shown that countries with more independent central banks have lower rates of inflation.

The latest experiment in large-scale central banking involves the creation of the European Central Bank (ECB). The ECB is to conduct monetary policy for the eleven member countries participating in the European Monetary Union. The structure of the ECB is similar to that of the U.S. Federal Reserve System, except that the eleven national central banks have considerable power within the ECB. The ECB has a mandate to focus on price level stability. However, many issues remain unresolved with respect to the actual conduct of monetary policy in the European Monetary Union.

Check List

When you finish this chapter, you should be able to:

- ✓ Understand the historical forces that led to the founding of the Federal Reserve.

- ✓ Understand why Congress established Federal Reserve Districts that mixed divergent geographical and economic groups.

✔ Describe the functions of each individual Federal Reserve bank.

✔ Understand the position of member banks and their role in the Federal Reserve System.

✔ Describe the composition of the Board of Governors.

✔ Describe the composition of the Federal Open Market Committee.

✔ Understand the relationship between the formal and informal structures of the Federal Reserve System.

✔ Explain the role of each component of the Federal Reserve System in monetary policy.

✔ Compare and contrast the public interest view and the principal-agent view of Federal Reserve behavior.

✔ Understand the issues that are involved in giving the Federal Reserve independence from political pressure.

✔ Compare central bank independence in other countries.

✔ Describe the basic structure and functions of the European Central Bank.

Self-Test

True or False

1. No state is served by more than one Federal Reserve bank.

2. Approximately one-half of all state-chartered banks are members of the Fed.

3. Members of the Board of Governors serve a nonrenewable term of 14 years.

4. The chairman of the FOMC is responsible for buying and selling securities for the Fed's account.

5. The Federal Reserve has greater influence in implementing monetary policy today than it did 75 years ago.

6. The political business cycle concept holds that economic activity should pick up shortly before an election.

7. Executive board members of the European Central Bank serve nonrenewable 14-year terms.

8. The Federal Reserve Act gave the Board of Governors authority to set reserve requirements.

9. A more independent central bank will usually result in a lower inflation rate in the home country.

Fill in the Blank

1. The Federal Reserve banks are owned by the _____ _____.

2. All _____ banks must be members of the Fed, but _____ banks have a choice.

3. Reserve requirements are set by the _____ within ranges set by _____.

4. The Board of Governors meets in _____.

5. Another name for the Full Employment and Balanced Growth Act of 1978 is the _____-_____ Act.

6. The Board of Governors of the Federal Reserve is appointed by the _____ and approved by the _____.

7. The Federal Reserve Act became law in _____.

8. The Federal Reserve Act divided the United States into _____ Federal Reserve districts.

Multiple Choice

1. The organizer of the Bank of the United States was
   a. Ben Franklin.
   b. Aaron Burr.
   c. Alexander Hamilton.
   d. John Adams.

2. The number of Federal Reserve districts created by the Federal Reserve Act was
   a. 5.
   b. 12.
   c. 20.
   d. 25.

3. The Federal Reserve System became law with the passage of the Federal Reserve Act in
    a. 1811.
    b. 1836.
    c. 1913.
    d. 1935.

4. The Federal Reserve chairman serves for _____ years as chairman.
    a. 2
    b. 4
    c. 10
    d. 14

5. The Board of Governors holds _____ seats on the Federal Open Market Committee.
    a. 5 out of the 10
    b. 7 out of the 10
    c. 5 out of the 12
    d. 7 out of the 12

6. Interdistrict bank mergers are approved by the
    a. Board of Governors.
    b. Federal Open Market Committee.
    c. Chairman of the Board of Governors.
    d. Secretary of the Treasury.

7. The _____ is always a voting member of the FOMC.
    a. President of the New York Federal Reserve Bank
    b. Secretary of the Treasury
    c. President of the United States
    d. Chairman of the House Banking Committee

8. The principal-agent view of motivation in bureaucratic organizations was developed by
    a. Buchanan and Tullock.
    b. Friedman and Becker.
    c. Keynes.
    d. Samuelson.

9. The proposed name for the central bank of the European Community is the
    a. Fed.
    b. European Central Bank.
    c. Bank of Europe.
    d. Bundesbank.

10. The name of the Treasury secretary in the Bush administration who argued that monetary policymaking should be placed in the hands of elected officials is
    a.   Alan Greenspan.
    b.   Lee Hamilton.
    c.   Nicholas Brady.
    d.   Sam Nunn.

11. Alan Greenspan is currently in his _____ term as Chairman of the Board of Governors.
    a.   first
    b.   second
    c.   third
    d.   fourth

12. Most of the Fed's earnings come from
    a.   interest on discount loans.
    b.   fees for check clearing.
    c.   The Fed does not have any earnings. It receives appropriations from Congress.
    d.   none of the above.

Essays

1. What is the role of the district Federal Reserve banks in monetary policy?

2. In 1980, the passage of DIDMCA changed the relationship between the Fed and nonmember banks.
    a.   During the 1970s, did the level of interest rates encourage or discourage state bank membership in the Fed?
    b.   Is your answer different for the 1990s? Why or why not?

3. Congress intended to keep the Fed independent of the executive and legislative branches of government. Discuss briefly some of the ways in which the legislation carried out that intent.

4. How does the Fed set the interest rate on U.S. Treasury securities?

5. The author presents two views that motivate the Fed's behavior. Discuss each view briefly.

6. If monetary policy were controlled by Congress rather than the Fed, the inflation rate would be higher. Comment.

7. Although the Fed is relatively independent compared to other government agencies, it is not completely independent. What are some factors that limit its independence?

8. Are the public interest view and the principal-agent view of Fed behavior mutually exclusive? That is, if one view is correct, must the other view necessarily be incorrect?

9. Generally, countries with relatively independent central banks enjoy less inflation. Why?

10. As part of a monetary union, Europeans negotiated the establishment of a European central bank. One way to structure the new central bank would be to use the Federal Reserve System as a model. Why might negotiators want to establish district boundaries that do not correspond to national boundaries?

11. Membership in the Federal Reserve declined until the late 1970s but has held steady since the early 1980s. Comment.

ANSWERS TO SELF-TEST

True or False

1. False. Several states are served by more than one Fed district. In fact, Missouri is headquarters to two Federal Reserve banks (St. Louis and Kansas city).
2. False. Only about one in seven state banks are members.
3. True.
4. False. The manager for domestic open market operations is the one responsible.
5. True.
6. True.
7. False. Executive board members serve nonrenewable 8 year terms.
8. False. The Board of Governors was given the authority to set reserve requirements in the 1930s.
9. True.

Fill in the Blank

1. member banks
2. national; state
3. Fed; Congress
4. Washington, D.C.
5. Humphrey-Hawkins
6. President; Senate
7. 1913
8. 12

Multiple Choice

1. c   2. b
3. c   4. b
5. d   6. a
7. a   8. a
9. b   10. c
11. c   12. d

Essays

1. The Federal Reserve district banks are involved directly through discount lending. They establish discount rates and lend to depository institutions. Indirectly, the district bank presidents are on the Federal Open Market Committee (FOMC), which sets guidelines for open market operations. Also, members of the Federal Advisory Council are selected by the district banks.

2. a. Before passage of DIDMCA, a major portion of the cost of belonging to the Federal Reserve System was the forgone interest on reserves that member banks had to hold but that nonmember banks did not have to hold. A lower interest rate made the cost of reserve requirements less, encouraging membership. In exchange for this membership, banks could borrow from the Fed and received check-clearing services.

   b. After the passage of DIDMCA in 1980, all banks faced the same reserve requirements, whether or not they were members of the Fed. Therefore lower interest rates would have a minimal impact in the 1990s.

3. Board members are appointed for long, nonrenewable terms. This reduces the need for them to try to please the President. Furthermore, the Fed generates its own funds through its earnings on the securities it holds, reducing the influence of Congress.

4. When interest rates start rising above the desired rate, the Fed buys securities, lowering the yield. When the interest rate falls below the desired rate, the Fed sells securities, raising the yield.

5. *The public interest view*: The Fed acts in the interest of its constituency (public) and seeks to achieve economic goals that are in the public interest. *The principal-agent view*: The Fed acts to increase its power, influence, and prestige as an organization, subject to constraints placed on it by principals such as the President and Congress.

6. Politicians would want to follow a more expansionary policy, particularly just before an election. To keep interest rates low Congress might increase the money supply. In Europe, the countries with the most independent central banks have the lowest inflation.

7. The President can usually influence the board through appointments because most members serve less than 14 years. Also, every four years, the President can appoint a new board chairman. Traditionally, the incumbent chairman resigns from the board when his term as chairman ends, freeing a position for the President to fill. Moreover, the Fed is a creature of Congress, which can amend the Federal Reserve Act, changing the Fed's power or even abolishing it.

8. They are not mutually exclusive. A good way for a bureaucracy such as the Fed to maximize its power, privileges, and prestige is by promoting the public interest.

9. Raising taxes or the national debt is often politically unpopular. Therefore politicians seeking reelection would be more likely to pressure the central bank to monetize the debt. The central bank's ability to resist this pressure depends on its independence.

10. If district boundaries correspond to national boundaries, individual countries might be able to pressure the district banks to pursue policies that are beneficial to the country but detrimental to Europe as a whole. By grouping several countries into one district and/or placing a single country in two or more districts, the conflicting interests of different countries can be balanced against each other. This approach minimizes the possibility of a single country dominating. *(Note*: This is the logic that Congress used when it grouped states into single districts and split states among several districts in the U.S. Federal Reserve System.)

11. Prior to passage of DIDMCA in 1980, nonmember banks had to hold fewer noninterest-bearing reserves. In the 1960s and 1970s, nominal interest rates rose, making the cost of Federal Reserve membership high. DIDMCA eliminated the advantage of nonmembership by imposing the same reserve requirements for member and nonmember banks.

20: MONETARY POLICY TOOLS

KEY CONCEPTS

In this chapter, we look in more detail at how the Fed uses its policy tools to influence the money supply. This is important because the Fed is the most important player in the money supply process. The Fed has three primary policy tools for influencing the money supply: open market operations, discount policy, and reserve requirements. We discuss each in turn.

Open market operations are the purchase or sale of Treasury securities by the Fed. An open market purchase increases the monetary base, and an open market sale decreases the monetary base. The FOMC is responsible for directing open market operations. Typically, the FOMC meets about eight times a year. At these meetings, a **general directive** is issued, which directs the **Trading Desk** as to what stance to take. Open market operations fall into two categories:

- **Dynamic transactions** are open market operations that are aimed at achieving desired changes in monetary policy, such as an increase or decrease in interest rates.

- **Defensive transactions** take place more frequently and are designed to offset fluctuations in the monetary base or in the money multiplier arising from changes in the currency-checkable deposit ratio or from changes in the excess reserve-checkable deposit ratio.

The second policy tool that is available to the Fed is **discount policy**. The **discount window** provides the most direct way for the Fed to act as a lender of last resort to the banking system. Discount policy affects the money supply by influencing the volume of discount loans. But beyond this, discount policy is important because it provides the most direct mechanism by which the Fed can direct funds to banks that face financial difficulties. Discount policy involves two components: setting the discount rate and setting the terms under which a bank can obtain a discount loan. Each Federal Reserve bank maintains its own discount window, and the district banks are responsible for the administration of discount policy. There are three types of discount loans:

- **Adjustment credits** are short-term loans that are made to a depository institution to help with temporary liquidity problems.

- **Seasonal credits** are short-term loans that are designed to help small banks with seasonal liquidity problems. They are typically made to depository institutions in agricultural or resort areas.

- **Extended credits** are longer-term loans that are made under exceptional circumstances to financial institutions suffering severe financial problems.

The Fed changes the discount rate infrequently. Consequently, Fed watchers pay close attention to announcements of changes in the discount rate because they believe that changes in the discount rate can signal a major change in Fed policy. This interpreting of the discount rate as a signal of Fed intentions is referred to as the **announcement effect**. For example, in late 1991, the Fed reduced the discount rate by a full percentage point. Fed watchers interpreted this announcement as a signal that the Fed wanted to reduce market interest rates.

The last of the Fed's policy tools are **reserve requirements**. Changes in reserve requirements work by changing the money multiplier. *Ceteris paribus*, an increase in the required reserve ratio reduces the money multiplier, decreasing the money supply. *Ceteris paribus*, a decrease in the required reserve ratio increases the money multiplier, increasing the money supply. The Board of Governors sets reserve requirements, within limits set by Congress. While historically reserve requirements imposed on different types of banks varied, the Depository Institution Deregulation and Monetary Control Act (DIDMCA) of 1980 changed this by establishing uniform reserve requirements for all depository institutions.

All three of the Fed's principal monetary policy tools influence the monetary base primarily through changes in the demand for or supply of reserves. Therefore, Fed watchers focus on the federal funds market. The idea is that the Fed's control of the monetary base gives it substantial control over the federal funds rate. Thus, changes in the federal funds rate signal changes in Fed policy:

- An increase in the federal funds rate relative to other interest rates signals the Fed's intention to raise interest rates and discourage spending in the economy.

- A decrease in the federal funds rate relative to other rates indicates an expansionary policy on the Fed's part.

Check List

When you finish this chapter, you should be able to:

✔ Describe how open market operations change the monetary base and hence the money supply.

✔ Understand the relationship between the FOMC, general directives, and the Open Market Trading Desk.

✔ Distinguish between outright purchase and sales and matched purchase-sales.

✔ Distinguish between defensive and dynamic transactions.

✔ Explain why open market operations play the leading role in monetary policy.

✔ Describe the two components of discount policy.

✔ Explain why the Fed must limit access to the discount window.

✔ Understand the relationship between discount lending and the lender-of-last resort function of the Fed.

✔ Describe how discount lending changes monetary base and hence the money supply.

✔ Distinguish among adjustment credits, seasonal credits, and extended credits.

✔ Describe how changes in reserve requirements change the money multiplier.

✔ Explain how the Fed determines compliance with reserve requirements.

✔ Understand why a change in reserve requirements is the least used policy tool.

✔ Understand that reserve requirements are equivalent to a tax.

✔ Give the arguments for and against the continuation of reserve requirements.

✔ Understand why Fed watchers focus on the Fed funds rate when trying to analyze the Fed.

✔ Use supply and demand analysis to analyze the effect of open market operations and changes in discount lending.

Self-Test

True or False

1. Open market operations are the main monetary policy tool in both the United States and Japan.

2. Most open market transactions are defensive transactions.

3. The Fed has greater control over open market operations than over the discount window.

4. The Fed usually sets the discount rate above market interest rates.

5. Discount lending is better suited to meeting the liquidity needs of individual banks than open market operations are.

6. Historically, country banks had higher reserve requirements than did city banks.

7. Reserve requirements are rarely used as a monetary policy tool.

8. The federal funds rate, like the discount rate, is considered a long-term rate.

9. The chairman of the Fed convenes the FOMC when he wishes to change the direction of monetary policy.

10. Fed policy can be easily discerned from the FOMC Domestic Policy Directive.

11. Borrowing from the Fed through the discount window would increase the monetary base.

12. The majority of banks meet their reserve requirements by holding deposits at the Fed.

13. A change in the discount rate would cause the borrowed reserve portion of the supply curve for reserves to flatten or steepen, depending on whether the discount rate increased or decreased.

Fill in the Blank

1. An open market purchase of securities by the Fed should _____ bank reserves.

2. Open market transactions used by the Fed to offset fluctuations in the monetary base arising from disturbances in portfolio preferences of banks and the nonbank public are called _____ transactions.

3. Decreases in the discount rate usually _____ decreases in short-term interest rates.

4. _____ banks hold a greater percentage of their reserves in the form of vault cash.

5. An open market sale of securities by the Fed would shift the reserve supply curve to the _____ and _____ the federal funds rate.

6. The discount rate is usually _____ _____ the federal funds rate.

7. The least often used monetary tool is _____ _____.

8. The vertical portion of the supply curve for reserves represents _____ _____.

9. The economist who suggested the notion of a 100% reserve requirement was
    _____ _____.

10. Borrowing from the Fed through the discount window became available to all
    depository institutions after _____.

Multiple Choice

1. Open market operations were first used as a monetary tool in the
    a. 1910s.
    b. 1920s.
    c. 1930s.
    d. 1940s.

2. The Federal Open Market Committee (FOMC) was created by Congress
    a. in the 1920s.
    b. in the 1930s.
    c. as part of the original Federal Reserve Act.
    d. and is a branch of the U.S. Treasury Department.

3. The number of times the FOMC meets each year is
    a. four.
    b. six.
    c. eight.
    d. twelve.

4. The oldest of the Federal Reserve policy tools is
    a. open market operations.
    b. reserve requirements.
    c. discount lending.
    d. All of the tools were developed at the same time.

5. The year in which discount lending was made available to all depository institutions
    was
    a. 1914.
    b. 1948.
    c. 1970.
    d. 1980.

6. The reserve requirement on time deposits as of 1996 was
    a. 0%.
    b. 3%.
    c. 10%.
    d. variable between 3% and 10%, depending on the amount of deposits held.

7. Loans that are made to a financial institution suffering from short-term liquidity problems are called
   a. seasonal credit loans.
   b. extended credit loans.
   c. reserve loans.
   d. adjustment credit loans.

8. The Fed monitors compliance with its reserve requirements by checking a bank's
   a. average daily liabilities against its average daily reserves over the previous week.
   b. daily deposits against the same day's reserves each day of the previous two weeks.
   c. daily liabilities against the same day's reserves each day of the previous two weeks.
   d. average daily deposits against its average daily reserves over the previous two weeks.

9. Generally, the percentage of reserves that large banks hold in the form of vault cash is
   a. the same as the percentage held by small banks.
   b. greater than the percentage held by small banks.
   c. less than the percentage held by small banks.
   d. No general statement can be made.

10. Just before its takeover by the FDIC in 1984, what kind of discount loan did Continental Illinois receive?
    a. adjustment credit
    b. seasonal credit
    c. extended credit
    d. rapid credit

11. The actual open market operations, the buying and selling of securities in financial markets, is done by the
    a. Board of Governors.
    b. traders at all 12 Federal Reserve banks.
    c. traders at the New York Federal Reserve bank.
    d. FOMC.

12. Most open market operations are
    a. defensive.
    b. dynamic.
    c. equally split between defensive and dynamic.
    d. neither defensive nor dynamic.

13. Which of the following is not a benefit of open market operations over other
    monetary policy tools?
    a. control
    b. flexibility
    c. ease of implementation
    d. cost

14. The reserve requirements for city and country banks is the same as a result of
    banking legislation passed in
    a. 1913.
    b. 1966.
    c. 1972.
    d. 1980.

15. If the supply curve for reserves is relatively flat, then an increase in demand for
    reserves would cause
    a. a small increase in both the federal funds rate and bank reserves.
    b. a large increase in both the federal funds rate and bank reserves.
    c. a small increase in the federal funds rate and a relatively large increase in bank
        reserves.
    d. a large increase in the federal funds rate and a relatively small increase in bank
        reserves.

Essays

1. What is meant by a contractionary monetary policy? How can that policy be
    achieved through open market operations?

2. Discuss briefly how open market operations are implemented.

3. An example of dynamic monetary policy would be the pumping of reserves into the
    banking system during Christmas time. Comment.

4. There are three advantages to using open market operations. Discuss each briefly.

5. One of the most important functions that the Fed performs is to act as lender of last
    resort.
    a. Some analysts believe that the existence of the Fed as lender of last resort
        encourages excessive risk taking by banks. Explain.
    b. Why can open market operations not be used to perform the lender of last resort
        function for individual banks?
    c. The Fed did use open market operations to meet its obligation as lender of last
        resort during the October 1987 stock market crash. What was different about
        this event compared to the more typical situations faced by a lender of last
        resort?

6. Reserve requirements for a week are based on an average of deposits held during the previous two-week period. What is the purpose of having this accounting lag?

7. The "tax" on bank deposits that results from reserve requirements would increase with higher inflation rates. Why?

8. One argument for reserve requirements is to maintain liquidity. How would having a more sophisticated financial system compromise this argument?

9. As a financial analyst, why might your compensation be tied to your ability to predict increases or decreases in the federal funds rate?

10. In 1990, the Fed lowered the reserve requirement ratios. Use supply and demand curves to assess the impact that this action had on the reserve position of banks and on the federal funds rate.

11. Economic data from the Labor Department indicates that the economy is slowing. In response to that news, the Fed decides to engage in an open market operation.
    a. Would the Fed purchase or sell securities? Explain.
    b. Would you classify the operation as defensive or dynamic? Explain.

12. Why do more countries not use open market operations as their major monetary policy tool?

ANSWERS TO SELF-TEST

True or False

1.   False. Open market operations are the major tool in the United States, but in Japan, a market for government securities did not exist until recently. Even today, the Treasury bill market in Japan is relatively small. To control the money supply, the Bank of Japan has used discount lending and interest rate controls.
2.   True.
3.   True.
4.   False. The discount rate is usually below the market rate. Even though the rate is low, banks still do not borrow much through the discount window.
5.   True.
6.   False. The National Banking Act (1863) and the Federal Reserve Act (1913) established lower reserve requirements for country banks.
7.   True.
8.   False. Both are considered short-term rates
9.   False. The FOMC meets eight times a year. The chairman does not call the meetings.
10. False. The Fed has been criticized for issuing vaguely worded directives.
11. True.
12. False. About 90% of banks meet their reserve requirements with vault cash.
13. False. The vertical portion of the curve would grow or shrink and hence the curve would shift up or down.

Fill in the Blank

1.   increase
2.   defensive
3.   precede
4.   Small
5.   left; raise
6.   less than
7.   reserve requirements
8.   nonborrowed reserves
9.   Milton Friedman
10. 1980

Multiple Choice

1. b   2. b
3. c   4. c
5. d   6. a

7. d   8. d
9. c   10. c
11. c   12. a
13. d   14. d
15. c

Essays

1. A contractionary monetary policy reduces the money supply, pushing up interest rates. An open market sale of securities by the Fed would achieve this objective.

2. The FOMC meets eight times a year and sets overall objectives for monetary policy. The account manager, an officer of the New York Fed, carries out the FOMC's instructions. The Open Market Trading Desk does the actual trading after the account manager accepts the best offer. The account manager confers with two members of the FOMC daily to make sure the FOMC's desired policy is achieved.

3. This action would be a defensive transaction by the Fed. The Fed is not trying to change the monetary aggregates. Instead, it is trying to offset fluctuations in monetary aggregates that would occur from people holding more cash (relative to checkable deposits) during the Christmas season.

4. *Control*: The Fed completely controls the volume of the open market operation. *Flexibility*: The Fed can make the open market operation as large or small as it wants. *Ease of implementation*: The Fed can implement its security transactions quickly, with no administrative delays.

5. a. This is an example of moral hazard. Because the Fed stands ready to help banks that have problems, bank managers are less concerned about taking risks. They take risks that they otherwise would not, knowing that the Fed will bail them out if necessary.
   b. There is no way to ensure that the reserves that are created through open market operations will be channeled to the bank that needs liquidity.
   c. The stock market crash created a generalized need for liquidity. That is, the entire financial system, not a specific bank, needed liquidity.

6. It gives the Fed time to analyze the reserve-deposit ratio and gives banks time to adjust their portfolios.

7. According to the Fisher effect, higher inflation rates should translate into higher interest rates. Because reserve requirements set limits on lending, the amount of foregone interest would increase.

8. A highly sophisticated financial system would allow banks to obtain financial assets that are quite liquid, such as securitized mortgages. A liquidity crisis would therefore become less likely.

9. If you are successful in predicting movements in the federal funds rate, you would also be somewhat successful in predicting movements in security prices and other interest rates that move in response to changes in the federal funds rate. Your employer would be able to profit by acting on your predictions. This ability should create profit for your firm, so your employer would compensate you on the basis of the accuracy of your predictions.

10.

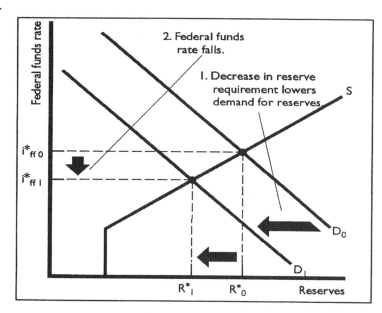

11. The Fed would purchase securities in an attempt to increase the money supply. It would be dynamic since it is an attempt to change monetary policy.

12. A possible reason other countries would not use open market operations is that they lack a market in government securities or that their financial markets are not as sophisticated.

KEY CONCEPTS

Most economists and policy makers agree that the aim of monetary policy should be to advance the economic well-being of a country's citizens. But how do we define well-being? To help determine economic well-being, the Fed has specified six **monetary policy goals**:

- The goal that has received the most emphasis in recent years is that of **price stability**. In a market economy, prices communicate important information to households and firms for use in making economic decisions. Inflation makes prices less reliable as signals for allocating economic resources.

- **High employment** is an important policy goal because a lack of jobs idles workers, underuses productive capacity, and lowers output (gross domestic product). Moreover, unemployment causes financial distress and decreases unemployed workers' self-esteem.

- Policymakers view steady **economic growth** as an important policy goal because economic growth raises household incomes and increases government revenues.

- **Financial market and institution stability** makes possible the efficient matching of savers and borrowers.

- **Interest rate stability** is a goal because interest rate fluctuations make household and business planning for the future difficult.

- Maintaining **foreign-exchange market stability** makes international transactions less risky, thereby promoting international trade.

Unfortunately, not all policy goals are mutually consistent. The classic example of conflicting goals is that of high employment and low inflation. The existence of conflicts among monetary policy goals means that achieving all goals simultaneously may not be possible. The Fed must choose which policy to make a priority.

The Fed cannot instantaneously observe changes in economic data such as GDP and inflation. Moreover, it takes time for policies, once adopted, to take effect. These information and impact lags make effective policymaking difficult, but the Fed cannot just give up in frustration. To overcome the lag problem, the Fed has adopted a strategy of intermediate targets. An **intermediate target** is an objective for a financial variable that the Fed believes is consistent with the ultimate policy goal.

The Fed controls intermediate target variables, such as interest rates and monetary aggregates, only indirectly. Private sector decisions also play a role in determining the value of intermediate target variables. For example, a change in the currency-checkable deposit ratio, which is controlled by the nonbanking public, can influence *M1* growth.

To help improve monetary control, the Fed uses **operating targets**, which are variables that the Fed can control and that are closely related to intermediate targets.

- It determines the value of its intermediate target consistent with achieving its monetary policy goals.

- It sets the operating target so as to achieve the intermediate target.

The advantage of this two-step targeting procedure is that the Fed can observe changes in operating targets quickly, thereby determining whether its interventions are having the desired effect.

In setting intermediate and operating targets, the Fed must choose between interest rates and money aggregates. It cannot successfully target both. The Fed uses three criteria in selecting a target:

- **Measurability**: The Fed must be able to measure precisely, in a timely manner, the target variable.

- **Controllability**: The Fed must have control of the target to be able to use it to influence the economy.

- **Predictable effect**: For an operating target to be effective, it must have a predictable effect on the intermediate target. For the intermediate target to be effective, it must have a predictable effect on the goal variable.

Check List

When you finish this chapter, you should be able to:

✔ Distinguish among the Fed's six policy goals and explain why the Fed seeks to pursue each.

✔ Understand that not all goals are consistent with one another.

✔ Explain why the Fed uses intermediate targets.

✔ Explain why the Fed uses operating targets.

✔ Understand why the Fed cannot pursue both an interest rate target and a monetary aggregate target simultaneously.

⌄ Use graphical analysis to illustrate why the Fed cannot pursue both an interest rate target and a monetary and credit aggregate goal simultaneously.

⌄ Apply the three criteria for selecting a target variable to interest rate targets and monetary aggregates in choosing intermediate targets.

⌄ Apply the three criteria for selecting a target variable to interest rate targets and reserve aggregates in choosing operating targets.

⌄ Discuss the major issues surrounding Fed policy during the periods 1951–1970, 1970–1979, 1979–1981, and since 1981.

⌄ Discuss major alternative targets that have been suggested.

Self-Test

True or False

1. The overall aim of monetary policy is to advance the economic well-being of the country's citizens.

2. Operating targets have longer lags than intermediate targets do.

3. Market interest rates rose in the early 1950s with the onset of the Korean War.

4. Monetarists believe that interest rate targets are the best way to conduct monetary policy.

5. During the 1970s, the primary operating target was short-term interest rates.

6. The federal funds rate was more volatile in the late 1970s than in the early 1980s because of the switch in operating targets that took place in 1979.

7. The time it takes for monetary policy changes to affect output, employment, or inflation is called impact lag.

8. The Fed has greater control over operating targets than it has over intermediate targets.

9. When setting monetary policy, the Fed attempts to target both the money supply and interest rates simultaneously.

10. Higher market interest rates would cause free reserves to increase.

Fill in the Blank

1. _____ is inflation at a rate of hundreds or thousands of percent per year.

2. According to the text, the Fed pursues _____ different policy goals.

3. Unemployment owing to workers moving into and out of the job market or workers who are between jobs is _____ unemployment.

4. _____ and _____ are two policy goals that are often in conflict with each other.

5. The inability of the Fed to observe changes in GDP instantaneously represents an _____ lag.

6. An increase in the value of the dollar relative to other currencies would make U.S. exported goods _____ attractive to foreigners and make foreign goods _____ attractive domestically.

7. To increase the exchange value of the dollar, the appropriate monetary policy would be to _____ interest rates through _____ monetary policy.

8. A Fed policy that amplifies rather than dampens economic fluctuations is called a(n) _____ monetary policy.

9. _____ _____ was appointed or reappointed chairman of the Federal Reserve by Presidents Reagan, Bush, and Clinton.

10. Beginning in October 1979, Fed Chairman Paul Volcker had the Fed target _____ _____ and let _____ _____ fluctuate.

Multiple Choice

1. Which of the following is NOT a goal of monetary policy?
    a. stabilize the price level
    b. high employment
    c. economic growth
    d. competitive markets

2. A country that had a very high inflation rate, over 100%, in the 1970s was
    a. Germany.
    b. Argentina.
    c. the United Kingdom.
    d. the United States.

3. The Humphrey-Hawkins Act addresses
    a. price level stability and employment.
    b. employment and economic growth.
    c. economic growth and foreign-exchange market stability.
    d. interest rates and unemployment rates.

4. Which of the following would be considered an intermediate Fed target?
    a. nonborrowed reserves
    b. federal funds
    c. *M2*
    d. full employment

5. Which of the following is NOT a criterion of an effective intermediate target?
    a. measurability
    b. controllability
    c. divisibility
    d. predictability

6. Which of the following is considered an operating target?
    a. monetary base
    b. *M1*
    c. AAA bond rate
    d. *M2*

7. Suppose total reserves in the banking system is equal to $60 billion and required and excess reserves are $50 billion and $10 billion, respectively. If nonborrowed reserves equal $58 billion, then free reserves would equal
    a. − $40 billion.
    b. +$40 billion.
    c. −$8 billion.
    d. +$8 billion.

8. Which of the following chairmen of the Board of Governors served during the 1980s?
    a. G. William Miller
    b. Arthur Burns
    c. William McChesney
    d. Paul Volcker

9. During the 1980s, critics of intermediate targets argued that indicator variables would be more appropriate than the intermediate targets that were being used. Which of the following was considered as a possible indicator variable?
    a. nominal GDP
    b. federal funds rate
    c. open market operations
    d. the three-month Treasury bill rate

10. According to the Humphrey-Hawkins Act, how many times each year must the Fed chairman testify concerning the Fed's conduct of monetary policy?
    a. once
    b. twice
    c. four times
    d. six times

11. The natural rate of unemployment currently stands at approximately
    a. 4%.
    b. 6%.
    c. 2%.
    d. 0%.

12. All of the following are mentioned as goals of monetary policy except
    a. balance of trade surplus.
    b. high employment.
    c. price stability.
    d. steady economic growth.

13. If the inflation rate is 6%, approximately how long will it take for prices to double?
    a. 6 years
    b. 10 years
    c. 12 years
    d. 20 years

14. The Federal Reserve-Treasury Accord of 1951 allowed the Fed to
    a. monetize the debt.
    b. reduce inflation to zero.
    c. peg interest rates at 3 percent.
    d. stop pegging interest rates.

15. The federal funds rate and reserve aggregates are examples of
    a. monetary tools.
    b. operating targets.
    c. intermediate targets.
    d. The federal funds rate is an operating target, and reserve aggregates are intermediate targets.

Essays

1. The Federal Reserve specifies six goals of monetary policy. Discuss each goal briefly.

2. What is meant by *impact lag*?

3. An investment tax credit is a tax break for businesses that buy new equipment. Which of the six monetary policy goals mentioned in essay question 1 would the tax credit help to achieve?

4. An important policy goal that the Fed pursues is high employment.
   a. What is meant by full employment?
   b. Does that mean zero unemployment?
   c. How would increased unemployment benefits affect the full employment rate of unemployment?

5. The Fed, in the hope of stabilizing the economy, sets short-term interest rates as an intermediate target.
   a. What would the money supply curve look like under this target?
   b. Could the Fed have *M2* as a target at the same time?

6. After February 1987, the Fed stopped announcing targets for *M1*. Why?

7. Recent economic data show that consumer confidence and industrial output are up. Assuming that the Fed uses interest rates as its operating target, what would likely happen to the money supply? Explain.

8. Economic data indicate that the economy is moving downward.
   a. What would happen to the levels of borrowed and free reserves if the Fed did not intervene?
   b. If the Fed wanted to maintain the level of borrowed and free reserves that existed prior to the downturn, what would be an appropriate policy?
   c. Would these actions by the Fed stabilize or destabilize the economy?

9. Suppose the Fed believes that shocks to money demand will be larger than shocks to the supply of money. Under these circumstances, the Fed should target the interest rate. Comment.

10. By setting operating targets, the Fed has been quite successful in dampening swings in inflation, output, and interest rates. Comment.

11. Political pressure forces the Fed to reduce the reporting requirement for banks from weekly to monthly. This means that data used in calculating *M2* are delayed. What are the implications of this delay for selecting an intermediate target?

ANSWERS TO SELF-TEST

True or False

1. True.
2. False. The reverse is true. In picking an operating target, the Fed wants something that is quickly measurable.
3. True.
4. False. Monetarists believe that money supply targets are the best way to conduct monetary policy and that interest rate targets are destabilizing.
5. True.
6. False. The federal funds rate was more volatile in the early 1980s because of the switch from the federal funds rate to nonborrowed reserves as an operating target.
7. True.
8. True.
9. False. The Fed can target one or the other but not both.
10. False. Free reserves are excess reserves minus reserves borrowed from the Fed. If interest rates go up, excess reserves would fall and reserves borrowed from the Fed would increase, causing free reserves to fall.

Fill in the Blank

1. Hyperinflation
2. six
3. frictional
4. Inflation; unemployment
5. information
6. less; more
7. increase; tight
8. procyclical
9. Alan Greenspan
10. monetary aggregates; interest rates

Multiple Choice

1.	d	2.	b
3.	a	4.	c
5.	c	6.	a
7.	d	8.	d
9.	a	10.	b
11.	b	12.	a
13.	c	14.	d
15.	b		

Essays

1. (1) *Stabilize the price level*: Inflation makes prices less useful as signals for resource allocation. Also, inflation can severely damage an economy's productive capacity.

   (2) *High employment*: Idle workers mean lower output and unemployment. Unemployment causes financial distress and loss of self-esteem.

   (3) *Economic growth*: With steady growth, households can enjoy higher incomes and greater well-being.

   (4) *Financial market and institutional stability*: The creation of the Federal Reserve and federal deposit insurance reduced the severity of bank panics.

   (5) *Interest rate stability*: Stability creates a favorable environment for savings and investment.

   (6) *Foreign-exchange stability*: A stable exchange rate simplifies planning for commercial and financial transactions. Changes in the exchange rate also affect exports and imports.

2. *Impact lag* refers to the time required for monetary policy changes to affect monetary goals.

3. (1) *Economic growth*: New equipment should allow businesses to grow more quickly and increase their output; economic growth would occur.

   (2) *High employment*: More output would mean more income. People would want to spend some of that income, which would lead to a greater demand for goods and services and an increase in employment.

4. a. Full employment occurs when there is no unemployment arising from business cycles. The full employment rate of unemployment coincides with an unemployment rate of approximately 6%.

   b. No. It recognizes that some people are going to be frictionally and structurally unemployed.

   c. With higher unemployment benefits, people would be willing to look for work longer. Frictional unemployment would rise, and the unemployment rate that coincides with full employment would increase.

5. a. The money supply curve would be horizontal at the targeted interest rate. Money supply and demand determine the interest rate. An increase or decrease in money demand would have to be matched by a similar change in money supply.

   b. The Fed could set the money supply or interest rates as a target, but not both. If the Fed sets the money supply as a target, interest rates will fluctuate in response to changes in the money demand.

6. Deregulation and financial innovation during the 1980s made *M1* less relevant as a measure of the medium of exchange.

7. The money supply should increase. Higher consumer confidence would probably lead to more consumer spending and less saving. Higher industrial output would lead to more investment spending. These two events would push up interest rates. To bring them back to the target level, the money supply would have to increase.

8. a. Without Fed intervention, interest rates would fall. Bank excess reserves (ER) would rise, and borrowed reserves (BR) would fall if the discount rate remained unchanged. Then, because free reserves equals excess reserves minus borrowed reserves, $FR = ER - BR$, free reserves would rise.
    b. The Fed could sell securities in open market transactions. This approach would raise interest rates, causing BR to fall and FR to rise.
    c. The open market sale by the Fed would worsen the downturn because it would take money out of the economy, raising interest rates. Therefore the Fed's policy would be procyclical.

9. Since targeting the interest rate is equivalent to picking a point along the money demand curve, if the money demand curve's position is unknown the Fed will have a very difficult time targeting the interest rate. If the Fed targets the interest rate, the economy will experience large fluctuations in the money supply. However, if the Fed instead targets the money supply, the economy will experience large fluctuations in interest rates. Consequently, when choosing which target to pursue the Fed must decide whether it is more acceptable (from an economic perspective) to endure large fluctuations in the money supply or large fluctuations in interest rates.

10. Reviewing the monetary policy record from the 1950s onward, we find that much of the Fed's monetary policy can best be described as procyclical. Therefore rather than dampening the swings, the Fed has exacerbated them.

11. The three criteria for selecting an intermediate target are measurability, controllability, and predictable impact on the goal variable. *M2* now performs poorly on the measurability criteria, given that banks report data less frequently. Therefore, it is more likely that the Fed will use an interest rate as a target.

22: THE INTERNATIONAL FINANCIAL SYSTEM AND MONETARY POLICY

KEY CONCEPTS

The previous chapters in Part V have dealt with the money supply process and monetary policy in the context of the domestic economy. This chapter extends the discussion to an economy with international trade. In so doing, it augments the list of domestic players that are important in the money supply process to the central banks, the banks, and the nonbanking public of other countries. Especially important are interventions by governments and central banks that are designed to influence the foreign-exchange rate. An open market purchase or sale of foreign assets by the central bank has the same effect on the money supply as does an open market operation involving domestic government bonds:

- A foreign-asset purchase increases the monetary base.

- A foreign-asset sale reduces the monetary base.

Central banks intervene in foreign-exchange markets because they are concerned about the effects of exchange rate depreciation and appreciation on their domestic economies.

- A depreciation of the domestic currency raises the cost of foreign goods and may lead to inflation. Central banks attempt to avoid this problem by buying their own currency in foreign-exchange markets.

- A domestic currency appreciation can make a country's goods noncompetitive in world markets. To offset this effect, central banks sell their own currency.

Although most foreign asset transactions are undertaken to influence the exchange rate, they can have undesired effects on the domestic economy. When a central bank allows the monetary base to respond to the sale or purchase of domestic currency, the transaction is called an **unsterilized foreign-exchange intervention**. In an attempt to insulate the domestic economy from the undesirable effects of foreign-exchange rate intervention, central banks sometimes undertake a **sterilized foreign-exchange intervention**.

The **balance of payments** measures the flow of private and government funds among countries. The balance of payments tracks both inflows and outflows of funds:

- Inflows of funds from foreigners to the domestic economy (e.g., from Mexico to the United States) are receipts and are noted with a plus sign (+).

- Outflows of funds from the domestic economy to foreigners (e.g., from the United States to Japan) are payments and are noted with a minus sign (−).

There are three major components of the balance of payments:

- The **current account** is the component of the balance of payments that summarizes purchases and sales of currently produced goods and services.

- The **capital account** measures trade in existing assets among countries. The capital account is in a surplus if we sell more assets to foreigners than we buy from them. The capital account is in a deficit if we buy more assets from foreigners than we sell to them.

- **Official reserve assets** are assets held by central banks for making international payments. Historically, gold was the leading official reserve asset. More recently, U.S. and other industrialized government securities, foreign bank deposits, and special drawing rights (SDRs) have been used as official reserve assets.

An **exchange rate regime** is the system by which exchange rates adjust. There are two basic types of exchange rate regimes:

- With a **flexible exchange rate system,** the exchange rate is determined by supply and demand in currency markets.

- The other type of exchange rate system is a **fixed exchange rate system**, in which exchange rates are determined and maintained at specified levels through government intervention.

Proponents of a fixed exchange rate argue that they promote international trade by lowering transactions costs involved in buying and selling across international borders. Fixed exchange rates also reduce uncertainty arising from exchange rate fluctuations. However, most analysts believe that foreign-exchange intervention has become increasingly ineffective, as the foreign-exchange market has expanded in volume to more than $1 trillion daily. Indeed, since the early 1970s, the United States has had a flexible exchange rate system.

Check List

When you finish this chapter, you should be able to:

- ✓ Understand how the buying and selling of foreign assets by domestic central banks changes the money supply.

- ✓ Distinguish between an unsterilized and a sterilized foreign-exchange intervention.

- ✓ Explain why sterilization is ineffective when foreign and domestic assets are perfect substitutes.

- Understand the roles of capital controls, information barriers, and political risk.

- Understand the motivation for intervening in foreign-exchange markets.

- Distinguish between flexible and fixed exchange rate regimes.

- Understand the relationship among the balance of payments, capital account, and changes in official reserves' transaction balance.

- Distinguish among the gold standard, the Bretton Woods system, and the post-Bretton Woods era.

Self-Test

True or False

1. A purchase of foreign assets by a central bank has the same effect on the monetary base as an open market purchase of government bonds does.

2. Economists generally believe that domestic and foreign securities are perfect substitutes.

3. Higher real interest rates in Japan should lead to a depreciation of the U.S. dollar.

4. The official settlement balance is often called the current account balance.

5. If Congress raises personal income taxes in the United States, the statistical discrepancy in the U.S. balance of payments would probably increase.

6. The gold standard existed from the 1800s until World War II.

7. If the central bank decided to buy domestic currency in the international market, we would expect domestic interest rates to increase, the value of the domestic currency to fall in the foreign-exchange market, and inflation in the home country to increase. Assume no offsetting open-market operation.

8. If the current account balance is in deficit, the trade balance must be in deficit also.

9. The Bretton Woods agreement led to the creation of the International Monetary Fund.

10. A central bank that decides to intervene in the foreign-exchange market to raise or lower the value of its currency will have to sacrifice some control of its domestic money supply.

Fill in the Blank

1. A foreign-exchange intervention by the Fed that causes a corresponding change in the monetary base is called a(n) _____ foreign exchange intervention.

2. A sterilized intervention by the Fed would leave the exchange rate unchanged if domestic and foreign assets are _____ substitutes.

3. Since the early 1970s, the United States has officially followed a(n) _____ exchange rate system.

4. A gold standard is an example of a(n) _____ exchange rate regime,

5. The _____ _____ and _____ were created under the Bretton Woods system to make loans to developing countries and to help stabilize exchange rates.

6. Speculative attack on a currency can occur if that currency is either _____ or _____.

7. In 1970, the IMF began issuing a paper substitute for gold known as _____.

8. A sale of foreign assets by the Fed has the same effect on the monetary base as an open market _____ of government bonds by the Fed.

9. Under the classical gold standard, if $20 equals 1 ounce of gold and DM50 (marks) equals 1 ounce of gold, the price of a $100 jacket would be _____ marks, and the exchange rate of dollars for marks would be _____.

10. To defend an undervalued currency, a central bank might follow a policy that would _____ the domestic short-term interest rate.

Multiple Choice

1. If the Fed sells foreign assets to purchase domestic currency, then
   a. international reserves will fall.
   b. the monetary base will fall.
   c. U.S. interest rates will rise.
   d. all of the above will occur.

2. A sterilized intervention by the central bank can affect exchange rates if
    a. domestic and foreign financial assets are perfect substitutes.
    b. capital controls exist in the economy.
    c. foreign assets are less liquid than domestic assets.
    d. either (b.) or (c.) occur.

3. The government agency that has primary authority in organizing exchange rate
    intervention is the
    a. Board of Governors of the Fed.
    b. FOMC.
    c. Treasury Department.
    d. Commerce Department.

4. A German family travels to Disney World. The family's expenditures would be
    reported in the U.S. balance of payments as a
    a. receipt with a positive sign.
    b. receipt with a negative sign.
    c. payment with a positive sign.
    d. payment with a negative sign.

5. U.S. exports of goods total $80 billion, and U.S. imports of goods total $77 billion.
    The net amount would show up in the
    a. merchandise account as a negative $3 billion.
    b. merchandise account as a positive $3 billion.
    c. capital account as a positive $3 billion.
    d. capital account as a negative $3 billion.

6. Which of the following would NOT appear in the U.S. current account?
    a. purchase of a U.S. computer by a Swiss firm
    b. interest income paid to a German citizen who purchased a U.S. government
        bond in an earlier year
    c. U.S. foreign aid to Somalia
    d. the opening of a Swiss bank account by a large U.S. firm

7. If the U.S. exports $50 m. of goods and imports $60 m., the _____
    _____ balance is –$10 m.
    a. merchandise trade
    b. capital account
    c. current account
    d. official settlements

8. Statistical discrepancies are reported in the
    a. current account.
    b. official settlement account.
    c. capital account.
    d. errors account.

9. Assuming a classical gold standard with $20 equaling 1 ounce of gold and 100 deutsche marks (DDA) equaling 1 ounce of gold, the exchange rate of dollars against deutsche marks is
   a. $1 = DM5.
   b. $1 = DM1.
   c. DM1 = $5.
   d. DM1= $20.

10. In the late 1800s and early 1900s, the dominant economy in the world market was that of
    a. the United States.
    b. Germany.
    c. France.
    d. the United Kingdom.

11. The Bretton Woods system functioned
    a. between World War I and World War II.
    b. between 1945 and 1971.
    c. from 1981 to the present.
    d. between 1865 and 1917.

12. Under the Bretton Woods system, dollars would be exchanged for gold at the rate of
    a. $10 for 1 ounce of gold.
    b. $22 for 1 ounce of gold.
    c. $35 for 1 ounce of gold.
    d. $100 for 1 ounce of gold.

13. The dominant reserve currency today is the
    a. U.S. dollar.
    b. German mark.
    c. SDR.
    d. Japanese yen.

14. At Maastricht, Holland, members of the European Community set a goal for completion of monetary union in Europe by
    a. 1995.
    b. 1999.
    c. 2001.
    d. 2010.

15. If the Federal Reserve allows the monetary base to respond to the sale or purchase of domestic currency in the foreign-exchange market, the transaction is called a(n) _____ foreign-exchange intervention.
    a. sterilized
    b. unsterilized
    c. compensated
    d. uncompensated

16. In an attempt to increase the value of the dollar, the Bundesbank purchases $5 billion in the foreign-exchange market. This will cause the monetary base in Germany to _____.
    a. remain unchanged
    b. decrease by $5 billion
    c. increase by $5 billion
    d. decrease by less than $5 billion

17. The sum of all receipts and payments in the balance of payments (current and capital account plus official settlements) is _____.
    a. greater than zero if the balance of payments is in surplus
    b. less than zero if the balance of payments is in deficit
    c. zero
    d. both (a.) and (b.)

18. The United States and other leading industrial countries have been under a floating exchange rate since
    a. the 1940s.
    b. the 1960s.
    c. the 1970s.
    d. None of the above. The exchange rate system that is now in place is fixed.

19. In December 1991, European Community countries met and agreed to a single currency and monetary policy that would take effect on January 1, 1999. The agreement is called the _____ treaty.
    a. Louvre
    b. Paris
    c. London
    d. Maastricht

Essays

1. Suppose that the value of the U.S. dollar has fallen to 108 yen. To reverse this slide, the Fed decides to sell Japanese securities and purchase domestic currency.
   a. What effect would these actions have on the U.S. monetary base?
   b. If the Fed decides that a sterilized foreign-exchange intervention is appropriate, what additional actions should the Fed undertake?
   c. Can the Fed successfully sterilize its intervention?

2. The United States is currently enjoying a low inflation rate but a high unemployment rate. As a policymaker, would you favor lowering or raising the exchange value of the dollar? Explain.

3. To correct a U.S. trade deficit, would you advocate a lower or higher U.S. interest rate?

4. Suppose that the United States suffers from a balance-of-payments deficit of $10 billion. What would happen to dollar assets held by foreign central banks?

5. The United States has been suffering a balance-of-payments deficit. Under a gold standard regime, what would likely happen?

6. What was the role of the International Monetary Fund (IMF) under the Bretton Woods system?

7. A country with a severe balance-of-payments problem might hesitate to devalue its currency. Why? In your answer, explain what a devaluation is.

8. In the first half of 1996, U.S. gross domestic product has grown at a 4% annual rate, which exceeds that of most of the U.S. trading partners. How should this strong growth rate affect the U.S. current account balance?

9. On January 1, 1999 the European Monetary Union officially began with the creation of the European Central Bank (ECB) and the trading of the Euro. Discuss the likelihood of the success of the ECB.

10. Explain the adjustments that would occur in Britain under the classical gold standard if there were an unexpected large increase in demand for British goods.

ANSWERS TO SELF-TEST

True or False

1. True.
2. False. Capital controls, information barriers, and for some countries the risk of seizure cause foreign and domestic assets to be imperfect substitutes.
3. True.
4. False. It is often called the balance of payments.
5. True.
6. False. The gold standard lasted until World War I, with a short period of revival between the two world wars.
7. False. The increase in the interest rate should increase the value of the domestic currency and bring down the inflation rate.
8. False. The current account balance is the sum of the trade balance, exports and imports of services, net investment income, and unilateral transfers. Therefore, the current account balance could be in surplus or deficit depending on what the values are for these other items.
9. True.
10. True.

Fill in the Blank

1. unsterilized
2. perfect
3. flexible
4. fixed
5. World Bank: IMF (International Monetary Fund)
6. undervalued; overvalued
7. SDRs (special drawing rights)
8. sale
9. 250; DM2.5 = $1
10. decrease

Multiple Choice

1.	d	2.	d
3.	c	4.	a
5.	b	6.	d
7.	a	8.	c
9.	a	10.	d
11.	b	12.	c
13.	a	14.	b

15. b   16. c
17. c   18. c
19. d

Essays

1. a. The U.S. monetary base would decrease.
   b. Under a sterilized foreign-exchange intervention, the monetary base should not change. To prevent a drop in the monetary base, the Fed could conduct an open market purchase of securities.
   c. Sterilization will not work if the assets of two countries are perfect substitutes. In the case of the United States and Japan, their financial systems are highly integrated, and many investors view the securities of the two countries as essentially equivalent. Therefore, sterilization is likely to be unsuccessful.

2. You would be more likely to recommend lowering the exchange rate. This action would make U.S.-produced goods more competitive in the world market, raising output and lowering unemployment. It could raise inflation rates by making foreign goods more expensive, but the U.S. government would likely be willing to risk this result because inflation is low.

3. A lower interest rate is the best recommendation. A lower interest rate should lower the value of the dollar and make U.S. goods more competitive.

4. To correct the deficit, the sum of additional dollar assets held by foreign central banks and the loss of U.S. international reserves would have be +$10 billion.

5. Gold would leave the United States. The U.S. money supply and prices of U.S. goods would fall. U.S. goods would become more competitive under the current fixed exchange rate, and the balance-of-payments problem would correct itself.

6. The IMF served as a lender of last resort. It helped countries to make short-run economic adjustments to balance-of-payments deficits and surpluses.

7. A devaluation of a currency is the lowering of the official value of a currency relative to other currencies. A government might be hesitant to do so because such actions raise the price of foreign goods, which is unpopular. Moreover, the government might face political charges that its domestic monetary policies were flawed.

8. The stronger output and therefore income numbers for the United States should lead to greater imports of goods in the United States relative to those of other countries and therefore should cause the trade balance and the current account balance to be in deficit.

9. The ECB, which is structurally similar to the Federal Reserve System, is supposed to be independent of each individual member country's wishes. However, it is possible that a dominant member, such as Germany, may impose its view of appropriate policies on other smaller countries. This may force smaller members to adopt policies that are inconsistent with their domestic agendas. In addition, if France, for example, is experiencing economic hardships, will the ECB be able to help France without causing undue duress to the rest of the system?

10. As a result of this increase in demand for British goods, gold would flow into Britain, and the British money supply would increase. There would be upward pressure on British prices, causing the demand for British goods to fall. The trade surplus in Britain would vanish, and the official value of the British pound would be restored.

KEY CONCEPTS

We now turn from the money supply process to a discussion of monetary theory. By developing an appreciation of monetary theory, you will be able to better understand the actions of the Federal Reserve and anticipate the impact of Fed policies on the economy. This chapter deals with money demand, which, together with money supply discussed in Part V, provides the basis for analyzing the market for money. People hold money because it is useful as a medium of exchange, a store of value, a unit of account, and a way to defer payment. But how much money should a business or household demand? The demand for money depends on the same factors that determine the demand for other assets. That is, the demand for money is explained by the theory of portfolio allocation.

One important role of money—the medium of exchange function—is to facilitate transactions. Thus desired money holdings depend on the volume of transactions. A key determinant of the volume of transactions is the price level, or average price. If the price level increases, more dollars are needed to buy the same quantity of goods. Households and businesses will want to hold larger money balances to finance their purchases. Thus changes in nominal money holdings are proportional to changes in the price level, so we can focus on the demand for **real money balances**.

Velocity is measured by dividing nominal GDP by the money supply:

$$V = \frac{1}{M} PY,$$

where V is velocity, P is the price level, Y is real national income, and M is the money supply. The **velocity of money** is the average number of times a dollar is spent on the purchase of goods and services during a period of time, usually a year.

The preceding equation is often rewritten as

$$MV = PY$$

and referred to as the **equation of exchange**. Based on the definition of velocity, V, the equation of exchange must be true and thus consistent with any observed event.

To convert the equation of exchange into an economic theory requires additional assumptions. For example, Irving Fisher, who first proposed the equation of exchange, assumed that velocity was constant. In effect, Fisher converted the equation of exchange into a **money demand function**, which relates the demand for real balances to its underlying determinants:

$$M = \frac{1}{V} PY.$$

Fisher's approach is called the **quantity theory of money**. As it turned out, Fisher was wrong: The velocity of money is not constant. In fact, the lack of predictability in velocity of *M1* led the Fed to shift from an *M1* target to an *M2* target in recent years. The velocity of money is important because the Fed uses monetary aggregate and interest rate targets to influence its policy goals. If velocity is unstable, the relationship between the money supply and policy goals will be weak. Several factors affect velocity:

- Velocity is determined in part by the **payments system factors**. An increase in the availability of money substitutes in the payments system reduces money demand.

- Converting assets into money involves a transactions cost. The transactions cost can be reduced by holding more money, but at the cost of forgone interest that could be earned on alternative assets. Therefore in determining the amount of real money balances to hold, households and businesses must weigh the transactions cost against interest forgone by holding real money balances. As the interest rate rises, the cost of forgone interest becomes more important, so less money is held. The transactions demand for money is inversely related to the interest rate.

- Because money is an asset as well as a medium of exchange, velocity also changes in response to portfolio allocation considerations. Particularly important is the relative return on other assets compared to money. As the return on other assets rises, the demand for money declines.

The demand for real money balances (M_d/P) is summarized by the following equation:

$$\frac{M_d}{P} = L(Y, S, i - i_m),$$

where Y is income, S is payment system factors, and $i - i_m$ is the relative return on other assets compared to money.

Check List

When you finish this chapter, you should be able to:

✓ Distinguish between the transaction motive and the portfolio allocation motive for demanding money.

✓ Understand that people care about real money balances, not nominal money balances.

✓ Understand the importance of the equation of exchange and velocity.

✓ Understand that changes in velocity are equivalent to changes in money demand.

✓ Explain why payments system factors and interest rates affect velocity.

✔ Relate the theory of portfolio choice and portfolio motive for money demand.

✔ Recognize the significance of John Maynard Keynes and Milton Friedman.

✔ Use the money demand relationship to explain the effect of Y, S, and $i - i_m$ on money demand.

Self-Test

True or False

1. If velocity were constant, the demand for real money balances would be proportional to the level of real transactions.

2. The *M1* velocity has been more stable than the *M2* velocity between 1950 and 1990.

3. In the late nineteenth century, most analyses considered only the transactions demand for money.

4. At high, above normal interest rates, the chances of a capital gain on bonds decreases.

5. In trying to explain the public's demand for money, Friedman examined *M2,* a broader measure of money than *M1*.

6. Everything else being equal, a decrease in the inflation rate should reduce the demand for real money balances.

7. Even with the introduction of computers, the Fed still has a great deal of difficulty in forecasting money demand.

8. A higher price level will cause a proportional increase in the nominal demand for money but not the real demand.

9. As the demand for money increases, the velocity of money also increases.

10. Velocity and the interest rate are inversely related.

11. Economists have been quite successful in developing models that predict the demand for real money balances accurately.

Fill in the Blank

1. The economist who introduced the concept of velocity was _____ _____.

2. The opportunity cost of holding money for transaction purposes is the _____ _____.

3. Holding money for unexpected situations is called the _____ motive for holding money.

4. The introduction of NOW accounts in the early 1980s _____ the demand for money.

5. If the price level doubles, all else being held constant, the amount of *real* money balances held for transaction purposes would _____ _____, but the amount of *nominal* money balances held for transaction purposes would _____.

6. You receive a one-time $10,000 bonus in 1996, raising your income for that year to $50,000. The increase in money demand under the Keynesian framework would be _____ than that under the Friedman approach because the change in temporary income will be _____ than the change in permanent income.

7. Steve Jones keeps $6,000 in a NOW account that yields a 2½% return. A short-term Treasury security has a 4½% return, and a high-risk corporate bond yields 9%. The convenience yield that Mr. Jones places on his checking account is at least _____.

8. _____ introduced the speculative motive as an additional reason that people demand money.

9. Casey Mulligan and Xavier Sala-i-Martin found that there was _____ relationship between the interest elasticity of money demand and the level of nominal interest rates.

Multiple Choice

1. Which of the following is NOT a reason that people hold money?
    a. medium of exchange
    b. hedge against inflation
    c. store of value
    d. means of deferred payment

2. What would the velocity of money be if the level of real transactions were $6000 billion, the money supply were $900 billion, the price level were 1.20, and the national debt in real terms were $3000 billion?
    a. 4
    b. 2.4
    c. 1.8
    d. 8

3. On the basis of the numbers from multiple choice question 2, what is the demand for real money balances?
    a. $900 billion
    b. $1080 billion
    c. $750 billion
    d. $5000 billion

4. Which of the following is NOT a determinant of asset demand according to the theory of portfolio allocation?
    a. income and wealth
    b. expected returns
    c. money supply
    d. risk and liquidity

5. The creation and subsequent use of ATM machines by economic agents would most likely lead to
    a. an increase in *M1* velocity.
    b. a decrease in the demand for real money (*M1*) balances.
    c. a decrease in *M1* velocity.
    d. both (a.) and (b.) occurring.

6. Market interest rates currently stand at 6%, and the velocity of money is 6. If market interest rates rise, everything else being equal, velocity will
    a. decrease.
    b. increase.
    c. remain unchanged.
    d. be undetermined. Each of the above has an equal possibility of occurring.

7. In the liquidity preference theory, Keynes assumed that wealth can be allocated among two assets: money and
    a. bonds.
    b. stocks.
    c. land.
    d. gold.

8. The liquidity preference theory states that the demand for holding real money balances is a function of
    a. income and wealth.
    b. interest rates and wealth
    c. income and interest rates.
    d. wealth and price level.

9. The money demand equation is more stable in Friedman's view than in Keynes's view because
    a. Friedman uses current income.
    b. Friedman uses permanent income.
    c. Friedman focuses only on interest rates.
    d. Friedman assumes that there are only two types of assets.

10. Which of the following statements is true about money demand?
    a. An increase in interest rates raises money demand.
    b. A decline in income raises money demand.
    c. An increase in the efficiency of the payments system reduces money demand.
    d. An increase in the return to money reduces money demand.

11. The person who is credited with developing the model that contained the velocity of money is
    a. Milton Friedman.
    b. Irving Fisher.
    c. Alfred Marshall.
    d. John Maynard Keynes.

12. If nominal GDP is $7.5 trillion and the quantity of money is $3 trillion, velocity is
    a. 1.75.
    b. 2.00.
    c. 2.50.
    d. 3.25.

13. The equation of exchange, $MV = PY$, is
    a. always true.
    b. true only when the money market is in equilibrium.
    c. true only at full employment.
    d. true when prices are constant.

14. Which of the following factors is (are) likely to increase velocity?
    a. an increase in the number of substitutes for money
    b. an increase in market interest rates
    c. a decrease in the convenience yield of money
    d. all of the above

15. Suppose that Wall Street expects stock prices and dividends will set new record highs this year. Holding all other factors constant, we would expect the demand for real money balances to
    a. increase.
    b. decrease.
    c. increase first, then decrease.
    d. remain unchanged.

Essays

1. Suppose that the consumer price index today is 140, meaning that what cost $100 in the base year now costs $140. If the amount of nominal money balances held for transaction purposes during the base year was $900 billion, how much money would have to be held today for that purpose?

2. The equation of exchange was developed by Irving Fisher.
    a. What is the equation of exchange?
    b. Because the equation of exchange is always true, it is NOT a scientific theory. Explain.
    c. How did Fisher convert the equation of exchange into a theory of money demand?

3. What impact did the introduction of credit cards have on the velocity of money? Why?

4. If the Fed were able to predict the value of V with great accuracy, its ability to conduct monetary policy would improve immensely. Comment.

5. The author lists three factors that cause variation in the velocity of money. Identify these factors and discuss each one briefly.

6. What is meant by money's *convenience yield*?

7. Assume that the conditions of the liquidity preference theory apply and that money supply and demand are both $900 billion. Now assume that interest rates increase from their equilibrium rate of 4% to 5%.
    a. What would happen to money demand?
    b. How could equilibrium in the money market be restored? Assume that the money supply is fixed.

8. Trish and Thomas are officials of the Federal Reserve. Trish argues for a monetary aggregate target, but Thomas argues for an interest rate target. Who is the Keynesian and who is the Friedmanite?

9. From the standpoint of monetary policy, the Fed prefers a velocity that is
    predictable. Why? Would you say that velocity has been predictable?

10. Suppose people become concerned about the stability of the financial system as Y2K
    approaches. Predict the likely effect on the demand for money.

ANSWERS TO SELF-TEST

True or False

1. True.
2. False. The reverse has been true.
3. True.
4. False. At above normal interest rates, the expectation is that rates will fall. When interest rates fall, bond prices will rise and a capital gain would be received.
5. True.
6. False. A lower inflation rate should increase the demand for real money balances because the opportunity cost of holding money would fall. Friedman argued that "expected inflation" reflects the return on durable goods.
7. True.
8. True.
9. False. If people want to hold more money, money turnover will decrease, and therefore so should velocity.
10. True.
11. False. The financial system changes over time in response to shifts in the cost of providing, the demand for, and the regulation of financial services. Effects of these changes on the demand for money make forecasting it a difficult task.

Fill in the Blank

1. Irving Fisher
2. interest rate
3. precautionary
4. increased
5. remain unchanged; double
6. greater; greater
7. 2%, or $120
8. Keynes
9. direct

Multiple Choice

1.	b	2.	d
3.	c	4.	c
5.	d	6.	b
7.	a	8.	c
9.	b	10.	c
11.	b	12.	c
13.	a	14.	d
15.	b		

Essays

1. $900 billion × 1.40 = $1260 billion (nominal balances held).

2. a. The equation of exchange is $MV = PY$.
    b. This equation must be true because of the way in which V is defined (i.e., $V = PY/M$). For something to qualify as a scientific theory, it must be falsifiable. Therefore, the equation of exchange is not a theory.
    c. Fisher made the equation of exchange falsifiable by assuming that velocity (V) was a constant. Then by dividing both sides of the equation of exchange by the price level (P), the left-hand side of the equation can be redefined as the demand for real money balance, and the right-hand side would be the level of real transactions divided by V, a constant. From this new equation, if the level of real transactions doubled, so would the demand for real money balances. (As it turns out, velocity is not constant; Fisher's theory was not only falsifiable but also false.)

3. Because credit cards can be used as a substitute for money, the demand for money declined. Therefore velocity of money increased. From the equation

    $$\frac{M}{P} = \frac{1}{V} Y,$$

    the introduction of credit cards should reduce M/P, money demand for transaction purposes. Assuming a given value of real GDP (i.e., Y), the value of $1/V$ would have to fall, which means that V would have to rise.

4. By knowing V, the Fed would know how much to change the money supply to achieve the desired policy goal.

5. (1) *Interest rates and transaction demand*: higher interest rates reduce the transaction demand for money, which in turn raises velocity.

(2) *Payments system factors*: The greater the number of substitutes for money, the less money is needed for transactions. Because $V = PY/M$, when M falls, V rises. An example of a substitute for M is credit cards. (See the answer to essay question 3, which offers an alternative explanation of why V would rise.)

(3) *Portfolio allocation decisions*: Changes in expected returns on money or in risk, liquidity, or information costs of money will change households' and businesses' demand for cash balances.

6. The convenience yield on money is the amount of interest that households and businesses are willing to sacrifice in return for the safety, liquidity, and low information costs of holding money.

7. a. The quantity of money demanded would fall because a higher interest rate means that the opportunity cost of holding money balances has increased.

   b. To restore equilibrium, either interest rates must fall to their previous level or income must rise. If income increases, the transactions demand for money would rise, as would precautionary demand. This increase in demand would offset the decrease in money demand caused by the higher interest rate.

8. Recall that if economic instability arises on the financial side, an interest rate target is most appropriate. If the economic instability arises on the real side, a monetary aggregate target is best. Keynesians believe that money demand is less stable than do Friedmanites, so a Keynesian is more likely to argue for an interest rate target. Therefore Thomas is the Keynesian, and Trish is the Friedmanite.

9. To conduct monetary policy, the Fed wants a velocity that is predictable. If velocity is predictable, the Fed would know how much to change M to achieve a desired change in nominal GDP. In the 1980s, *M1*'s velocity was unstable, causing the Fed to target *M2* rather than *M1*. *M2*'s velocity was stable from 1957 to 1989, but in the 1990s it has not been stable.

10. In general, people will demand more money for precautionary purposes. As a result, the demand for currency will be especially high. In addition, people may convert stocks and bonds into cash because of their fears about the safety of their financial assets.

24: LINKING THE FINANCIAL SYSTEM AND THE ECONOMY: THE *IS-LM-FE* MODEL

KEY CONCEPTS

The economy is a very complex set of social institutions. Markets for goods, services, and assets are all interrelated; a change in supply or demand in one market can affect equilibrium in many other markets. If we are to understand how the economy works, we need to develop a simplified model that will allow us to grasp the essential features of the economy without being overwhelmed in details. One such model is the *IS-LM-FE* model, which is developed in this chapter. This model simplifies economic analysis by using the trick of letting one representative market stand in for a number of related markets. In particular, the *IS-LM-FE* model combines all markets into three:

- the **goods market**, which is the market for currently produced goods and services;

- the **money market**, which involves trade of assets used as the medium of exchange;

- the **nonmoney asset market**, which is the market for assets other than money, such as commercial paper and equities.

We turn first to a discussion of the goods market. In a closed economy, the total quantity of goods demanded, called aggregate demand, is the sum of **desired national consumption**, C; **desired national investment**, I; and **desired government purchases**, G. In equilibrium, the total **current output** of goods, Y, must equal demand, or

$$Y = C + I + G.$$

Rearranging this equation gives

$$Y - C - G = I$$

The term on the left-hand side of this equation is the amount of output that is not consumed by households or used by government. That is, it is savings. Therefore in equilibrium, $Y - C - G = S$, or

$$S = I.$$

The equilibrium of investment and savings is summarized by the *IS* **curve**. That is, points on the *IS* curve are combinations of interest rates and income that are consistent with saving equaling investment. The *IS* curve slopes downward because when current output rises, saving increases. As a consequence, the interest rate must fall so that saving and investment are again equal.

To finish the discussion of the goods market, we need to establish the level of current output. For simplicity, we assume **full employment output** regardless of the interest rate. That is, output is at a constant level, Y^*, that is consistent with full employment. Therefore the output curve is a vertical line, which we called the **full employment (*FE*) line.**

We assume that there are only two financial markets: the money market and the nonmoney asset market. With just two asset markets, the money market will be in equilibrium only if the nonmoney market is also in equilibrium. The reason this is true is that excess demand in one asset market must be the same as excess supply in the other market. After all, if you have an excess demand for nonmoney assets and want to buy them, you must be willing to supply dollars to the seller of bonds to do so. If the money market is in equilibrium, there is no excess demand or supply of money. Therefore there will be no excess demand or supply in the nonmoney asset market either, and the nonmoney asset market must also be in equilibrium. Knowing that one asset market is in equilibrium means that the other asset market is also in equilibrium. Therefore, we need to keep track of equilibrium in only one market. Moreover, because monetary policy is a focus of policymaking, it is the money market we focus on.

The ***LM* curve** depicts the relationship between current output and the real interest rate in asset markets. Equilibrium in the money market (hence also in the nonmoney asset market) is reached when the quantity of real money supplied is the same as the demand for real money balances. To describe the relationship between the expected real interest rate, r, and output, Y, we hold the other factors constant. That is, on a given *LM* curve, nominal money, the price level, expected inflation, and the nominal return on money balances are held constant. The *LM* curve slopes upward because when income increases, money demand also increases. Therefore for a given money supply, the expected real interest rate must increase to restore equilibrium in the money market.

The financial system and the goods market are both in equilibrium when the *IS* curve, the *FE* line, and the *LM* curve all intersect. A shift in the *IS* curve, the *FE* line, or the *LM* curve changes the equilibrium in the economy.

- Changes in desired consumption, desired investment, or government purchases, other than those caused by a change in the expected real interest rate, cause the *IS* curve to shift.

- Anything that changes productivity, such as changes in technology, shifts the *FE* curve.

- A change in nominal money balances, the price level, expected inflation, or the nominal return to money balances causes a change in equilibrium in the money market. Therefore if any of these variables change, the *LM* curve will shift.

Shifts in the *IS* curve, the *FE* line, or the *LM* curve shift the short-run equilibrium of the economy. However, changes in the price level cause the *LM* curve to adjust so that the economy returns to long-run equilibrium at full employment.

Check List

When you finish this chapter, you should be able to:

✔ Understand the importance of developing a model of the economy.

✔ Describe the assumptions underlying general equilibrium models.

✔ Explain how the *IS-LM-FE* model combines all markets into three.

✔ Relate the *IS* curve to the goods market equilibrium and explain why it is downward sloping.

✔ Identify the three major components of the *IS* curve.

✔ Distinguish between a closed economy *IS* curve and an open economy *IS* curve.

✔ Identify the factors that cause a shift in the *IS* curve.

✔ Relate the *LM* curve to asset market equilibrium and explain why it is upward sloping.

✔ Identify the factors that cause a shift in the *LM* curve.

✔ Relate the *FE* curve to full employment and explain why it is vertical.

✔ Use the *IS-LM-FE* diagram to illustrate equilibrium.

✔ Use the *IS-LM-FE* diagram to show what happens to equilibrium in response to shifts in *IS*, *LM,* and *FE*.

Self-Test

True or False

1. The goods market is in equilibrium when current output supplied equals the current amount demanded.

2. An increase in the government deficit as a result of higher government spending would not affect national savings.

3. An increase in the real interest rate would cause the *IS* curve to shift downward.

4. The *IS* curve for a large open economy is flatter than that for a closed economy.

5. Referring to the *IS-LM-FE* model, the author shows that if we start from a point of equilibrium in all three markets and then disturb that equilibrium by causing one of the curves to shift, we can at best restore equilibrium in two of the markets.

6. A decline in the price level, nominal money balances being held constant, will cause the *LM* curve to shift to the right.

7. The full-employment line determines the level of output in the *IS-LM-FE* model.

8. If we have equilibrium in the nonmoney market that does not mean we have equilibrium in the money market.

Fill in the Blank

1. Points above the *IS* curve represent an excess _____ of goods.

2. The *IS* curve for a small open economy is _____ at the world real rate of interest.

3. Another name for money demand is _____ _____.

4. The _____ curve shows the combinations of interest rates and income levels that are consistent with equilibrium in financial markets.

5. The _____ _____ is vertical because of the assumption that the economy is at _____ employment.

6. The reduction in private consumption and investment resulting from the high real interest rates caused by an increase in government purchases is called

   _____ _____.

7. If money is _____, changes in money supply have no effect on real variables, such as the real interest rate and real GDP.

8. A positive relationship has been found to exist between the elasticity of money demand and nominal interest rates. Holding prices fixed, we can conclude from the above relationship that the *LM* curve will become _____ as real interest rates increase.

Multiple Choice

1. Nominal interest rates remain unchanged despite a drop in expected inflation. If the level of savings before the drop in expected inflation is $100 billion in real terms, savings after the drop will be
   a. less than $100 billion.
   b. $100 billion.
   c. more than $100 billion.
   d. changed in an unpredictable way.

2. The curve that relates aggregate demand for current output to the real interest rate is the
   a. *LM* curve.
   b. *IS* curve.
   c. *AD* curve.
   d. *FE* line.

3. OPEC countries meet and decide to raise the price of a barrel of oil. What impact will this decision have on the U.S. *FE* line?
   a. Shift it left
   b. Shift it right
   c. Cause an upward movement along the curve
   d. Cause a downward movement along the curve

4. Goods market equilibrium is represented by the intersection of the
   a. *LM* and IS curves.
   b. C + I + G line and the *IS* curve.
   c. *LM* curve and the *FE* line.
   d. *IS* curve and the *FE* line.

5. Which of the following variables does NOT appear in the money demand equation?
   a. real income
   b. interest rate on nonmoney assets
   c. return on money
   d. labor productivity

6. Equilibrium in the money market is represented by
   a. the *IS* curve.
   b. the *LM* curve.
   c. both the *IS* and *LM* curves.
   d. the *FE* line.

7. As a result of new innovations in banking, money demand becomes more sensitive to changes in the interest rate. The most likely consequence of this increased sensitivity is a
    a. flatter *IS* curve.
    b. steeper *IS* curve.
    c. flatter *LM* curve.
    d. steeper *LM* curve.

8. You would expect the increased integration of global financial markets that has occurred since 1980 to result in
    a. a flatter *LM* curve.
    b. a steeper *IS* curve.
    c. a flatter *IS* curve.
    d. a steeper *LM* curve.

9. In the derivation of the *LM* curve, the level of
    a. real money balances is assumed to be fixed.
    b. nominal money balances is assumed to be fixed.
    c. real output is assumed to be fixed.
    d. real interest is assumed to be fixed.

10. Holding all other factors constant, an increase in the nominal return on money _____ the demand for real money balances and shifts the LM curve to the _____.
    a. increases; right
    b. increases; left
    c. decreases; right
    d. decreases; left

11. Assuming a three-sector economy—households, business, and government—with the goods market in equilibrium, then equilibrium national savings equals
    a. Y
    b. $Y - G$
    c. $G + C - Y$
    d. $Y - G - C$

12. If the goods market is not in equilibrium, which of the following statements is true?
    a. We are on the *IS* curve.
    b. We are on the *LM* curve.
    c. We are not on the *IS* curve.
    d. None of the above.

13. On the basis of the author's discussion of the *IS* curve, we would expect which country to have the least control over the real interest rate?
    a. United States
    b. Germany
    c. Belgium
    d. With international capital mobility, all three countries would lose control.

14. An increase in the real interest rate will cause
    a. the *IS* curve to shift to the right.
    b. the *IS* curve to shift to the left.
    c. the *IS* curve to become flatter.
    d. none of the above

15. Assuming money neutrality, any increase in the money supply to stimulate the economy will leave the level of real output unchanged because
    a. the price level will increase by the same amount as the money supply.
    b. a crowding out effect will occur due to higher nominal interest rates.
    c. real interest rates will increase.
    d. the velocity of money will fall by an amount equal to the money supply increase

Answer questions 16 and 17 using the following information. The government increases spending for job training programs by $100 billion. These programs increase worker productivity. Money supply and the price level do not change.

16. This program will shift
    a. both the *LM* and *IS* curves to the right.
    b. both the *IS* curve and the *FE* line to the right.
    c. the *LM* curve to the right and leave the *FE* line and the *IS* curve unaffected.
    d. the *IS* curve to the right and leave the *FE* line and the *LM* curve unaffected.

17. As a result of the program,
    a. real interest rates and the output level increase.
    b. real interest rates decrease and output increases.
    c. real interest rates remain unchanged and output increases.
    d. real interest rates increase and output remains unchanged.

Essays

1. New economic data show a larger than expected drop in unemployment. What impact would this change have on national savings? Explain.

2. Because of the large number of individuals who do not have health care, the government decides to require all employers to provide health care insurance for their employees. What impact will this have on investment? Explain.

3. Explain why the *IS* curve has a negative slope.

4. Intel develops a new computer chip that is twice as fast as existing computer chips and costs no more. What impact would this development have on the *IS* curve, the *FE* line, and the *LM* curve? Give an economic explanation.

5. Would a point below the *LM* curve represent an excess supply of money or an excess demand for money? Explain.

6. Congress passes a law requiring credit card companies to reduce the interest rate charged on outstanding balances. If there is no reduction in the availability of credit cards as a result of this legislation, how will the *LM* curve be affected? Explain.

7. In an attempt to balance the budget, the government raises taxes.
    a. Using the *IS-LM-FE* diagram, show what the impact will be on real interest rates and output. Assume that the price level is flexible.
    b. Explain your result.

8. What is meant by the *neutrality of money*?

9. If money is neutral, persistent increases in the money supply will only result in inflation. Explain.

10. One of the many statistics put out by the federal government is the level of consumer confidence. If consumer confidence increases, how should this affect national savings? Explain.

ANSWERS TO SELF-TEST

True or False

1. True.
2. False. National savings would fall. If the goods market is in equilibrium, savings equals investment, and $I = Y - C - G$. If consumption, C, does not change in response to an increase in government spending, G, and assuming equilibrium, an increase in G would reduce I and therefore S.
3. False. The curve would not shift; the movement would be along the curve.
4. True.
5. False. The statement is true if we hold the determinants of the three curves constant. The author shows that equilibrium can be restored in all three markets simultaneously if we allow the price level to vary.
6. True.
7. True.
8. False. Equilibrium in one market means equilibrium in the other market. $M_d - M_s = N_s - N_d$.

Fill in the Blank

1. supply
2. horizontal
3. liquidity preference
4. *LM*
5. *FE* line; full
6. crowding out
7. neutral
8. flatter

Multiple Choice

1.	c	2.	b
3.	a	4.	d
5.	d	6.	b
7.	c	8.	c
9.	a	10.	b
11.	d	12.	c
13.	c	14.	d
15.	a	16.	b
17.	a		

Essays

1. Current income levels rise, pushing up saving. However, the data would have a positive impact on expectations of future income, which should reduce current saving. Therefore the change in saving is ambiguous, although the first effect likely would dominate the second effect.

2. Investment will decrease. The expected future profitability of capital will decline because the need to provide health care insurance raises the cost of production.

3. A lower real interest rate increases both investment and consumption. The demand for goods is therefore increased. For equilibrium to exist in the goods market, the current level of output would have to increase to match the higher demand. The *IS* curve represents equilibrium in the goods market and is graphed with real interest rates on the vertical axis and current output on the horizontal axis, so it must have a negative slope.

4. Labor productivity would increase. The *IS* curve would shift to the right (see Table 24.1 in the main text). The *FE* line would shift to the right (see Table 24.2 in the main text). The *LM* curve would adjust so as to restore equilibrium.

5. An excess demand for money. At a point below the *LM* curve, the interest rate is lower than the equilibrium interest rate, income held constant. A lower interest rate means a higher money demand. Therefore money demand is greater than money supply.

6. The *LM* curve will shift to the right and downward. The demand for money as a result of this legislation will fall. To restore equilibrium in the money market, real interest rates on nonmoney assets have to fall.

7.   a.

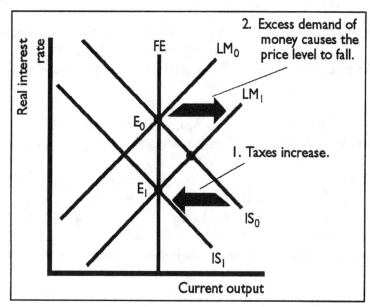

b.   The *IS* curve shifts to the left. The price level will fall as people try to increase
      the amount of real money balances held because of the lower real interest rate.
      The *LM* curve will shift to the right to restore equilibrium, from E_0 to E_1.

8.   A one-time change in the nominal money supply affects only nominal variables such
      as nominal output or the price level. Real output and the real interest rate remain
      unaffected by a one-time increase or decrease in the nominal money supply.

9.   If money is neutral, an increase in the money supply has no effect on real variables
      but can affect nominal variables. An increase in the money supply causes the *LM*
      curve to shift to the right. This causes excess demand for real goods at the new
      lower interest rate. The price level rises, shifting *LM* back to the left and restoring
      equilibrium, but at a higher price. If the money supply persistently increases, the
      price level must also continuously increase; that is, inflation occurs.

10.   If consumer confidence increases, people are more confident about the future, which
      includes future income. People would consume more out of current income, driving
      down national savings.

25: Aggregate Demand and Aggregate Supply

KEY CONCEPTS

In the previous chapter, we developed the *IS-LM-FE* model, which allowed us to focus on the interaction of interest rates and current income. In this chapter, we develop another model of the economy that economists commonly use. This one, based on **aggregate demand** and **aggregate supply**, allows us to focus on the price level and economic activity.

The **aggregate demand curve** (*AD*) shows the relationship between aggregate demand and the price level. The aggregate demand curve slopes downward because, for a given level of nominal money supply, an increase in the price level reduces real money balances. Lower real money balances cause the real interest rate to rise. The rise in the real interest rate, in turn, reduces aggregate demand in three ways:

- Because the real interest rate is the opportunity cost of funds, an increase in the real interest rate reduces businesses' desired investment.

- An increase in the real interest rate increases desired saving and reduces desired consumption.

- An increase in the real interest rate causes the exchange rate to appreciate and reduces net exports.

A shift in the aggregate demand curve reflects a change in aggregate demand at a given price level. Therefore anything that causes a change in consumption, investment, government spending, or net exports (other than a change in the price level) shifts *AD*. A shift to the right in the aggregate demand curve is expansionary; a shift to the left is contractionary.

The **aggregate supply curve** (*AS*) illustrates the relationship between the output that businesses are willing to supply and the price level. Understanding aggregate supply requires distinguishing between the short run and the long run. The **short-run aggregate supply curve** (*SRAS*) shows the relationship between the price level and output in the short run. An increase in the price level is associated in the short run with an increase in the quantity that businesses are willing to supply. The short-run aggregate supply curve slopes upward, but exactly why it does so is a source of disagreement among economists. In fact, there are two competing theories concerning the slope of the aggregate supply curve:

- The **new classical approach** argues that imperfect information about the actual state of the economy explains why the aggregate supply curve slopes upward. *SRAS* slopes upward because producers confuse changes in the general price level (inflation) with changes in relative prices.

- In the **new Keynesian approach**, if aggregate demand increases, businesses would like to respond by increasing prices but cannot because prices are rigid. Instead, the increased aggregate demand is met by increasing production. Therefore, *SRAS* slopes upward because a rise in aggregate demand means that output will increase as a result of rigid prices.

The **long-run aggregate supply curve** (*LRAS*) shows the relationship between the price level and output in the long run. Both the new classicals and the new Keynesians argue that the long-run aggregate supply curve is vertical at the full-employment level of output, *Y**.

- In the **new classical approach**, firms eventually learn that the price level is changing in response to changes in current output. Therefore, expected prices and actual prices will eventually align, and output will return to the full employment level, *Y**.

- In the **new Keynesian approach**, even though prices are sticky in the short run, all firms eventually adjust prices. Therefore, output returns to its full employment level in the new Keynesian approach as well.

Changes in production costs shift the short-run aggregate supply curve. Three factors significantly affect production costs. Particularly important are changes in labor costs, changes in nonlabor costs, and changes in the expected price level. An increase in full employment output causes the long-run aggregate supply curve to shift to the right. Factors that can shift the long-run aggregate supply curve include increases in capital and labor available and increases in productivity.

Short-run equilibrium is determined by the intersection of the aggregate demand curve and the short-run aggregate supply curve. Because *SRAS* slopes upward, a shift in *AD* can influence the economy in the short run. This outcome is true for both the new classical and new Keynesian views. Therefore monetary policy can influence the economy in the short run.

Long-run equilibrium occurs at the intersection of the aggregate demand curve and the long-run aggregate supply curve. During periods of high unemployment, wages tend to fall, shifting *SRAS* to the right. During periods of low unemployment, wages tend to rise, shifting *SRAS* to the left. Therefore, the economy tends toward full employment and, in the long run, output is given by full employment. The price level, however, can take on any value. Therefore changes in aggregate demand brought about by changes in the money supply can change the price level but have no effect on real variables in the long run, an example of **monetary neutrality**.

Check List

When you finish this chapter, you should be able to:

- ✔ Understand the significance of aggregate demand.

- ✔ Identify the components of aggregate demand.

- ✔ Explain why the aggregate demand curve is downward sloping.

- ✔ Identify factors that can shift the aggregate demand curve.

- ✔ Understand the effects of a change in money supply and a change in money demand on aggregate demand.

- ✔ Understand the effects of changes in consumption, government spending, and net exports on aggregate demand.

- ✔ Understand the significance of aggregate supply.

- ✔ Distinguish between the new classical and new Keynesian views of the *SRAS*.

- ✔ Understand the significance of price misperception.

- ✔ Understand the significance of sticky prices.

- ✔ Explain why the *LRAS* is vertical according to the new classical view and according to the new Keynesian view.

- ✔ Understand the effects of a change in labor costs, other input costs, and the expected price level on the *SRAS*.

- ✔ Understand the effect of increases in capital and labor and increases in productivity on the *LRAS*.

- ✔ Graphically illustrate the short-run equilibrium using *AD-SRAS*.

- ✔ Describe and graphically illustrate how the economy adjusts to the long-run equilibrium.

- ✔ Understand the role of short-run productivity shocks in the real business cycle view.

- ✔ Use *AD-AS* to describe economic fluctuations in the United States during the periods 1964–1969, 1973–1975, and 1990–1991.

Self-Test

True or False

1. With the money supply held constant, a higher price level in the United States will increase real interest rates, reducing aggregate demand.

2. In monopolistically competitive markets, sellers are price takers and buyers are price setters.

3. The early 1970s was a period of low inflation in the United States.

4. Higher inflation expectations cause costs to rise because workers demand higher nominal wages to maintain their real wages.

5. New Keynesians and new classicals agree about the short-run aggregate supply but disagree about aggregate demand.

6. Many analysts believe that a reduction in bank credit contributed to the 1990-1991 recession.

7. The aggregate demand curve and the demand curve for individual goods are negatively sloped for the same reasons.

8. Points on the aggregate demand curve represent combinations of the price level and current output for which the goods market and asset market are in equilibrium at the same time.

9. The short-run aggregate supply curve has a positive slope until full employment is reached and then becomes vertical.

Fill in the Blank

1. With a fixed money supply, an increase in the average price level will _____ the real interest rate, _____ aggregate demand.

2. A reduction in the U.S. average price level, the money supply being held constant, would _____ the exchange rate value of the dollar.

3. In the short run, the amount of output supplied will exceed the full employment level of output if the _____ price level is above the _____ price level.

4. Anything that changes _____ _____ will shift the short-run aggregate supply curve.

5. Most economists agree that in the long run, the equilibrium level of output is
    _____ _____ _____.

6. In the real business cycle model, short-term changes in output are explained
    primarily by temporary shocks to _____.

7. Between 1973 and 1975, the economy suffered from _____, when
    increasing prices were accompanied by falling output.

8. A decrease in expected future income causes a decline in desired consumption,
    reducing aggregate demand. As an official of the Fed, you would recommend a(n)
    _____ in the money supply to restore full employment.

9. An increase in the productivity of workers will shift the _____ curve to
    the _____.

10. The new classical view of aggregate supply was based on work done by
    _____ _____ and is also known as the _____ theory.

11. Strict adherence to the Keynesian view would imply a _____ aggregate
    supply curve and _____ inflation.

12. A reduction in the cost of raw materials will shift the _____ run aggregate
    supply curve to the _____.

Multiple Choice

1. Suppose output in the economy increases from $5000 billion to $5200 billion while
    real interest rates rise from 3% to 4%. Everything else being equal, you would
    expect
    a. money demand to increase.
    b. money demand to decrease.
    c. money demand to remain unchanged.
    d. money demand to either increase or decrease.

2. An increase in investment sensitivity to changes in the interest rate would result in a
    a. steeper aggregate demand curve.
    b. flatter aggregate demand curve.
    c. shift to the right in the aggregate demand curve.
    d. shift to the left in the aggregate demand curve.

3. The new Keynesian approach argues that
    a. the short-run aggregate supply curve is horizontal.
    b. the short-run aggregate supply curve is vertical.
    c. the short-run aggregate supply curve has a positive slope.
    d. the short-run aggregate supply curve has a negative slope.

4. The long-run aggregate supply curve
    a. is horizontal at the equilibrium price level.
    b. is vertical at full employment output.
    c. has a positive slope according to the new Keynesian approach.
    d. has a positive slope according to the new classical approach.

5. The largest component of production costs is typically
    a. raw materials.
    b. rent.
    c. advertising.
    d. labor.

6. An increase in the price of raw materials, according to the new Keynesian view, will
    a. shift the short-run supply curve to the right and the long-run supply curve to the left.
    b. shift the short-run supply curve to the left and leave the long-run supply curve unaffected.
    c. shift the long-run supply curve to the left and the short-ran supply curve to the right.
    d. not cause either the long-run or short-run supply curve to move.

7. All else being held constant, an unexpected decrease in aggregate demand will
    a. cause a recession.
    b. cause inflation.
    c. have no effect on output.
    d. eventually result in a depression.

8. Kenny does not believe that anticipated changes in money growth can affect the economy. He is probably a
    a. monetarist.
    b. traditional Keynesian.
    c. new Keynesian.
    d. new classical.

9. Marisa believes that monetary policy can be effective in shortening recessions but that expectations are important. She is probably a
    a. monetarist.
    b. traditional Keynesian.
    c. new Keynesian.
    d. new classical.

10. An increase in oil prices will shift the _____ curve to the left causing prices to _____.
    a. *SRAS*; rise
    b. *SRAS*; fall
    c. *AD*; rise
    d. *AD*; fall

11. The aggregate demand curve has a
    a. negative slope because higher prices cause higher interest rates, which in turn reduce aggregate demand.
    b. negative slope because firms will charge higher prices as output increases.
    c. negative slope because the demand for individual goods has negative slope and the aggregate demand is simply the sum of the individual demand curves.
    d. positive slope because higher prices increase income, which in turn increases aggregate demand.

12. The more interest elastic is the money demand, the
    a. flatter the aggregate demand curve.
    b. steeper the aggregate demand curve.
    c. flatter the aggregate supply curve.
    d. steeper the aggregate supply curve.

13. A change in the tax laws forces businesses to depreciate equipment less quickly, and at the same time the demand for money increases because banks make it more difficult to obtain a credit card. How will the aggregate demand curve be affected by these two events?
    a. Both of these events will lead to a shift to the right in the aggregate demand curve.
    b. Both of these events will lead to a shift to the left in the aggregate demand curve.
    c. The increase in money demand will cause a rightward shift, and the change in the depreciation law will cause a leftward shift.
    d. The increase in money demand will not cause the curve to shift, and the change in the depreciation law will cause the curve to shift rightward.

14. According to the new classical view, aggregate output will be at full employment in the short-run when
    a. there is no inflation.
    b. aggregate supply equals aggregate demand.
    c. the expected and actual price level are the same.
    d. aggregate output will never be at full employment.

15. The long run aggregate supply curve (*LRAS*) is
    a. vertical at the full employment output level.
    b. only vertical if all markets are noncompetitive.
    c. upward sloping and steeper than the short-run aggregate supply curve.
    d. horizontal at the equilibrium price level.

Essays

1. As a result of a hurricane that hits the eastern seaboard, the prices of fruits and vegetables increase.
    a. What effect will this increase have on output?
    b. What will happen to interest rates?

2. U.S. and Japanese negotiators meet and agree to allow goods to flow more freely between the two countries. How will this agreement affect the U.S. aggregate demand curve?

3. According to the new classicals, would an overestimation of the general price level increase or decrease short-run aggregate supply? Why?

4. Economists disagree about short-run aggregate supply.
    a. How would a traditional Keynesian economist draw the short-run aggregate supply curve? Explain.
    b. How would an economist who followed the new Keynesian approach draw the short-run aggregate supply curve? Explain.

5. What is the effect of an investment tax credit, which reduces the cost of investment to businesses, on the short-run and long-run aggregate supply curves?

6. Suppose that the government wants to promote small business by encouraging bank lending.
    a. Recommend a policy that would accomplish this objective.
    b. What would be the effect of such a policy on aggregate demand and aggregate supply?

7. Explain why the aggregate demand curve is negatively sloped.

8. What is the Ricardian equivalence proposition, and how does it relate to aggregate demand?

9. To raise tax revenues, the government decides to impose a value-added tax on producers. A value-added tax is a tax imposed on producers at each stage of the production process. How will the equilibrium price and output level in the economy be affected in the short and long run?

ANSWERS TO SELF-TEST

True or False

1. True.
2. False. Sellers are the price setters because there are only a few sellers of each product. Buyers are price takers.
3. False. The early 1970s was a period of high inflation caused by the oil price shocks.
4. True.
5. False. New Keynesians and new classicals disagree about short-run aggregate supply.
6. True.
7. False. In looking at a particular good, an increase in the price of that good raises its relative price and causes individuals to find substitutes. In the case of the aggregate demand curve, we are not considering the price of a particular good but the overall price level. The increase in the price level causes real money balances to fall in turn leading to higher interest rates and lower aggregate demand.
8. True.
9. False. The short-run aggregate supply curve has a positive slope throughout.

Fill in the Blank

1. raise; lowering
2. lower
3. actual; expected
4. production costs
5. full employment output
6. productivity
7. stagflation
8. increase
9. *LRAS*; right
10. Robert Lucas; misperception
11. horizontal; zero
12. short; right

Multiple Choice

1.	d	2.	b
3.	c	4.	b
5.	d	6.	b
7.	a	8.	d
9.	c	10.	a
11.	a	12.	b
13.	b	14.	c
15.	a			

Essays

1. a. Adverse weather is an example of a price shock, which shifts short-run aggregate supply to the left.

    b. Higher prices reduce real money balances, causing real interest rates to rise. By the way, the rise in real interest rates causes consumption, investment, and net exports to decline, which is a movement along the *original* aggregate demand curve.

2. Both exports and imports will increase. Therefore the effect on net exports is ambiguous. If net exports increase, the aggregate demand curve will shift to the right. If net exports decrease, the aggregate demand curve will shift to the left.

3. It would cause aggregate supply to decrease. Producers believe that the relative price of the goods they are producing is lower than it actually is, which would cause them to cut back on production.

4. a. The traditionalist would draw short-run aggregate supply as flat, viewing prices as sticky in the short run.

    b. A follower of the new Keynesian approach would draw the curve with a positive slope, recognizing two types of firms: firms that continuously change their prices on the basis of the current level of output and firms with sticky prices that set their prices in advance on the basis of their expectations of economic conditions. The steepness of the short-run aggregate supply curve would therefore depend on the percentage of sticky-price versus flexible-price firms.

5. The short-run curve would shift to the right because the cost of production would decline. The long-run curve would shift to the right because the tax credit would encourage capital formation.

6. a. There are several possible answers. One idea would be to ease supervision by bank regulators (e.g., the FDIC). Of course, an unfortunate by-product of such a policy might be increased moral hazard problems.

b. The aggregate demand curve would shift to the right. Also, the short-run aggregate supply curve would shift downward because the cost of production to small business would drop. The resulting increased output would place upward pressure on prices. Eventually, the aggregate supply curve would shift to the left, restoring full employment.

7. As the price level, P, rises, real money balances (M/P) fall. Real interest rates rise to reduce the demand for real money balances and restore equilibrium in the money market. A higher real interest rate increases savings and reduces consumption demand. The higher real interest rate will also reduce the demand for investment. The higher real interest rate causes the value of the dollar to increase in the foreign-exchange market, which reduces net exports, NX. Aggregate demand is, therefore, lower.

8. The Ricardian equivalence proposition states that a reduction in taxes will not lead to an increase in aggregate demand. The public realizes that a tax cut today will increase the government deficit, and this deficit will have to be paid back in the future with interest. The tax cut today is offset by higher taxes in the future.

9. The tax represents a cost of production and will cause the $SRAS$ curve to shift to the left, lowering output and raising unemployment. In the long run, high unemployment will put downward pressure on wages, shifting $SRAS$ back to its original position.

KEY CONCEPTS

In this chapter, we look at changes in money and economic activity over time to see whether there is a link between the two. As it turns out, the growth of the money supply is **procyclical**, meaning that money growth increases during booms and declines during recessions. Some economists believe that changes in the money supply actually are responsible for subsequent changes in economic activity. Others believe that changes in money supply reflect, rather than cause, business cycles. There are three competing views about the relationship between money and economic activity: the real business cycle model, the new Keynesian model, and the new classical model. Each of the three leading economic theories proposes a different explanation as to why money growth is procyclical.

We turn first to a discussion of the real business cycle model. Proponents of this view believe that prices are flexible even in the short run, so the economy is at full employment all the time. Fluctuations in output in the short run arise primarily from changes in productivity, such as changes in the availability of raw materials, changes in government regulation, and technological innovations.

Money plays no role in determining economic activity, according to the real business cycle model. Instead, most proponents of the real business cycle model argue that there is **reverse causality**. That is, they believe that current and anticipated changes in economic activity affect the demand for money, not the supply. If the Fed passively responds to changes in demand by supplying more money, money will appear to be procyclical. Therefore causality runs from economic activity to money, not from money to economic activity. Unfortunately for real business cycle model proponents, the empirical evidence developed by Friedman and Schwartz strongly suggests that, in fact, money does influence economic activity.

Proponents of the new classical model attribute the link between money and economic activity to imperfect information. Wages and prices fail to adjust fully to current market conditions when workers and business managers misperceive the price level. A change in the price level that is anticipated has no effect on output. An important determinant of the expected price level is the money supply. Therefore in the new classical model, the effect of a change in money supply growth depends crucially on whether the change is expected or not expected:

- If the change in monetary policy is anticipated, workers and business managers will change their expectation of the price level, and monetary policy will not affect economic activity.

- If the change in monetary policy is unanticipated, workers and business managers will not change their expectation, and monetary policy will have a short-run effect on economic activity.

Therefore in the short-run, an unanticipated increase in money growth will cause economic activity to expand, and an unanticipated decrease in money growth will cause economic activity to decrease.

Is the new classical approach supported by the empirical evidence? Available evidence suggests that both expected and unexpected changes in the nominal money supply affect current output. Therefore, the new classical approach does not seem to be supported by the evidence.

Proponents of the new Keynesian model believe that prices are not completely flexible in the short run. Even if households and businesses correctly forecast the price level, because they are inflexible in the short run, wages and prices cannot fully adjust to current market conditions. Therefore even anticipated monetary policy can influence economic activity in the short run. An increase in money growth causes economic activity to expand and a decline in money growth causes the economy to contract. However, to the extent that households and businesses can adjust wages and prices, an anticipated change in policy is less effective than an unanticipated change.

The linkage between money and economic output has important policy implications. If the nominal money supply is not neutral, policymakers can try to use changes in money supply to smooth the business cycle. For example, the Fed could expand money supply when it wants to stimulate the economy. A policy that is designed to smooth short-run fluctuations in output is known as a **stabilization policy**. The real business cycle model places no value on stabilization policies because of the assumption that only supply shocks affect output. Economists who advocate the new classical approach also are critical of stabilization policy. They stress that only unexpected changes in policy have any real effect. Moreover, in practice, unanticipated policies must be random (otherwise, people would be able to anticipate them). Because they are random, unanticipated policies introduce uncertainty, causing random fluctuations in output. Therefore stabilization policies either are ineffective or counterproductive. The reason for this result is the assumption that the public has **rational expectations**, which is the assumption that people base their expectations on all available information, including changes in money growth. In the new Keynesian approach, stabilization policy can be effective. The reason is that both expected and unexpected changes in money supply affect output. Therefore policymakers can systematically affect output by changing the money supply, even if people have rational expectations. Thus, monetary policy can be used to stabilize the economy. However, the existence of lags in policy making and implementation implies that policymakers should not attempt to fine-tune every disturbance in aggregate demand; stabilization policy should be reserved for major economic downturns.

Check List

When you finish this chapter, you should be able to:

- ✔ Understand what it means for money to be procyclical.

- ✔ Understand the significance of reverse causality.

- ✔ Explain why real business cycle theory proponents believe that causality runs from economic activity to money.

- ✔ Understand the significance of "independent" changes in the money supply.

- ✔ Distinguish between anticipated and unanticipated changes in the money supply.

- ✔ Explain why anticipated changes in monetary policy have no effect on real economic activity according to the new classical view.

- ✔ Explain why unanticipated changes in monetary policy can affect real economic activity but must be random, and therefore counterproductive, according to the new classical view.

- ✔ Use an *AD-AS* diagram to illustrate the effect of anticipated and unanticipated monetary policy in the new classical view.

- ✔ Explain why both anticipated and unanticipated changes in monetary policy can influence real economic activity according to the new Keynesian view.

- ✔ Use an *AD-AS* diagram to illustrate the effect of anticipated and unanticipated monetary policy in the new Keynesian view.

- ✔ Describe the channels through which monetary policy influences aggregate demand according to the new Keynesian approach.

- ✔ Distinguish among the views about stabilization policy of real business cycle proponents, new classicals, and new Keynesians.

- ✔ Use *AD-AS* diagrams to explain economic events during the 1980s and 1990s.

Self-Test

True or False

1. Economists have found that changes in the growth rate of the nominal money supply tend to precede changes in economic activity.

2. A conclusion of the old classical model is that money is neutral in the short run.

3. Although new classicals believe that whether a policy is anticipated or not is important to understanding how the policy will affect the economy, new Keynesians believe that anticipated and unanticipated policies have the same effect.

4. New Keynesians believe that stabilization policies should always be used to fine-tune the economy.

5. Evidence about the effects on output of monetary and fiscal policies during the 1980s and early 1990s is more supportive of the new classical approach than of the new Keynesian approach.

6. In a perfectly competitive market with perfect information, a basic assumption of the new classical model would be violated.

7. Milton Friedman and Anna Schwartz found evidence that supported the real business cycle view.

8. A belief that used to be widely accepted is that money supply changes affected real output only with a long and variable lag. Economists now believe that with improved technology, these lags are minimal.

Fill in the Blank

1. Friedman and Schwartz found that money affects output with a _____ and _____ lag.

2. New classical economists believe that output will increase as a result of an increase in the money supply that causes the actual price level to exceed the _____ price level.

3. The early 1980s was a period of _____ monetary policy and _____ fiscal policy.

4. The Fed chairman during the early part of the 1990s was _____ _____.

5. The early 1990s was a period of _____ monetary policy and
    _____ fiscal policy.

6. According to the real business cycle model, money is _____ in the short
    run.

7. An expected increase in the money supply would cause both real output and the
    price level to increase in the _____ _____ model.

Multiple Choice

1. Business cycles have been a feature of modern economics since
    a. the Industrial Revolution
    b. the U.S. Civil War.
    c. World War I.
    d. the Renaissance.

2. The low point of the business cycle is called the
    a. bottom.
    b. trough.
    c. recession.
    d. depression.

3. Friedman and Schwartz found that the peak in the nominal money supply growth
    precedes the peak in output on average by
    a. one month.
    b. six months.
    c. sixteen months.
    d. three years.

4. An expected change in the money supply in the short run will
    a. cause NO change in output in the new classical and new Keynesian models.
    b. cause a change in output in the new classical model but NOT in the new
        Keynesian model.
    c. cause a change in output in the new Keynesian model but NOT in the new
        classical model.
    d. cause a change in output in BOTH the new Keynesian and new classical
        models.

5. Economists belonging to which school would be the most likely to endorse a
    monetary policy aimed at stabilizing economic activity?
    a. new Keynesian
    b. new classical
    c. real business cycle
    d. Economists from all three schools would endorse a stabilization policy.

6. According to the new Keynesian view, an expansionary monetary policy would cause a gradual shift of
   a. the aggregate demand curve to the right as prices rise.
   b. the aggregate demand curve to the right as interest rates rise,
   c. the aggregate supply curve to the left as prices rise.
   d. the aggregate supply curve to the left as interest rates rise.

7. Senator Tommy, a candidate for President, argues that stabilization policies are either ineffective or counterproductive. You would conclude that he is most likely a
   a. real business cycle proponent.
   b. new Keynesian.
   c. new classical.
   d. traditional Keynesian.

8. Senator David, Senator Tommy's opponent, argues that stabilization policies are completely ineffective and inconsequential. You would conclude that he is most likely a
   a. real business cycle proponent
   b. new Keynesian.
   c. new classical.
   d. traditional Keynesian.

9. Bush administration officials complained during 1991 that slow but steady money growth was responsible for the slow economic recovery. To stimulate economic growth, they wanted the Fed to increase money supply growth. You would conclude that the Bush administration officials were
   a. new Keynesians because they believed that anticipated policies do influence the economy.
   b. new Keynesians because they believed that anticipated policies do NOT influence the economy.
   c. new classicals because they believed that anticipated policies do influence the economy.
   d. new classicals because they believed that anticipated policies do NOT influence the economy.

10. During the 1992 campaign, Bill Clinton proposed reducing the federal deficit by lowering government spending and raising taxes. He believed that his proposed changes would have a dampening effect on the economy. To offset the effect of his fiscal policies, Mr. Clinton called on the Fed to implement an expansionary policy. You would conclude that Mr. Clinton was a
    a. new Keynesian because he believed that anticipated policies do influence the economy.
    b. new Keynesian because he believed that anticipated policies do NOT influence the economy.
    c. new classical because he believed that anticipated policies do influence the economy.
    d. new classical because he believed that anticipated policies do NOT influence the economy.

11. According to the new Keynesian view, a decrease in the U.S. money supply will cause
    a. interest rates to rise, foreign investment in the United States to increase, the value of the U.S. dollar to rise, and net exports to decrease.
    b. interest rates to rise, foreign investment in the United States to decrease, the value of the U.S. dollar to fall, and net exports to increase.
    c. stock prices to fall, financial wealth to decrease, and consumption and investment to decrease.
    d. both a and c.

12. According to the real business cycle model, fluctuations in real output in the short run are due to
    a. productivity shocks.
    b. money supply changes.
    c. aggregate demand.
    d. government spending decisions.

13. In the short run, expected changes in the money supply would
    a. affect real output only in the new classical model.
    b. affect real output only in the new Keynesian model.
    c. affect real output only in the new classical and Keynesian models.
    d. not affect real output in any of the models. Only unexpected changes affect real output.

14. Price flexibility is greatest in the _____ _____ model and least flexible in the _____ _____ model.
    a. new classical; new Keynesian
    b. real business; new classical
    c. new Keynesian; real business
    d. real business; new Keynesian

Essays

1. According to the real business cycle model, the short-run and long-run aggregate supply curves have the same shape. Comment.

2. A drought in the Southeast substantially reduces agricultural output, causing the short-run aggregate supply curve to shift to the left. The consequence is a recession. Indicate the appropriate monetary policy for each of the following approaches:
   (a.) Real business cycle model
   (b.) New classical
   (c.) New Keynesian

3. Both new Keynesian and new classical economists believe that a change in the money supply can lead to a change in real output. How does each group support this conclusion?

4. For new Keynesians, an anticipated change in monetary policy will have less of an effect than an unanticipated change will. Why?

5. Policy lags make fine-tuning the economy difficult. Explain.

6. You are about to graduate from college and are interviewing for jobs. One of the recruiters is from the Federal Reserve. The Fed is interested in hiring an economist who would work in the economic stabilization division. You decide to decline the offer because you believe that all changes in the money supply are ineffective. Your friend, however, is eager to work in this position because he is a firm believer in the effectiveness of monetary policy. Of the three models discussed in this chapter, which one is most consistent with your view and which one is most consistent with your friend's? Explain.

7. Advocates of the real business cycle model argue that a change in the money supply affects real output in the short run. Comment.

Use the following information to answer questions 8 through 10. In Chapter 1, the author emphasized that the best way to evaluate an economic theory is to apply the economic approach.

8. How can the economic approach be used to decide among the real business cycle model, the new classical approach, and the new Keynesian approach?

9. On the basis of information presented in the main text, which theory—real business cycle, new classical, or new Keynesian—is best?

10. Given your answer to essay question 9, why do economists continue to debate which model best explains the data?

ANSWERS TO SELF-TEST

True or False

1. True.
2. True.
3. False. New Keynesians believe that unanticipated policies have a greater effect on the economy than do anticipated policies.
4. False. Policy lags make fine-tuning impossible.
5. False. The reverse is true; evidence from the 1980s and 1990s supports the new Keynesian view.
6. True.
7. False. According to the real business cycle model, money is neutral. Friedman and Schwartz concluded that changes in money growth cause business fluctuations. They came to this conclusion by examining money supply and output data from the Civil War to 1960.
8. False. Economists still believe that there are numerous lags in the policy and implementation process. The author mentions five: data lag, recognition lag, legislative lag, implementation lag, and impact lag.

Fill in the Blank

1. long; variable
2. expected
3. tight; easy
4. Alan Greenspan
5. easy; tight
6. neutral
7. new Keynesian

Multiple Choice

1.	a	2.	b
3.	c	4.	c
5.	a	6.	c
7.	c	8.	a
9.	a	10.	a
11.	d	12.	a
13.	b	14.	d

Essays

1. Proponents of the real business cycle model assume that prices are flexible and information is perfect, even in the short run. Therefore, the short-run aggregate supply curve is vertical at the full employment level. The shape of the aggregate supply curve in both the short run and the long run is the same.

2. (a.) *Real business cycle model*: No policy intervention will work. Monetary policy is ineffective.
   (b.) *New classical*: No policy intervention will work. If the policy is anticipated (e.g., an increase in money supply growth), it will be ineffective. If it is unanticipated, it must be random and therefore counterproductive.
   (c.) *New Keynesian*: An increase in money supply growth will shift *AD* to the right, returning the economy to full employment more rapidly.

3. *New classical*: New classical economists argue that an unexpected increase in the money supply will cause the actual price level to be above the expected price level. Firms are fooled into thinking that the relative prices of their products have increased, and they increase their output. An expected change in the money supply will not cause a change in output.
   New Keynesian: New Keynesian economists argue that prices are not completely flexible in the short run. For unanticipated changes in monetary policy, the story is much the same as for a new classical. On the other hand, an anticipated increase in the money supply will cause the aggregate demand curve to shift to the right. Because of long-term contracts and imperfect competition, not all prices rise. The aggregate supply does not completely adjust so output increases. Therefore, both anticipated and unanticipated monetary policy can be effective.

4. New Keynesians assume that prices are not completely flexible. However, prices are partially flexible. An unanticipated change in monetary policy has no effect on households' and businesses' expectations about the price level. So *SRAS* does not shift, and monetary policy can influence economic activity. An anticipated change in monetary policy will cause households and businesses to revise their expectations about prices. To the extent that they are able, given existing contracts and commitments, workers will demand higher wages and businesses will charge higher prices, shifting the short-run aggregate demand curve to the left. However, the curve will not shift so far as to be at full employment because workers and businesses are limited in their ability to change wages and prices.

5. Lags make it difficult to design policies to offset short-term and/or mild economic fluctuations. By the time a policy is implemented, the economy will often have corrected itself. For example, a stimulative policy that is designed to offset a small increase in unemployment might as likely cause the economy to become overheated as to correct the problem for which it was designed. Therefore attempting to fine-tune the economy will not work.

6. Your position is most consistent with that of the real business cycle model. Economists who follow this view place no value on monetary policy's ability to stabilize the economy. They believe that productivity disturbances cause fluctuations. Your friend is most likely a new Keynesian. Economists who follow this school believe that changes in the money supply can change real output, employment, and interest rates in the short run. Money supply changes affect real interest rates in the short run, which in turn lead to changes in consumption, investment, and net exports. The aggregate demand curve would shift and equilibrium output would be affected, as would the price level.

7. Advocates of this view argue that an anticipated increase in economic activity increases demand for money. The increase in demand causes the Fed to increase the money supply. Money would be neutral in the short run as well as the long run because prices are flexible in both the short and long run. Real output would be unaffected.

8. Economic analysis is the development and testing of an economic theory's predictions to determine the theory's usefulness. Economic analysis involves setting out what is to be explained (the problem), what you believe to be the explanation (the theory), and the evaluation of the theory by examining actual data. Deciding which theory is best involves three criteria: (1.) Are the assumptions of the theory reasonable? (2.) Does the theory generate predictions that you can verify with actual data? (3.) Do the data corroborate the predictions?

9. According to the information provided in the text, the new Keynesian model is best supported by the data. The real business cycle model's assertion that changes in output cause changes in money growth is not supported by the work of Friedman and Schwartz. The new classical model's contention that anticipated monetary policy is ineffective is not supported by the events of the 1980s and 1990s. On the other hand, the new Keynesian prediction that both anticipated and unanticipated monetary policy is effective is supported by the data.

10. Economics is a nonexperimental science that must rely on history to provide it with data. Usually, the data are confounded by factors that make a clean test of a theory difficult. Although the new Keynesian model has received the most support from the data, the results so far have been inconclusive.

27: Information Problems and Channels for Monetary Policy

KEY CONCEPTS

In the previous chapter, we discussed how changes in the money supply can influence economic activity. In this chapter we look in more detail at exactly how money influences real economic variables. Our goal is to develop a model of the macroeconomy and the role of the financial system that is more realistic. We can then use that model to make more accurate predictions about the effects of monetary policy on economic activity.

Asymmetric information can make it difficult to match borrowers and lenders. This can be especially true for small businesses. Banks specialize in gathering information about the creditworthiness of borrowers and in monitoring borrowers' activities after loans are made. Therefore banks can often provide funds to small businesses more cheaply than can financial markets. For this reason, a majority of lending occurs through financial intermediaries rather than directly through financial markets. However, because many bank customers have no alternative sources of funds, if they are turned down for a bank loan, then they will have to forgo their investment opportunity. Therefore, changes in the availability of bank credit can affect overall investment and economic activity.

Asymmetric information can also affect business decisions about the use of internal versus external funds. High information costs may affect the cost of using internal funds rather than external funds. Therefore a business's net worth is also an important determinant of its ability to invest. Businesses with greater net worth have greater access to internal funds and can more readily finance investment opportunities that arise. Moreover, a high net worth acts as a signal to potential lenders about a firm's prospects, thus reducing the cost of external financing.

There are two important sources of shifts in bank lending and net worth:

- **Financial panics** are episodes that are characterized by bank runs, fluctuations in financial markets, widespread business bankruptcies, and lower output.

- **Credit controls and credit crunches** also cause banks to cut back on lending.

There are three channels through which monetary policy can influence the economy:

- **The money channel**: This mechanism works by reducing interest rates. When the Fed supplies additional reserves to the banking system, banks use the funds to expand lending. But to induce borrowing, banks lower interest rates, inducing additional investment and consumption. Alternatively, banks can use reserves to buy securities. This bids up security prices, reducing interest rates.

- **The bank lending channel**: With this mechanism, a monetary expansion increases banks' ability to lend, allowing bank-dependent borrowers to spend more, stimulating the economy.

- **The balance sheet channel**: This mechanism assumes that monetary policy works through changes in net worth and liquidity. Specifically, an expansionary monetary policy, which reduces interest rates, increases businesses' net worth by reducing the cash flow necessary for debt service. This reduces the cost of borrowing for businesses that face high information costs.

The bank lending and balance sheet channels differ from the money channel in that they predict that monetary policy should have different effects on different individuals and firms. In particular, individuals or businesses that depend on bank loans should be disproportionately affected by changes in monetary policy if the bank lending channel is valid, while low-net-worth firms should be disproportionately affected if the balance sheet channel is valid. In fact, both of these predictions have been verified.

Check List

When you finish this chapter, you should be able to:

✔ Explain the importance of asymmetric information for the financial system.

✔ Understand the role of financial intermediation in overcoming information problems.

✔ Distinguish between internal and external financing and understand why the cost of external funds is often higher than the cost of internal funds.

✔ Understand the role of net worth in dealing with information problems.

✔ Use an *AD-AS* diagram to illustrate the effects of a drop in bank lending and net worth.

✔ Understand the importance of financial panics, credit controls, and credit crunches.

✔ Distinguish among the money channel, the bank lending channel, and the balance sheet channel and indicate the public policy implications of each.

Self-Test

True or False

1. For small firms, internal funds are usually a cheaper source of finance than are external funds.

2. The local supermarket would be more adversely affected by restrictions imposed on bank lending than the local appliance store would.

3. Financial panics are less common today than they were 100 years ago.

4. In the money channel, borrowers consider all sources of funds to be close substitutes for one another.

5. The likelihood of households and businesses experiencing financial distress increases as their access to credit from financial institutions increases.

6. A credit crunch would have more of an impact on small firms than on large firms.

7. The money channel and the bank lending channel are mutually incompatible.

8. Financial intermediaries are particularly important for businesses that have high information costs.

9. Spending by small firms is more sensitive to changes in monetary policy than is spending by large firms.

10. Spending by firms with strong balance sheets is more sensitive to changes in monetary policy than is spending by firms with weak balance sheets.

Fill in the Blank

1. Financial panics cause the money supply to _____.

2. _____ is the loss of deposits by banks because of their inability to pay competitive market interest rates.

3. _____ _____ are regulations that limit the availability of credit.

4. The money, bank lending, and balance sheet channels all predict that an increase in money supply will _____ spending, shifting *AD* to the _____.

5. The _____ channel takes the position that borrowers are indifferent to how or from whom they raise funds and that borrowers regard alternative sources of credit as close substitutes.

6. The _____ _____ channel argues that, for many borrowers, there is no close substitute for bank credit.

7. The _____ channel assumes that a rise in interest rates reduces aggregate demand.

8. Financial regulations, like _____ _____, have caused credit crunches in the past.

9. The Carter credit controls resulted in a _____ _____.

10. _____-_____-_____ borrowers are disproportionately affected by a tightening of monetary policy under the balance sheet channel.

Multiple Choice

1. What is the role of asymmetric information in the bank lending channel?
    a. High-information-cost borrowers must borrow from banks.
    b. High-information-cost borrowers find internal funds less expensive than external funds.
    c. High interest rates reduce spending by businesses and households.
    d. All of the above are true.

2. What is the role of asymmetric information in the balance sheet channel?
    a. High-information-cost borrowers must borrow from banks.
    b. High-information-cost borrowers find internal funds less expensive than external funds.
    c. High interest rates reduce spending by businesses and households
    d. All of the above are true.

3. The money channel is a part of the _____ model.
    a. new classical
    b. new Keynesian
    c. real business cycle
    d. new Marxist

4. New government regulations restrict the type of information that credit bureaus can report. You would expect
    a. businesses' cost of funds to rise and their investment spending to fall.
    b. businesses' costs of funds to fall and their investment spending to rise.
    c. no impact on the cost of funds or investment spending.
    d. an increase in the use of external funds relative to internal funds as a source of financing by larger firms.

5. Regulatory restrictions on bank lending are called
    a. credit controls.
    b. financial panics.
    c. credit rationings.
    d. liquidity premiums.

6. Suppose that a new banking regulation reduces paperwork on new bank loans. What type of borrower(s) would most benefit?
    a. Small businesses and households
    b. Large businesses and households
    c. Large and small businesses
    d. Only small businesses

7. Banking panics have a tendency to
    a. lower the real interest rate on both safe and risky securities.
    b. raise the real interest rate on both safe and risky securities.
    c. lower the real interest rate on risky securities and raise the real interest rate on safe securities.
    d. lower the real interest rate on safe securities and raise the real interest rate on risky securities.

8. Interest rate ceilings on deposits existed prior to the 1980s. The Fed regulation that set these limits was
    a. Regulation A.
    b. Regulation I.
    c. Regulation Q.
    d. Regulation W.

9. The credit crunch that occurred at the beginning of the 1990–1991 recession was in large part caused by
    a. interest rate ceilings on deposits that reduced bank deposits.
    b. banks' concern about the strength of borrowers' balance sheets.
    c. the Fed imposing limits on lending.
    d. banks leaving the Federal Reserve System.

10. The lack of an efficient operating bank sector in the former Soviet Union means that
    a. the money channel is invalid.
    b. monetary authorities must deal directly with businesses.
    c. information problems are more difficult.
    d. World Bank officials pressure Russian officials to establish new bank
        regulations.

11. In a credit crunch the bank lending channel would indicate that there would be
    a. an overall decline in borrowing, with large businesses showing the largest
        decline.
    b. an overall decline in borrowing, with small businesses showing the largest
        decline.
    c. an overall decline in borrowing, with small and large businesses showing an
        equal decline.
    d. no overall decline in borrowing because businesses and individuals would take
        advantage of the lower interest rates caused by the weakened economy.

12. According to the balance sheet channel, an increase in borrower net worth will shift
    the aggregate demand curve to the _____ and the money demand curve to
    the _____.
    a. right; right
    b. right; left
    c. left; right
    d. left; left

13. Suppose U.S. products account for a substantial percentage of the budget of Mexican
    households and businesses. In December 1994, the Mexican peso depreciated
    against the U.S. dollar, thereby sharply increasing the Mexican cost of U.S. products.
    The balance sheet channel would indicate that in Mexico, there would be
    a. an overall decline in borrowing, with large businesses showing the largest
        decline.
    b. an overall decline in borrowing, with small businesses showing the largest
        decline.
    c. an overall decline in borrowing, with small and large businesses showing an
        equal decline.
    d. no overall decline in borrowing because businesses and individuals would take
        advantage of the lower interest rates caused by the weakened economy.

14. Loans made by financial institutions
    a. are crucial to understanding the impact of monetary policy in the bank lending
        channel.
    b. play no special role in the money channel.
    c. are not considered important in the balance sheet channel.
    d. are characterized by both (a.) and (b.).

Essays

1. Why might it be unwise for a saver to lend to a borrower who is willing to pay an above-market interest rate?

2. Suppose that the economy suffers a financial panic.
   a. What impact does the panic have on the components of *M1*?
   b. What is the impact on the yield spread between high- and low-risk securities?

3. Credit controls on banks should lower both the real interest rate and the nominal interest rate. Explain.

4. A contractionary monetary policy by the Fed that decreased bank reserves would have a greater impact on small businesses under the bank lending channel than under the money channel.
   a. Why?
   b. Illustrate your answer using an *AD-AS* diagram.

5. In October 1987, stock prices had their biggest one-day decline on record.
   a. This decline increased the probability of financial distress. Explain.
   b. Explain the difference in the effect of the October 1987 stock market crash under the money channel and under the balance sheet channel.
   c. Illustrate your answer to (b.) using the *AD-AS* diagram.
   d. After the crash, the Fed announced that, in its capacity as lender of last resort, it stood ready to provide liquidity to the financial system. Would such an action be necessary under the balance sheet channel? Under the money channel? Explain.

6. The money channel and the bank lending channel are observationally equivalent in that both predict that a contractionary monetary policy will shift the aggregate demand curve to the left. However, small and large businesses would be affected differently under each channel. Explain.

7. The three criteria for selecting among competing theories are: (1.) Are the assumptions of the model reasonable? (2.) Does the model generate a testable hypothesis? (3.) Are the model's predictions verified by the actual data?
   a. On the basis of the information given in the main text, how well do the money channel, bank lending channel, and balance sheet channel stand up under the three criteria?
   b. On the basis of your answer to (a.), which of the three channels should a model of the economy include?

8. World Bank officials recently released a study that found that countries with more even land distribution have experienced more rapid economic growth in the post-World War II period. These officials further speculated that the reason for this more rapid growth was better access to financial markets. Explain their reasoning.

9.   George Goterari, an official of a small Latin American country, complains that the biggest obstacle to growth is the lack of a well-developed banking sector. Comment.

Answers to the Chapter 27 Self-Test appear on page 346.

CHAPTERS 1-16: MIDTERM EXAMINATION 2

Self-Test

True or False

1. There is no guarantee that if a theory satisfies the three criteria for choosing a useful economic theory it will be the best theory for understanding the particular workings of the economy.

2. Currently in the United States, a ten-dollar bill is convertible into ¼ ounce of gold.

3. Long-term bond prices are more sensitive than short-term bond prices to changes in the interest rate.

4. Historically in the United States, interest rates tend to fall during business cycle expansions and rise during business cycle contractions.

5. A bond with a rating of "AA" has less default risk than a bond with a rating of "A".

6. In a spot market transaction, settlement occurs at a future date at a price agreed upon today.

7. The imposition of circuit breakers has increased the liquidity of stock markets.

8. Mutual funds are an example of a contractual saving institutions.

9. Loan loss reserves are the part of net worth set aside for anticipated future loan losses.

10. State-chartered banks that are members of the Federal Reserve System are supervised the Office of the Comptroller of the Currency.

Fill in the Blank

1. The financial system _____ funds from those who have excess funds to those who are in need of funds.

2. _____ _____ were the largest financial asset classification held by savers in 1998.

3. The _____ for loanable funds is equivalent to the _____ of bonds.

Essays

1. It might be unwise because of adverse selection. Borrowers who are willing to pay above-market interest rates are more likely to be unable or unwilling to repay their loans.

2. a. The currency component of *M1* should increase, and the deposit component of *M1* should decrease.
    b. Individuals will try to buy low-risk securities, reducing low-risk security yields, and avoid buying high-risk securities, raising their yield. The yield spread between high- and low-risk securities will widen.

3. Credit controls reduce the availability of funds to borrowers, reducing spending. This condition causes aggregate demand to fall, which in turn causes money demand to fall, reducing the real interest rate. The inflation rate will fall because of the reduction in aggregate demand. The nominal interest rate is the sum of the real interest rate and the expected inflation rate. Both the real interest rate and the inflation rate fall, so the nominal interest rate will fall also.

4. a. According to the bank lending view, the aggregate demand curve will shift to the left, owing to the initial rise in interest rates resulting from the decrease in money supply, and also because bank-dependent borrowers must reduce their spending.

    b.

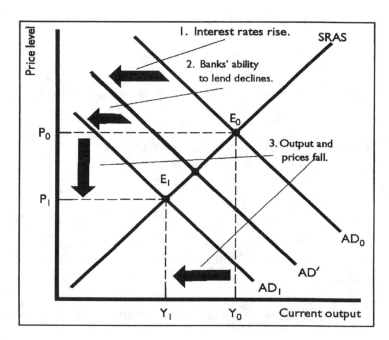

5. a. The likelihood of financial distress is inversely related to the liquidity in an individual's or business's balance sheet and to net worth, or assets minus liabilities. Both of these factors fell with a decline in stock prices. (Keep in mind that stocks are a major type of liquid asset.)

   b. Under the money channel, the stock market crash would have no effect on overall economic activity. Under the balance sheet channel, the reduction in liquidity and the decline in net worth reduce the borrowing capacity of low-net-worth borrowers, reducing their consumption and/or investment demand. This causes the aggregate demand curve to shift to the left. A recession would result, all else being constant.

   c.

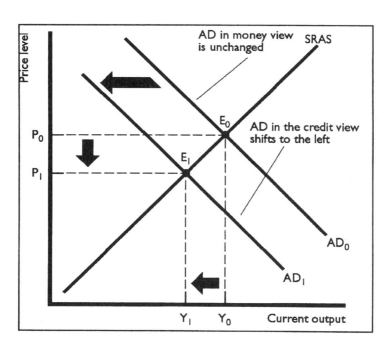

   d. By promising to provide liquidity, the Fed limits the possibility of financial distress. Limiting financial distress is not important under the money channel but is crucial for preventing a recession under the balance sheet channel. (By the way, the Fed's actions prevented the immediate collapse of the investment firm of E. F. Hutton. After the fact, many analysts pointed to the short-term survival of Hutton as important in preventing further economic disruption after the crash. When Hutton eventually did merge with another firm, the transaction was completed in an orderly manner and did not disrupt financial markets.)

6. Although both channels predict a shift in aggregate demand to the left, the bank lending channel predicts that the impact of monetary policy will disproportionately affect small businesses and other bank-dependent borrowers. The money channel predicts that the impact of a contractionary policy will be more symmetric, affecting all businesses simultaneously. Therefore, by looking at the changes in spending by small versus large businesses, it is possible to distinguish between the money and bank lending mechanisms.

7. a. The assumptions underlying all three channels are reasonable. The money channel predicts that a decrease in the money supply will cause interest rates to rise, thereby reducing spending. This prediction is consistent with the data. The bank lending channel predicts that bank-dependent borrowers will be more sensitive to changes in monetary policy, which has been found to be true. The balance sheet channel predicts that low-net-worth borrowers will be more sensitive to changes in monetary policy, which is consistent with actual findings.

    b. The three criteria are met by all three channels, so a complete model of the economy will incorporate all three mechanisms.

8. They are applying the balance sheet channel. In less-developed countries, land is the most common form of collateral for bank loans. If there is more equal land distribution, collateral is more widely available, and so information problems are less. Therefore, entrepreneurs with worthwhile projects are more likely to be able to find financing.

9. In less-developed countries, asymmetric information problems are particularly acute, as nearly all indigenous businesses are small. Therefore the lack of a well-developed banking sector is particularly troublesome.

KEY CONCEPTS

In Chapter 1, to motivate your interest in money, the financial system, and the economy, we argued that one reason for studying money is because changes in money are associated with changes in important economic variables such as economic activity and inflation. Now, in the final chapter of the book, we come full circle and turn to a discussion of money and inflation. Economists have identified three sources of short-term inflation:

- Aggregate demand could rise in response to an increase in nominal money supply growth.

- Aggregate demand could increase because of short-run increases in velocity arising from increased government spending, consumer spending, or investment spending growth.

- Even if aggregate demand does not increase, the growth rate of aggregate supply could fall.

There are limits, however, to changes in velocity or aggregate supply. Therefore the cause of sustained long-term inflation is sustained growth in the nominal money supply at a rate faster than the growth rate of output less velocity.

Inflation imposes costs on society. The nature of these costs differs depending on whether inflation is expected or unexpected. When inflation is expected, financial and other contracts can be modified to minimize inflation costs. Nevertheless, even when inflation is expected, not all costs can be avoided:

- When people anticipate inflation, they seek to economize on the amount of money they hold. As a consequence, they must convert assets into money more often, incurring more **shoe leather costs** in the process.

- Another cost from expected inflation occurs because the U.S. tax system is defined in nominal terms. For example, inflation causes the nominal value of assets to increase. When these assets are sold, capital gains taxes must be paid even when the real values of the assets have not increased.

- The third cost from expected inflation involves **menu costs**, which are the costs to businesses of changing prices.

When inflation is unexpected, it is not possible to modify financial or other contracts to minimize inflation costs. Therefore unexpected inflation also imposes costs on society:

- Unexpected inflation can redistribute wealth among lenders and borrowers. Higher than expected inflation benefits borrowers at the expense of lenders. Lower than expected inflation benefits lenders. Although the loss to one person arising from unexpected inflation is a gain to someone else, unexpected inflation is still undesirable. For fear of redistribution of wealth from unexpected inflation, investment decisions will be distorted as borrowers and lenders enter contracts that are designed to avoid inflation costs.

- The expense that households and businesses incur in attempting to forecast inflation is another cost of unexpected inflation.

- In a market economy, changes in relative prices communicate information about the scarcity of resources. When inflation fluctuates significantly, relative prices may change in response to general price-level changes, distorting the value of prices as signals about market conditions. Variations in relative prices cause households and businesses to waste resources investigating price differences.

Despite the tremendous costs arising from inflation, governments still pursue inflationary monetary policies. They do so to maintain low unemployment. Two types of inflation can arise when the government pursues a goal of low employment:

- **Cost-push inflation** is caused by workers pushing for higher wages. To avoid high unemployment after a successful wage push, the government must expand the money supply so as to maintain adequate aggregate demand.

- **Demand-pull inflation** occurs when policymakers attempt to maintain economic activity above the long-run full-employment level. In this case, output would fall unless the government continuously expanded the money supply.

Suppose that, for whatever reason, policymakers decide to disinflate. The type of costs that the economy will incur depends on whether the new classical or new Keynesian approach is correct:

- Because new classicals believe that wages and prices adjust quickly to changes in expectations, they advocate a disinflation policy of **cold turkey**. Such an approach has the advantage of quickly changing expectations.

- New Keynesians argue that long-term contracts and menu costs slow the adjustment of wages and prices to changes in expectations. New Keynesians therefore advocate a disinflation policy of **gradualism**, which allows people to adjust prices, so the overall cost to the economy is less.

For both new classicals and new Keynesians, the cost of disinflation is less if the public expects lower inflation. However, merely announcing a disinflationary policy may not be enough to convince people of the Fed's intention to disinflate. An additional crucial factor is **central bank credibility**. Many economists and policymakers believe that the key to central bank credibility is the adoption of a **rules strategy**, which requires the central bank to follow specific publicly announced guidelines in setting monetary policy.

As an alternative to disinflation, the government could impose **price controls**. However, such an action is not advisable for at least two reasons:

- Price controls interfere with the operation of markets, reducing economic efficiency. Typically, with price controls, shortages and surpluses develop in various markets. Because prices cannot adjust, there is no means to eliminate these.

- If the public expects the price controls to be removed in the future, inflation can be suppressed in the short run, but in the long run, it will burst out again. Therefore price controls do not provide a long-run solution to inflation.

Check List

When you finish this chapter, you should be able to:

✔ Use the equation of exchange to identify the sources of short-run inflation.

✔ Explain why long-run inflation is a monetary phenomenon.

✔ Use an *AD-AS* diagram to illustrate the short-run effect of changes in the money supply or changes in velocity on the price level.

✔ Use an *AD-AS* diagram to illustrate the effect of a shift in *SRAS* on the price level.

✔ Use an *AD-AS* diagram to illustrate the long-run effect of changes in the money supply on the price level.

✔ Identify the costs of expected inflation.

✔ Identify the costs of unexpected inflation and explain the importance of inflation uncertainty.

✔ Distinguish between cost-push inflation and demand-pull inflation and use an *AD-AS* diagram to illustrate both.

✔ Distinguish between a cold turkey and a gradual approach to disinflation.

✔ Understand the role of credibility in disinflation.

✔ Explain the significance of rules versus discretion.

✔ Understand why most economists argue against price controls as a means for controlling inflation.

Self-Test

True or False

1. Since the 1950s, inflation rates have continually increased from one decade to the next.

2. An example of a supply shock would be a one-time increase in the price of a barrel of oil that caused the aggregate supply curve to shift to the left.

3. A supply shock affects the price level in both the short run and the long run.

4. To keep the real after-tax return on an investment constant, the nominal interest rate would have to increase by more than the inflation rate.

5. If inflation takes a sudden unexpected jump owing to an oil price shock, a lender will be adversely affected.

6. Cost-push inflation can be sustained in the long run without an accommodating expansionary policy, whereas demand-pull inflation cannot.

7. Central bank credibility is important for achieving disinflation at low cost.

8. Cost-push inflation is characterized by a shift of *SRAS* to the left.

9. New classical economists usually advocate gradualism.

10. According to the theory of purchasing power parity, rapid inflation should cause a country's currency to appreciate.

Fill in the Blank

1. $MV = PY$ is called the _____ _____ _____.

2. Extreme cases of inflation in which the rate of inflation is in the hundreds or thousands of percent per year are called _____.

3. The _____ rate of unemployment is the rate of unemployment that exists when the economy produces at the full-employment level of output.

4. Letting the money supply grow at 4% per year, year after year, is consistent with a(n) _____ _____.

5. _____ _____ are government regulations that prevent prices from changing.

6. Former Federal Reserve Chairman Paul Volker implemented a(n) _____ policy that resulted in a substantial reduction in inflation during the early 1980s.

7. When people believe that the Fed will fight inflation, the Fed is said to have _____.

8. _____ _____ _____ occur when excessive transactions must be executed to avoid inflation losses.

9. One way to build credibility is to follow a _____ strategy rather than a _____ strategy.

10. New classical economists often argue for a _____ _____ approach, whereas new Keynesians argue for a _____ approach for reducing inflation.

11. High unemployment accompanies _____-_____ inflation, whereas low unemployment is associated with _____ - _____ inflation.

Multiple Choice

1. A market basket of goods in year 1 cost $88. In year 2, the exact same market basket cost $147. Between year 1 and year 2, prices rose
   a. 47%.
   b. 147%.
   c. 67%.
   d. 167%.

2. The money supply is growing at 3% per year, real output is growing at 2% per year, velocity is constant, and the nominal interest rate is 7%. Inflation is
   a. 0%.
   b. 5%.
   c. 1%.
   d. 12%.

3. An anticipated decrease in money supply growth, according to the new classical approach, will
   a. lower inflation and real output in the short run.
   b. lower inflation and real output only in the long run.
   c. lower inflation in the short run but leave real output unchanged in the short run.
   d. lower inflation in the short run but increase real output in the long run.

4. When we say that money is neutral in the long run, we mean that
   a. it leaves velocity unchanged in the long run.
   b. it leaves prices unchanged in the long run.
   c. it increases the price level and real output by the same amount in the long run.
   d. it leaves real output unchanged in the long run.

5. What would be the expected real after-tax return on a security that pays a 9% interest rate if the expected inflation rate is 3% and the individual faces a marginal tax rate of 25%? (Remember, taxes are paid on nominal interest income.)
   a. 3.75%
   b. 4.5%
   c. 6.00%
   d. 2.25%

6. The natural rate of unemployment is equal to the
   a. frictional minus the structural rate of unemployment.
   b. frictional plus the structural rate of unemployment.
   c. frictional rate of unemployment.
   d. structural rate of unemployment.

7. To reduce the rate of inflation,
   a. the new classicists advocate a cold turkey approach, whereas the new Keynesians advocate a policy of gradualism.
   b. the new Keynesians advocate a cold turkey approach, whereas the new classicists advocate a policy of gradualism.
   c. the new Keynesians and new classicists both advocate a cold turkey approach.
   d. the new Keynesians and the new classicists both advocate a policy of gradualism.

8. According to new Keynesians, the cost of reducing the inflation rate is
   a. higher interest rates.
   b. lost jobs and output.
   c. greater government spending.
   d. greater trade deficits.

9. An unanticipated increase in the money supply shifts
   a. *AS* to the right and leaves *AD* unchanged.
   b. both *AD* and *AS* to the right.
   c. *AD* to the right and *AS* to the left.
   d. *AD* to the right and leaves *AS* unchanged.

10. Price controls were last used in the United States during the
    a. mid-1960s.
    b. mid-1970s.
    c. early 1970s.
    d. early 1980s.

11. Many economists argue against price controls because
    a. price controls are unconstitutional in the United States.
    b. price controls have been used to establish credibility.
    c. shortages often arise.
    d. price controls can be used only during a war.

12. An unanticipated decrease in the money supply, according to the new Keynesian approach, will
    a. lower the price level and real output in the short run.
    b. lower the price level and real output only in the long run.
    c. lower the price level in the short run but leave real output unchanged in the short run.
    d. have the same effect on the price level and real output in the short run and the long run.

13. Which of the following is NOT an example of a policy rule?
    a. The Fed pursues a policy of 6% nominal GDP growth.
    b. The Fed responds to the stock market crash by expanding the money supply.
    c. The money supply expands at a constant 3% per year.
    d. The Fed sets a target of no inflation.

14. In the 1980s, Paul Volker pursued a policy of rapid disinflation. This indicates that Federal Reserve officials' views were most likely influenced by
    a. monetarists.
    b. new Keynesians.
    c. new classicals.
    d. real business cycle theorists.

15. Under the leadership of Alan Greenspan, the Federal Reserve has pursued a policy of slow gradual disinflation. This indicates that Federal Reserve officials' views are most likely influenced by
    a.   monetarists.
    b.   new Keynesians.
    c.   new classicals.
    d.   real business cycle theorists.

Essays

1.   What is inflation and what are the three most commonly used indexes to measure inflation?

2.   One cost of inflation arises from the fact that the U.S. tax system is not perfectly indexed for inflation.
     a.   In the late 1970s, the federal income tax system was structured so that income tax revenues increased faster than the inflation rate. Explain.
     b.   How can the government prevent this inequity from occurring?

3.   Suppose that the economy is suffering from hyperinflation.
     a.   Why will workers want to receive a paycheck each day, even though this demand would impose extra costs on their employer?
     b.   Would you be surprised to learn that workers are negotiating pay raises every day?
     c.   Given your answers to (a.) and (b.), what will happen to economic efficiency?

4.   Contrast cost-push inflation and demand-pull inflation.

5.   Nobel laureate Milton Friedman has argued that inflation is everywhere and always a monetary phenomenon. Do you agree? Why or why not?

6.   Compare the rules strategy to a discretionary strategy for monetary policy.

7.   For the rules strategy to be effective, what has to be true?

8.   With the collapse of communism, price controls were relaxed by the governments of the former Soviet Union. What happened as a consequence?

9.   Arthur Burns, Fed chairman under President Nixon, often stated that the Fed was pursuing a policy of hard money, meaning that the Fed was taking a hard line on inflation. Simultaneously, the money supply continued to expand at historically high levels. Ultimately, Burns argued for the adoption of wage and price controls. Comment.

10. Between 1987 and 1995, during the tenure of three presidents, Alan Greenspan, a Republican who was originally appointed by President Reagan, consistently argued for a policy aimed at moderating inflation. When it came time again in 1995 to consider whom to appoint as Fed chairman, President Clinton felt obligated to reappoint Greenspan. Explain how the need to maintain the Fed's credibility made this reappointment politically necessary.

ANSWERS TO SELF-TEST

True or False

1. False. Inflation rates rose in the 1960s and 1970s and fell in the 1980s.
2. True.
3. False. A supply shock affects the price level only in the short run.
4. True.
5. True.
6. False. Neither can be sustained in the long run without an accommodating expansionary policy.
7. True.
8. True.
9. False. New classicals usually advocate a cold turkey approach.
10. False . The theory of purchasing power parity assumes that the exchange rate will adjust so that prices are the same in all countries. So if prices rise in one country (i.e., there is inflation), then the exchange rate must fall.

Fill in the Blank

1. equation of exchange
2. hyperinflation
3. natural
4. rules strategy
5. Price controls
6. disinflationary
7. credibility
8. shoe leather costs
9. rules; discretionary
10. cold turkey; gradualist
11. cost-push; demand-pull

Multiple Choice

1.	c	2.	c
3.	c	4.	d
5.	a	6.	b
7.	a	8.	b
9.	d	10.	c
11.	c	12.	a
13.	b	14.	c
15.	b		

Essays

1. Inflation is the rate of increase in the price level. The three most commonly used measures are the following: (1.) *Consumer price index (CPI)*: Uses a market basket purchased by a typical consumer. (2.) *Producer price index (PPI)*: Includes items purchased by the producer in the production process. (3.) *GDP deflator*: Considers prices of goods and services that are included in GDP.

2. a. This condition is the result of bracket creep as inflation pushes people into higher tax brackets. For example, suppose that in year 1, Cathy Johnson makes $50,000 and on average pays 15% of her income in taxes. Her total tax liability would be $50,000(0.15) = $7500. Suppose that the inflation rate during the year is 10% and that Cathy's income keeps up with inflation. Her income in year 2 would be:

    $$\$50,000(1.10) = \$55,000.$$

    With bracket creep, the average amount of taxes that Cathy pays is now 16%, making her total tax liability:

    $$\$55,000(0.16) = \$8800.$$

    To keep up with inflation, the government would have to collect only:

    $$\$7500(1.10) = \$8250 < \$8800.$$

    Therefore inflation led to an increase in the real average tax rate.

    b. The government could index income taxes. That is, brackets could be adjusted to reflect inflation. If Cathy had an average tax rate of 15% in year 2, the amount of tax she would have paid is:

    $$\$55,000(0.15) = \$8250 = \$7500(1.10)$$

3. a. During hyperinflation, the value of money falls rapidly. Therefore every day you wait to be paid reduces the purchasing power of your salary, so you want to be paid each day.
    b. You should not be surprised. The uncertainty associated with hyperinflation makes long-term contracting difficult. In the extreme, wage contracts would have to be negotiated every day.
    c. The costs associated with issuing daily paychecks and conducting daily wage negotiations would reduce the efficiency of the economy.

10-3

4.   Cost-push inflation occurs when the cost of production rises, causing firms to raise the prices of their output. The short-run aggregate supply curve (*SRAS*) shifts to the left. Demand-pull inflation occurs when policymakers attempt to raise the level of output above the level corresponding to the natural rate of unemployment. The aggregate demand curve (*AD*) shifts to the right, causing prices to rise. The *SRAS* curve shifts upward as wages and prices adjust and the level of output falls back to a level that is consistent with the natural rate of unemployment.

5.   Strictly speaking, inflation can arise from several sources. For example, short-term inflation can result from changes in *m*, *v*, or *y*. This point is made clear by the equation of exchange:

$$\pi = \dot{m} + \dot{v} - \dot{y}.$$

However, if what is referred to is sustained long-term inflation, which is what Friedman was talking about, only money supply growth can sustain inflation, and Friedman's statement is correct.

6.   A rules strategy for monetary policy suggests that the central bank follow specific and publicly announced guidelines. A discretionary monetary policy suggests that the central bank adjusts monetary policy as it sees fit to achieve goals for economic growth, inflation, and other economic variables.

7.   For the rules strategy to be effective, the central bank must avoid the temptation of trying to fine-tune the economy.

8.   The relaxation of price controls allowed rapid inflation. During the Soviet era, shortages of consumer goods resulted in accumulation of large money balances. With the elimination of price controls, these balances were spent, bidding up prices. The consequence was inflation.

9.   Given the inconsistency between the Fed chairman's words and the Fed's actions, the only way to reestablish credibility was through wage and price controls.

10.   Greenspan had developed a reputation as an inflation fighter. Failure to reappoint him would have sent a signal to Wall Street that the Clinton administration was not serious about fighting inflation, thereby undermining the credibility of the Fed.

Self-Test

True or False

1. Financial markets channel funds directly between borrowers and savers, whereas financial intermediaries are engaged in indirect finance.

2. If Kyle deposits a $50 bill that he was hiding in the cookie jar into his passbook savings account at the Polar Cap Bank, then initially *M1* will decrease but *M2* will remain the same.

3. For a discount bond, the current yield is greater than the yield to maturity when the price of the bond is less than its face value.

4. According to the Purchasing Power Parity Theory, if domestic inflation exceeds foreign inflation, the nominal exchange rate should appreciate.

5. In a small open economy, if the domestic real interest rate is less than the expected real world interest rate, domestic residents will lend their money in domestic markets.

6. Holding all other factors constant, an increase in wealth will increase the demand for all financial assets equally.

7. Venture capital firms overcome the free-rider problem by restricting trade in shares of the companies they invest in.

8. The FDIC usually uses the payoff method when handling the failure of a large bank.

9. Financial innovation on the part of banks increases the ease with which government regulators can oversee the banking system.

10. The Riegle-Neal Interstate Banking and Branching Efficiency Act of 1994 allowed foreign banks to operate branches in any state outside of its home state as long as domestically owned banks could branch under the same circumstances.

Fill in the Blank

1. The _____ price is the price you must pay to purchase a 20-year U.S. Treasury bond from a securities dealer.

2. _____ _____ is the risk that cannot be diversified away.

3. In the loanable funds model, an increase in expected inflation will _____ the equilibrium interest rate, but the effect on the equilibrium quantity of loanable funds will be _____.

4. In the _____ _____ _____ of the term structure, bonds are not substitutes at all.

5. _____ _____. _____ involves the daily settlement of trading positions in futures markets.

6. Market participants who use all information available to them when making investment decisions are said to have _____ _____.

7. _____ _____ are the costs that savers incur to determine the creditworthiness of borrowers and to monitor how borrowers use their acquired funds.

8. _____ _____ are financial intermediaries that specialize in writing contracts to protect their policyholders from the risk of financial loss associated with particular events.

9. A _____ _____ occurs when a bank cannot pay its depositors in full and still have enough reserves left to meet its reserve requirements.

10. An _____ _____ can transfer funds from abroad into the United States and make loans in the United States.

Multiple Choice

1. In a barter system
   a. an individual must find someone that wants a good he has and has a good he wants.
   b. an individual must keep track of the relative prices of many goods.
   c. a society can easily specialize in the production of goods for which they are most suited.
   d. both (a.) and (b.) apply.

2. Ice cream would probably not be useful as money because
   a. almost anyone can make ice cream.
   b. it deteriorates quickly unless special precautions are taken.
   c. it is cumbersome to make large purchases with ice cream.
   d. all of the above apply.

3. In the absence of secondary markets,
   a. firms would have a difficult time raising money through issuing stocks and bonds.
   b. the government would lose an important source of tax revenue.
   c. the public would easily to be able to hold a diversified portfolio of assets.
   d. stock mutual funds would become more popular.

4. Suppose Scott and Rachel wish to start a business. Their bank offers to loan them $10,000 today if they agree to repay a lump sum of $15,000 in three years' time. What is the yield to maturity on this loan?
   a. 8.25%
   b. 10.51%
   c. 14.47%
   d. 16.67%

5. Consider a $10,000 face value coupon bond with an annual coupon payment of $750. If the current price of this bond is $11,500, then the yield to maturity is
   a. less than 7.5%.
   b. equal to 7.5%.
   c. equal to 8%.
   d. greater than 8%.

6. Suppose that P.J., ruler of the country of FP-LAND, announces that from this moment on anyone wishing to sell a FP-LAND government bond will have to fill out an application and wait six weeks for approval. Holding all other factors constant, this announcement should
   a. decrease the liquidity of FP-LAND's government bonds.
   b. increase the yield on FP-LAND's government bonds.
   c. increase the price of FP-LAND's government bonds.
   d. lead to both (a.) and (b.) occurring.

7. If an avocado costs $1.67 in the United States, 4 pesos in Mexico, and the exchange rate is 9.570 pesos/dollar, the real exchange rate is approximately
   a. 0.25 Mexican avocados per U.S. avocado.
   b. 4.00 Mexican avocados per U.S. avocado.
   c. 4.00 U.S. avocados per Mexican avocado.
   d. 9.57 U.S. avocados per Mexican avocado.

8. A put option contract involves asymmetric rights and obligations because
   a. the option seller is obligated to buy the underlying asset.
   b. the option seller is obligated to sell the underlying asset.
   c. the option buyer is obligated to buy the underlying asset.
   d. the option buyer is obligated to sell the underlying asset.

9. According to the efficient markets hypothesis
    a. traders and investors use all available information in forming expectations of future rates of return.
    b. there should be no unexploited profit opportunities in the market.
    c. the equilibrium price of an asset equals the market's optimal forecast of its fundamental value.
    d. all of the above are true.

10. In which of the following ways can lenders decrease adverse selection?
    a. by subscribing to an information gathering service
    b. by forcing borrowers to pledge assets as collateral
    c. by lending to borrowers with high net worth
    d. all of the above

11. To avoid moral hazard insurance companies
    a. charge risk-based premiums to policyholders.
    b. use restrictive covenants, which limits the risky activities of the insured.
    c. can require the policyholder to pay a deductible.
    d. can use both (b.) and (c.) of the above.

12. The largest source of funds for commercial banks at the end of November 1998 was
    a. checkable deposits.
    b. cash items in process of collection.
    c. borrowings from the Federal Reserve.
    d. nontransaction deposits.

13. Comparing the size of U.S. banks, the number of U.S. banking firms, and the concentration of assets held by U.S. banks with banks in other large economies as of 1998, we can conclude that
    a. only three U.S. banks are ranked among the top ten largest banks in the world when ranked by total assets.
    b. the U.S. banking industry has a large number of banking firms.
    c. the U.S. banking industry is not as concentrated as those in other countries.
    d. all of the above are true.

14. Regulations that were intended to limit competition between banks were intended to
    a. maintain the overall stability of the banking system.
    b. reduce the likelihood of bank runs.
    c. reduce the chance of moral hazard in banks' behavior.
    d. do all of the above.

15. Euromarkets are
    a. stock markets located in European cities.
    b. markets for time deposits denominated in a currency other than that of the issuing domestic financial center.
    c. the European equivalent of the federal funds market.
    d. can only be used by banks located in European countries.

Essays

1. After the introduction of federal deposit insurance, stricter regulation of insured banks became necessary. Why?

2. Using the three theories of the term structure of interest rates, explain why the yield curve **can** slope upward. Is one of the three theories preferred to the others? Explain.

3. Suppose that market participants expect productivity growth in the United States to rise relative to that of Japan. *Ceteris paribus*, this should lead to a depreciation of the yen/dollar exchange rate and a rise in U.S. net exports. Comment.

ANSWERS TO SELF-TEST

True or False

1. True.
2. True.
3. False. A discount bond does not make coupon payments and hence has no current yield.
4. False. The nominal exchange rate should depreciate.
5. False. Domestic residents will lend their funds abroad at the higher real world interest rate.
6. False. The demand for all financial assets will rise, however, the amount of the increase will depend on the wealth elasticity of demand.
7. True.
8. False. The FDIC uses the purchase and assumption method for handling large bank failures.
9. False. Financial innovation requires regulators to spend more time and effort monitoring the behavior of banks.
10. True

Fill in the Blank

1. asked
2. Market (Systematic) risk
3. increase; indeterminate
4. segmented markets theory
5. Marking to market
6. rational expectations
7. Information costs
8. Insurance companies
9. bank failure
10. agency office

Multiple Choice

1.	d	2.	d
3.	a	4.	c
5.	a	6.	d
7.	b	8.	a
9.	d	10.	d
11.	d	12.	d
13.	d	14.	d
15.	b		

Essays

1. Asymmetric information makes screening and the ongoing monitoring of banks crucial in minimizing adverse selection and moral hazard. However, the introduction of federal deposit insurance reduced the incentive for depositors to monitor banks. Therefore, banks could engage in more risky activities. Thus, federal regulation of insured banks is necessary.

2. *Expectations Hypothesis*: The interest rate on a long-term bond equals an average of the short-term interest rates expected to occur over the life of the long-term bond. If market participants expect higher future short-term interest rates, the yield curve will slope upward. *Segmented Markets Hypothesis*: The market for each bond with a different maturity is a separate market. When the demand for short-term bonds is high relative to the supply, the yield on short-term bonds will be low. When the demand for long-term bonds is low relative to the supply, the yield will be high. Thus, the yield curve will slope upward. *Preferred habitat theory*: The interest rate on a long-term bond equals an average of the short-term interest rates expected to occur over the life of the long-term bond plus a term premium. If market participants prefer short-term bonds, the yield curve can slope upward under a wide variety of expectations of future short-term interest rates. The preferred habitat theory better satisfies the conditions for an acceptable economic theory as described in Chapter 1.

3. Higher future expected productivity in the U.S. relative to Japan should lead market participants to expect the dollar to appreciate in the future. This expected appreciation of the exchange rate lowers the expected foreign rate of return relative to the U.S. rate of return. Investors will wish to purchase U.S. denominated assets, which will increase the actual exchange rate. As the dollar gets stronger, U.S. exports should fall, U.S. imports should rise and net exports should fall.

CHAPTERS 1-16: MIDTERM EXAMINATION 2

Self-Test

True or False

1. There is no guarantee that if a theory satisfies the three criteria for choosing a useful economic theory it will be the best theory for understanding the particular workings of the economy.

2. Currently in the United States, a ten-dollar bill is convertible into ¼ ounce of gold.

3. Long-term bond prices are more sensitive than short-term bond prices to changes in the interest rate.

4. Historically in the United States, interest rates tend to fall during business cycle expansions and rise during business cycle contractions.

5. A bond with a rating of "AA" has less default risk than a bond with a rating of "A".

6. In a spot market transaction, settlement occurs at a future date at a price agreed upon today.

7. The imposition of circuit breakers has increased the liquidity of stock markets.

8. Mutual funds are an example of a contractual saving institutions.

9. Loan loss reserves are the part of net worth set aside for anticipated future loan losses.

10. State-chartered banks that are members of the Federal Reserve System are supervised the Office of the Comptroller of the Currency.

Fill in the Blank

1. The financial system _____ funds from those who have excess funds to those who are in need of funds.

2. _____ _____ were the largest financial asset classification held by savers in 1998.

3. The _____ for loanable funds is equivalent to the _____ of bonds.

4. The _____ _____ _____ of the term structure can explain why yield curves usually slope upward.

5. Holding all other factors constant, when the U.S. dollar _____, U.S. consumers are able to purchase foreign-made goods and services for a lower price in terms of dollars.

6. The _____ _____ and the _____ - _____ _____ are examples of pricing anomalies.

7. Although _____ _____ _____ are not financial intermediaries, they do help to match savers and borrowers in the financial system.

8. In Germany, _____ _____ allows banks to carry out traditional banking services and many nonbanking activities within a single firm.

9. Congress created the Federal Reserve System to be the _____ _____ _____ _____ for the banking system.

10. The Foreign Bank Supervision Enhancement Act of 1991 was passed as a result of the failure of the _____ _____ _____ _____ _____ _____.

Multiple Choice

1. Which of the following is NOT a part of economic analysis?
   a. defining the problem
   b. proposing a theory to explain the problem
   c. examining actual data to evaluate the theory
   d. creating data to better fit the theory

2. Which of the following statements about *M1* is true?
   a. *M1* includes all deposits against which market participants can write a check.
   b. *M1* is the broadest monetary aggregate.
   c. *M1* is the narrowest definition of money.
   d. *M1* includes 3-month U.S. Treasury bills.

3. Depository institutions provide liquidity services to depositors by
   a. offering checkable deposits that can be converted into cash quickly.
   b. issuing five-year Certificates of Deposit.
   c. providing a physical location where brokers and dealers can trade stocks and bonds.
   d. gathering information on prospective borrowers.

4. Suppose that Arnold and Patricia purchase a twenty five-year $100,000 face value, 10 percent coupon bond. If the yield to maturity was 10 percent when they purchased the bond, what was the purchase price of the bond?
    a. $57,000
    b. $75,000
    c. $100,000
    d. $112,500

5. According to the theory of portfolio allocation, which are the following is NOT a determinant of asset demand?
    a.   wealth
    b.   the expected return on one asset relative to another
    c.   the risk of one asset relative to another
    d.   the current age of the saver

6. Holding all other factors constant, an increase in the expected return on bonds relative to other assets should increase the _____ for bonds and _____ the interest rate.
    a.   demand; increase
    b.   demand; decrease
    c.   supply; increase
    d.   supply; decrease

7. According to the preferred habitat theory, if the short-term interest rates expected to occur over the next three years are 5%, 6%, and 7% and people prefer to hold one-year bonds, the interest rate on a three-year bond today will
    a.   equal 5.0%.
    b.   equal 5.5%.
    c.   equal 6.0%.
    d.   be greater than 6%.

8. Suppose that U.S. residents expect the dollar to depreciate against the British pound over the course of the next year. Holding all other factors constant, this expected depreciation should
    a.   increase the nominal foreign rate of return.
    b.   increase the demand for pounds relative to dollars.
    c.   result in a depreciation of the pound/dollar exchange rate.
    d.   result in all of the above occurring.

9. In the United States, nonfinancial corporations raise most of their funds for investment purposes from
    a.   commercial banks.
    b.   financial markets.
    c.   current and accumulated profits.
    d.   investment banks.

10. From the lender's perspective, moral hazard involves
    a. the verification that borrowers are using their funds as intended.
    b. distinguishing the good-risk applicants from the bad-risk applicants before making an investment.
    c. the elimination of default risk.
    d. lending funds to all those who wish them.

11. A defined contribution pension plan
    a. can be either fully funded or under-funded.
    b. promises an assigned benefit based on earnings and length of service.
    c. determines retirement income based on the value of the funds in the plan.
    d. is best characterized by plans such as the Social Security System.

12. When Karen deposits a $100 bill into her checking account at the Grizzly Bank
    a. both the bank's assets and liabilities fall by the same amount.
    b. the bank's assets rise, but the bank's liabilities fall.
    c. the bank's assets fall, but the bank's liabilities rise.
    d. both the bank's assets and liabilities rise by the same amount.

13. The Glass-Steagall Act of 1933
    a. was designed to protect depositors of commercial banks from risky investment activities of banks.
    b. separated investment banking from commercial banking.
    c. created federal deposit insurance.
    d. did both (a.) and (b.) of the above.

14. The Depository Institutions Deregulation and Monetary Control Act of 1980
    a. permitted depository institutions to offer federally insured money market deposit accounts.
    b. eliminated the FSLIC.
    c. instituted risk-based deposit insurance premiums.
    d. provided for uniform reserve requirements and access to Federal Reserve facilities.

15. Which of the following services do international banks provide?
    a. risk-sharing
    b. liquidity
    c. information services
    d. all of the above

Essays

1. There has been much discussion in the 1980s and 1990s over reforming the current tax system. Specifically, politicians have debated the merits of replacing the current progressive tax system with a flat tax or a national sales tax. Predict what would happen to the spread between municipal bonds and U.S. Treasury bonds if Congress eliminates the current tax system and replaces it with a national sales tax.

2. When banks are faced with asymmetric information, how do they overcome the free-rider problem?

3. Discuss the problems associated with the FDIC's too-big-to-fail policy as it relates to the banking system.

ANSWERS TO SELF-TEST

True or False

1. True.
2. False. Federal Reserve Notes are the definitive money in the United States.
3. True.
4. False. Evidence from U.S. data indicates that interest rates generally rise during economic upturns and fall during economic downturns.
5. True.
6. False. In a spot market transaction, settlement occurs immediately.
7. False. The existence of circuit breakers makes it harder to sell securities when the market is experiencing extreme fluctuations.
8. False. Mutual funds are investment institutions.
9. True.
10. False. These banks are supervised by the Fed.

Fill in the Blank

1. channels
2. Pension reserves
3. demand; supply
4. preferred habitat theory
5. appreciates
6. January effect; small firm effect
7. securities market institutions
8. universal banking
9. Lender of Last Resort
10. Bank of Credit and Commerce International

Multiple Choice

1.	d	2.	c
3.	a	4.	c
5.	d	6.	b
7.	d	8.	d
9.	c	10.	a
11.	c	12.	d
13.	c	14.	d
15.	d		

Essays

1. Currently interest income on municipal bonds is tax-exempt. Replacing the current tax system with a national sales tax makes interest income on all bonds tax-exempt. Since U.S. Treasury bonds are safer, more liquid, and have lower information costs than municipal bonds, there should be an increase in demand for U.S. Treasury bonds and a decrease in demand for municipal bonds. The prices of U.S. Treasury bonds will rise and the yields will fall. The prices of municipal bonds will fall and the yields will rise. The spread between the yields on municipal bonds and U.S. Treasury bonds will widen.

2. The free-rider problem refers to the fact that once information is made public, anyone can use the information without paying for it. Therefore, a private company that gathers information on a potential borrower must find a way to profit from the information without making it public. Banks do this by retaining the loans that they make in their own portfolio. If they do a good job of screening potential borrowers, they will avoid lending to poor credit risks, thereby profiting from their collected information.

3. The too-big-to-fail policy is essentially a statement that some large U.S. banks would not be allowed to fail because failure would cause unwanted economic consequences. The policy implies that all deposits at large U.S. institutions will be insured regardless of the size of the deposit. This type of implicit deposit insurance can cause large banks to undertake too much risk. If these banks fail, the FDIC will ensure that all depositors receive the full value of their deposits. Smaller banks are also influenced by this policy. Since smaller banks will be allowed to fail, large depositors will typically not deposit their funds with small banks making it more difficult for smaller banks to raise large pools of funds for investment purposes.

Self-Test

True or False

1. The *M2* money supply is less sensitive than *M1* to shifts in the nonbank public's portfolio preferences.

2. An increase in the federal budget deficit will always increase the monetary base.

3. When the Fed wishes to offset temporary fluctuations in the monetary base, it uses a dynamic open market operation.

4. In theory, the sum of the current account balance and the capital account balance equals zero.

5. For the closed economy version of the *IS-LM-FE* model, national saving can exceed investment in long-run equilibrium.

6. According to the new Keynesian view, only unanticipated monetary policies affect output in the short run.

7. If the sum of the growth rates of the nominal money supply and velocity exceeds the growth rate of real output, inflation is occurring.

Fill in the Blank

1. Holding all other factors constant, if deposit outflows become harder to predict, banks will hold _____ excess reserves and the money multiplier will _____ .

2. Generally speaking, countries that have more independent central banks have _____ inflation rates.

3. _____ _____ _____ is the most often stated goal of Federal Reserve monetary policy.

4. The _____ of money is the average number of times a dollar is spent in the economy each year to purchase goods and services.

5. The _____ _____ _____ _____ explains short-term changes in output that result from temporary shocks to productivity.

6. The _____ _____ _____ illustrates how a change in the supply of bank loans affects bank-dependent borrowers, changing their spending and aggregate demand.

7. _____ is a decrease in the rate of inflation.

Multiple Choice

1. Assume that the Woodlands Bank has no initial excess reserve holdings. Suppose the required reserve ratio on checkable deposits is 100% and Margie deposits $50 cash into her personal savings account at the Woodlands Bank. The Woodlands Bank can make new loans up to a maximum amount equal to
    a. $0.
    b. $50.
    c. $100.
    d. $500.

2. Suppose that the Fed purchases new computers for its staff members. Holding all other factors constant,
    a. the monetary base will fall.
    b. the monetary base will rise.
    c. the *M1* money supply will fall.
    d. the *M1* money multiplier will rise.

3. Which of the following activities are not carried out by **all** Federal Reserve district banks?
    a. issuing new Federal Reserve Notes
    b. examining state member banks
    c. conducting open market operations
    d. making discount loans

4. The benefits of using open market operations as a policy tool include
    a. the Fed's ability to control the volume of open market operations.
    b. the ease of implementation of open market operations.
    c. the Fed's ability to adjust the size of open market operations as needed.
    d. all of the above.

5. Monetary policy is procyclical if
    a. the money supply decreases when the economy is expanding.
    b. the money supply increases when the economy is contracting.
    c. the money supply decreases when the economy is contracting.
    d. the money supply increases regardless of the current state of the economy.

6. If the Fed makes an unsterilized foreign-exchange market intervention,
    a. the domestic money supply will change.
    b. the domestic interest rate will change.
    c. the equilibrium exchange rate will change.
    d. all of the above will occur.

7. An increase in the efficiency of the payments system
    a. decreases the demand for money and increases the velocity of money.
    b. decreases the demand for money and decreases the velocity of money.
    c. increases the demand for money and increases the velocity of money.
    d. increases the demand for money and decreases the velocity of money.

8. In the *IS-LM-FE* model, an improvement in the efficiency of the payments system, assuming that prices are perfectly flexible, results in
    a. a decrease in the demand for real money balances and a higher long-run equilibrium price level.
    b. an increase in the demand for money and a higher long-run equilibrium interest rate.
    c. an increase in the demand for money and a higher long-run equilibrium output level.
    d. both (b.) and (c.) occurring.

9. According to the New Classical view, the short-run aggregate supply curve slopes upward because
    a. market participants fail to correctly distinguish between a movement in the general price level and a movement in relative prices.
    b. price are completely flexible.
    c. of the existence of long-term nominal contracts and imperfect competition.
    d. of the existence of price controls in the U.S. economy.

10. Using monetary policy to fine-tune the economy is difficult because
    a. there may be long and variable lags in the policymaking and implementation process.
    b. the Federal Reserve is motivated by self-interest.
    c. the Congress can never agree on an appropriate monetary policy.
    d. the U.S. Treasury cannot control its spending.

11. Suppose that there is a drop in borrowers' net worth. The short-run effect on the economy is
    a. to raise information costs and reduce the ability of firms and households to borrow.
    b. to reduce consumer and investment spending.
    c. to lower the current levels of output and prices.
    d. likely to include all of the above.

12. To reduce inflation at a low cost in terms of lost output and jobs in the United States,
    a.   the public's expectation of the inflation rate must be reduced.
    b.   the public must believe that the central bank will carry out its disinflationary policy.
    c.   the President must announce his desire for lower overall prices.
    d.   both (a.) and (b.) must occur.

Essays

1. Suppose that the federal funds rate is 6 percent and the Fed wants to permanently lower the rate to 4 percent. Describe the most likely action the Fed would use to lower the federal funds rate. Now suppose that once the rate is 4 percent, the U.S. Treasury unexpectedly transfers funds from the commercial banking system into its General Account. Assuming that the Fed does not react to the Treasury's action, what is likely to happen to the federal funds rate? Finally, if the Fed does not wish the federal funds rate to change in response to the Treasury's action, describe a policy the Fed could undertake.

2. Suppose that the Fed discards its currently used targeting procedure and switches to an inflation-targeting regime. Discuss the costs and benefits of such a change in Federal Reserve policy.

3. Suppose that the U.S. economy is currently in a recession. Compare and contrast the likely policy proposals for eliminating the recession through the use of monetary policy from the Real Business Cycle, New Classical, and New Keynesian points of view.

ANSWERS TO SELF-TEST

True or False

1. True.
2. False. An increase in the federal budget deficit will only increase the monetary base if the Fed monetizes the debt.
3. False. The Fed uses defensive open market operations to offset temporary fluctuations in the monetary base.
4. True.
5. False. In equilibrium national saving must equal investment.
6. False. In the new Keynesian view, both unanticipated and anticipated monetary policy affect output in the short run, but the effect is not symmetrical.
7. True.

Fill in the Blank

1. more; decrease
2. lower
3. Price level stability
4. velocity
5. real business cycle model
6. bank lending channel
7. Disinflation

Multiple Choice

1.	b	2.	b
3.	c	4.	d
5.	c	6.	d
7.	a	8.	a
9.	a	10.	a
11.	d	12.	d

Essays

1. The Fed can make a dynamic open market purchase of Treasury securities. The open market purchase would increase the quantity of nonborrowed reserves in the system and decrease the federal funds rate. If the Treasury unexpectedly transfers funds from the commercial banking system into its General Account, the amount of nonborrowed reserves in the economy will decrease and the federal funds rate will increase. If the Fed wishes to offset the Treasury's action, it could make a defensive open market purchase of securities to temporarily increase the level of nonborrowed reserves in the economy.

2. Inflation-targeting would most likely involve the Fed setting policy according to some type of monetary rule. The benefits of such a policy include: focusing the public's attention on what the Federal Reserve can achieve in practice (by announcing explicit inflation targets); providing an anchor for inflationary expectations; helping to institutionalize good U.S. monetary policy; and providing accountability for Federal Reserve actions. The costs of such a policy include: diminishing the flexibility of monetary policy to address other policy goals; requiring the Fed to depend on uncertain forecasts of future inflation; holding the Fed accountable only for a goal of low inflation may make it difficult to monitor the Fed's support for good economic policy overall; and, making economic decisions in the presence of an inflation target is hampered by uncertainty about the future levels of output and employment. Do the costs outweigh the benefits? Very few countries actually target inflation and as such there is no definitive answer regarding whether the costs outweigh the benefits.

3. Real Business Cycle proponents do not believe in the efficacy of policy to influence the current state of the economy. Thus, Real Business Cycle theorists would not prescribe any type of policy to help the economy. New Classical theorists believe that only unanticipated policies have real short-run effects on the economy. However, unexpected changes in monetary policy introduce uncertainty with respect to households' and businesses' decisions, leading to random output fluctuations. Thus, New Classical economists would not suggest any monetary policy to eliminate the recession. New Keynesian theorists believe that both anticipated and unanticipated monetary policies can influence the economy. Thus, a New Keynesian might suggest expansionary monetary policy to stimulate aggregate demand, forcing output back to its long-run level.

Self-Test

True or False

1. Holding all other factors constant, an increase in wealth increases the currency-checkable deposit ratio (C/D).

2. Members of the Board of Governors of the Federal Reserve System are chosen by the President of the United States and confirmed by the Congress.

3. The Fed can rarely achieve all six of its monetary policy goals simultaneously.

4. Increases in the general price level increase the demand for nominal money balances and decrease the demand for real money balances.

5. The long-run aggregate supply curve is horizontal because prices are perfectly flexible.

6. For most firms, economists have found that external funds are a cheaper source of financing than internal funds.

7. If the sum of the growth rates of the nominal money supply and velocity equals the growth rate of real output, inflation is occurring.

Fill in the Blank

1. Federal Reserve notes are _____ of the Federal Reserve System.

2. There are _____ Federal Reserve districts.

3. The most often used tool of monetary policy is _____ _____ _____.

4. The _____ _____ _____ equals the net increase in a country's official reserve assets.

5. A point below the *LM* curve represents an excess _____ for money.

6. According to the New Classical view only _____ policy will affect the level of output in the short run.

7.   A one-time change in government spending cannot by itself produce
     _____.

Multiple Choice

1.   Suppose Shawn deposits $100 cash into his checking account. Assume that the
     required reserve ratio on checkable deposits is 20 percent, banks do not hold excess
     reserves, and, the nonbank public's holdings of currency do not change. What is the
     maximum potential change in the money supply?
     a. $100
     b. $250
     c. $400
     d. $500

2.   Which of the following increases the monetary base?
     a.   Federal Reserve float falls.
     b.   The U.S. Treasury sells bonds to the nonbank public.
     c.   The Bundesbank deposits $5 million into its account at the Fed.
     d.   The Fed makes a discount loan to the Glacier Bank.

3.   The Federal Open Market Committee
     a.   has twelve members and is the focal point of Fed policy.
     b.   meets about eight times per year to discuss monetary policy.
     c.   sets the required reserve ratios.
     d.   satisfies both (a.) and (b.) of the above.

4.   When the Fed makes a dynamic open market purchase
     a.   the level of nonborrowed reserves increases.
     b.   the equilibrium federal funds rate increases.
     c.   the supply curve for federal funds shifts to the left.
     d.   all of the above occur.

5.   Which of the following is not a goal of monetary policy?
     a.   high employment
     b.   income equality
     c.   financial market stability
     d.   foreign-exchange market stability

6.   Milton Friedman's view of money demand
     a.   does not separate money demand into specific motives as Keynes' does.
     b.   focuses on a broader definition of money than *M1*.
     c.   uses two measures of the opportunity cost of holding real money balances.
     d.   incorporates all of the above.

7. In a sterilized foreign-exchange market intervention,
   a. the domestic money supply can either rise or fall depending upon the type of intervention.
   b. the domestic money supply remains unchanged regardless of the type of intervention.
   c. the exchange rate will remain unchanged if domestic assets and foreign assets are perfect substitutes.
   d. both (b.) and (c.) of the above occur.

8. In the *IS-LM-FE* model, suppose that there is a reduction in consumer and business confidence. Assuming that prices are perfectly flexible,
   a. the *IS* curve will shift right and the long-run equilibrium price level will rise.
   b. the *IS* curve will shift left and the long-run equilibrium price level will fall.
   c. the *IS* curve will shift right and the long-run equilibrium output level will rise.
   d. the *LM* curve will shift left and the long-run equilibrium interest rate will rise.

9. According to the New Keynesian view, the short-run aggregate supply curve slopes upward because
   a. prices are completely inflexible.
   b. price are completely flexible.
   c. of the existence of long-term nominal contracts and imperfect competition.
   d. of the existence of price controls in the U.S. economy.

10. In studying the business cycle, economists have found that in the short run
    a. the growth rate of the money supply is procyclical, but lags the growth of output by many months.
    b. the growth rate of the money supply is procyclical and changes in the nominal money supply precede the fluctuations in output.
    c. the growth rate of the money supply is anticyclical and lags the growth of output by many months.
    d. the growth rates of the nominal money supply and real output are not related.

11. Suppose that the federal government places a moratorium on bank lending. The likely short-run effect on the economy is
    a. to reduce spending on consumer durables or on business plant and equipment by bank-dependent borrowers.
    b. to shift the aggregate demand curve to the left.
    c. to lower the current levels of output and prices.
    d. likely to include all of the above.

12. Which of the following benefit from unanticipated inflation?
    a. people on fixed incomes
    b. lenders
    c. companies that have issued bonds
    d. individuals who have purchased bonds

<u>Essays</u>

1. Briefly describe the structure of the Federal Reserve System. Is today's system consistent with the original blueprint of the designers of the Fed? Explain.

2. An examination of the Fed's monetary policy record since 1951 shows that the Fed has preferred to use interest rates as operating targets to achieve its monetary policy goals. Explain how interest rate targeting can result in procyclical monetary policy.

3. Compare and contrast the effects of monetary policy with respect to the bank lending channel and the balance sheet channel. How are these transmission mechanisms similar? How are they different?

ANSWERS TO SELF-TEST

True or False

1. False. As wealth increases, the proportion of wealth held as checkable deposits grows relative to currency. Hence, the currency-checkable deposit ratio falls.
2. False. Board of Governor members are confirmed by the Senate.
3. True.
4. True.
5. False. The long-run aggregate supply curve is vertical when prices are free to adjust.
6. False. For most firms, internal funds are a cheaper source of financing than external funds.
7. False. The equation of exchange in growth rate form shows that if the sum of the growth rates of the nominal money supply and velocity equals the growth rate of real output, prices are not changing.

Fill in the Blank

1. liabilities
2. twelve
3. open market operations
4. official settlements balance
5. demand
6. unanticipated
7. inflation

Multiple Choice

1.	c	2.	d
3.	d	4.	a
5.	b	6.	d
7.	d	8.	b
9.	c	10.	b
11.	d	12.	c

Essays

1. The Federal Reserve System has a pyramid structure with much power concentrated at the top and lesser amounts of power at the bottom. The basic structure includes four main parts: The Board of Governors, the Federal Open Market Committee (FOMC), the Federal Reserve district banks, and member banks of the Federal Reserve System. At the top of the pyramid are seven Board of Governors of the Federal Reserve System. Each governor is chosen by the President, confirmed by the Senate, and serves a fourteen year nonrenewable term. One of the Governors acts as the Chairperson of the Board of Governors and serves a renewable four-year term. The FOMC is the policy making arm of the Federal Reserve System. The FOMC has twelve members: the seven Board of Governors and five of the twelve district bank presidents. The president of the New York Fed is always a member of the committee; the remaining eleven presidents serve on a rotating basis. There are twelve Federal Reserve district banks. Each bank is responsible for carrying out duties related to the Fed's roles in the payments system, monetary control, and financial regulation for the banks in its district. Finally, at the bottom of the pyramid are the member banks of the Federal Reserve System.

   The Federal Reserve System was essentially created to be the Lender of Last Resort. However, over time Congress has given the Fed the ability to set reserve requirements and more importantly to conduct open market operations. The system was designed to diffuse power across geographical and political lines to ensure that one group of individuals did not unduly influence the monetary economy. The creators of the Fed probably did not anticipate that the power of the Federal Reserve System would lie in the hands of the Board of Governors and the FOMC. However at the same time, the Fed still successfully acts as the Lender of Last Resort.

2. When the Fed targets the interest rate it must supply enough money to ensure that the quantity demanded of money equals the quantity supplied of money at the chosen interest rate. During business cycle expansions, income rises and so does the demand for money. This increase in the demand for money causes upward pressure on the interest rate. To alleviate this upward pressure, the Fed must supply more money. Thus, during business cycle expansions the Fed increases the money supply and so monetary policy is procylclical.

3. Both the bank lending channel and the balance sheet channel predict that expansionary monetary policy will ultimately increase aggregate demand. However, the two channels differ on the reasons for the increase. In the bank lending channel there are borrowers that are dependent on banks for external financing. An increase in the money supply lowers market interest rates and increases banks' ability to lend. In the short-run, aggregate demand in the economy increases for two reasons: the increase in households' and businesses' spending through a drop in the interest rate and the increased availability of bank loans. In the balance sheet channel the liquidity of balance sheet positions is a determinant of spending on business investment, housing, and consumer durables. An increase in the money supply lowers market interest rates and increases the value of firms' assets. This rise in net worth lowers the cost of external financing and enhances the ability of firms to invest in plant and equipment. In the short-run, aggregate demand in the economy increases for two reasons: the response of households' and businesses' spending to the decline in the interest rate, and, the increased ability of borrowers to obtain funds because of higher net worth and liquidity.

GLOSSARY

Accommodating policy Actions to stimulate aggregate demand to restore output and jobs, but at the cost of greater inflation. (28)

Adverse selection The problem of distinguishing good-risk applicants from bad-risk applicants before making a loan or providing insurance. (11, 12)

Agency office A foreign bank office in the United States that cannot take deposits from U.S. residents, although it can transfer funds from abroad to the United States and make loans in the United States. (16)

Agents Managers who control (but do not own) the assets of a firm or organization. (11)

Aggregate demand The sum of demands for an economy's goods and services for consumption, investment, government purchases (not including transfer payments), and net exports. (25)

Aggregate demand (_AD_) curve The graph of the relationship between the aggregate demand for goods and services and the aggregate price level. (25)

Aggregate supply The total amount of output that producers in the economy are willing to supply and sell at a given price level. (25)

Aggregate supply (_AS_) curve The graph of the relationship between the aggregate output that firms in the economy are willing to supply and the aggregate price level. (25)

Announcement effect A signal to financial markets by the Fed of its policy intentions through changes in the discount rate. (20)

Appreciation An increase in the value of a currency against another currency. (8, 22)

Asset A thing of value that can be owned; a use of funds and a claim on a borrower's income. (2, 3)

Asymmetric information A condition that occurs when borrowers have some information about their opportunities or activities that they do not disclose to lenders, creditors, or insurers. (3, 11)

Auction market A secondary financial market in which prices are set by competitive bidding by a large number of traders acting on behalf of individual buyers and sellers. (3)

Automated teller machines Electronic devices for performing banking transactions. (2, 13)

Balance-of-payments accounts An accounting device for measuring private and government flows of funds between a country and foreign countries. (22)

Balance sheet A statement showing an individual's or firm's financial position at a point in time. It lists assets, liabilities, and net worth. (13)

Balance sheet channel A description of ways in which interest rate changes from monetary policy affect borrowers' net worth and spending decisions. (27)

Bank A financial institution that accepts deposits from savers and makes loans to borrowers. (12, 13)

Bank assets Cash items and funds used in securities investments, loans, and other asset holdings by the bank. (13)

Bank failure A situation in which a bank cannot pay its depositors in full and still have enough reserves to meet its reserve requirements. (13)

Bank holding company A large firm that holds many different banks as subsidiaries. It was originally used by banks to get around branching restrictions. (14)

Bank lending channel A description of ways in which monetary policy influences spending decisions of bank-dependent borrowers. (27)

Bank liabilities Funds acquired by the bank from savers. (13)

Bank net worth The excess of the value of bank assets over the value of bank liabilities. (13)

Bank reserves The sum of an institution's vault cash and deposits with the central bank. (13)

Bank run A sequence of events in which depositors lose confidence in a bank, for real or imagined reasons, and make withdrawals, exhausting the bank's liquid funds. (14)

Bankers' acceptances Time drafts that establish credit between parties who do not know each other, facilitating international trade. (3, 16)

Banking panics Waves of severe bank runs that cause contractions in credit availability, often culminating in business recessions. (14)

Barter The exchange of goods and services by trading output directly with one another. (2)

Basis risk The imperfect correlation of changes in the price of a hedged instrument and changes in the price of the instrument actually traded in the futures market. (9)

Beta A measure of the response of a security's expected return to changes in the value of the market portfolio. (5)

Board of Governors The Board of the Federal Reserve System, made up of seven members, appointed by the President, who administer monetary policy and set the discount rate. (19)

Bond rating A single statistic summarizing the assessment of a firm's net worth, cash flow, and prospects—in short, its likely ability to meet its debt obligations. (7)

Borrowed reserves (BR, discount loans) A component of the monetary base consisting of reserves borrowed from the central bank. (17)

Borrowers Demanders of funds for consumer durables, houses, and business plant and equipment. (3)

Borrowings Nondeposit liabilities of a bank, including short-term loans in the Fed funds market, loans from the bank's affiliates, and discount loans. (13)

Branches Individual banking offices in different locations owned by the same banking firm. (13, 14)

Branching restrictions Geographical limitations on banking firms' ability to open more than one office, or branch. (14)

Bretton Woods system A fixed exchange rate system that permitted smoother short-term economic adjustments than were possible under the gold standard, based on the convertibility of U.S. dollars into gold at a price of $35.00 per ounce. (22)

Brokered deposits A financial innovation in which a depositor with an amount to invest over the deposit insurance limit goes to a broker who buys certificates of deposit in different banks, giving the depositor insurance on the entire amount. (15)

Brokers Individuals who earn commissions by matching buyers and sellers in a particular market. (12)

Bubble A situation in which the price of an asset is more than its fundamental value. (10)

Budget deficit The excess of government spending over tax revenue. (5, 18)

Business cycle The periodic fluctuations in aggregate output, consisting of expansion (a boom) followed by contraction (a recession). (1, 26)

Call option The right to buy an underlying asset, which is obtained by the buyer of the call option. Sellers have an obligation to sell. (10)

Capital account The balance-of-payments account that measures trade in existing assets among countries. (22)

Capital account balance A country's capital inflows minus its capital outflows. (22)

Capital controls Government-imposed barriers to foreign savers' investing in domestic assets or to domestic savers' investing in foreign assets. (22)

Capital inflow The flow of funds into a country to buy domestic assets. (22)

Capital markets Financial markets for trading debt instruments with a maturity greater than one year and equity instruments. (3)

Capital outflow The flow of funds from a country to buy foreign assets. (22)

Cash markets Markets in which actual claims are bought and sold with immediate settlement. (3)

Central bank A special governmental or quasi-governmental institution within the financial system that regulates the medium of exchange. (2)

Central bank credibility The belief by the public that central bank announcements reflect its true policy intentions. (28)

Certificate of deposit (CD) A fixed-maturity instrument, sold by a bank to depositors, that pays principal and interest at maturity, with a penalty for early withdrawal. (3)

Checkable deposits Accounts that grant a depositor the right to write checks to individuals, firms, or the government. (13)

Checks Promises to pay definitive money on demand; checks are drawn on funds deposited with a financial institution. (2)

Circuit breakers Interventions that are designed to restore orderly securities markets. (10)

Closed economy An economy of a country that neither borrows from nor lends to foreign countries. (5) **Closed-end mutual fund** A fund that sells a fixed number of nonredeemable shares, which are then traded over-the-counter like common stock. The price fluctuates with the value of the underlying assets. (12)

Coinsurance An insurance option that requires the policyholder to pay a certain fraction of the costs of a claim, in addition to the deductible. (12)

Cold turkey Reducing inflation all at once, rather than gradually. (28)

Collateral Assets that are pledged to pay for a loan in the event of default on the loan. (11, 13)

Commercial bank(s) The largest group of depository institutions, which offer risk-sharing, liquidity (checking accounts), and information services that benefit savers and borrowers. (3, 12, 13)

Commercial bank loan A loan to businesses or consumers that is made by banks and financial companies. (3)

Commercial paper A liquid, short-term investment for savers that is used by high-quality, well-known firms and financial institutions to raise funds. (3, 13)

Commodity money Physical goods (particularly precious metals) that are used as the medium of exchange. (2)

Compensating balance A required minimum amount in a checking account that is used as a form of collateral in commercial loans. (13)

Compounding Earning interest on interest as savings are accumulated over a period of time. (4)

Consol A (perpetual) coupon bond with an infinite maturity; its price is based on the present value of the coupon payments. (4)

Consumer price index (CPI) An index of prices of a marketbasket of goods purchased by urban consumers. It is a commonly used measure of inflation. (2, 28)

Contagion The spreading of bad news about one bank to other banks. (14)

Contractual saving institutions Financial institutions (insurance companies and pension funds) that allow individuals to transfer risk of financial hardship and accumulate funds for retirement. (12)

Corporate bonds Intermediate and long-term obligations issued by large, high-quality corporations in order to finance plant and equipment spending. (3, 7)

Corporate control A contest for ownership and control of a firm that pits shareholders against managers in an effort to direct the firm's resources to their highest-valued use. (11)

Corporate restructuring firms Investors that raise equity capital to acquire shares in other firms to reduce free-rider problems and moral hazard. (11)

Cost-push inflation Price increases resulting from workers' pressure for higher wages. (28)

Coupon bond A credit market instrument that requires multiple payments of interest on a regular basis, such as semiannually or annually, and a payment of the face value at maturity. (4)

Coupon rate An interest rate equal to the yearly coupon payment divided by the face value. (4)

Credit controls Regulatory restrictions on bank lending. (27)

Credit crunch A decline in either the ability or the willingness of banks to lend at any given interest rate. (14, 26, 27)

Credit market instruments Methods of financing debt, including simple loans, discount bonds, coupon bonds, and fixed payment loans. (4)

Credit rationing The restricting of credit by lenders such that borrowers cannot obtain the funds they desire at the given interest rate. (11, 13)

Credit risk (default risk) The probability that a borrower will not pay in full promised interest, principal, or both. This characteristic of a credit market instrument influences its interest rate. (7, 13)

Credit-risk analysis The examination of a borrower's likelihood of repayment and general business conditions that might influence the borrower's ability to repay the loan. (13)

Credit union A financial intermediary that takes deposits from and makes loans to individuals who work at the same firm or in the same industry. (12)

Crowding out The reduction in private consumption and investment that accompanies an increase in government purchases in a closed economy. (24)

Currency A type of money, such as dollar bills and coins. (2)

Currency-deposit ratio The relationship of currency, C, held by the nonbank public to checkable deposits, D. (17)

Currency in circulation Federal Reserve Notes (official currency) held by the nonbank public. (17)

Currency premium A number that indicates investors' collective preference for financial instruments denominated in one currency relative to those denominated in another. (8, 22)

Currency swap An exchange of expected future returns on debt instruments denominated in different currencies. (16)

Current account A balance-of-payment account that summarizes transactions among countries for purchases and sales of currently produced goods and services. (22)

Current account balance The sum for a country of the trade balance, services balance, net investment income, and unilateral transfers. (22)

Current output The output of goods and services produced in the economy in the immediate period. (24)

Current yield The coupon payment divided by the current price of a bond. (4)

Dealers Individuals who hold inventories of securities and sell them for a price higher than they paid for them, earning the spread between the bid and the asked price. (12)

Debt A claim that requires a borrower to repay the amount borrowed (the principal) plus a rental fee (interest). (3)

Debt deflation A decrease in prices that raises the real value of households' and firms' outstanding debt, reducing their net worth and their ability to finance desired spending. (11, 27)

Deductible A specified amount to be subtracted from a policyholder's loss when a claim is paid by the insurance company. (12)

Default The inability to repay all or part of an obligation. (3)

Default risk (credit risk) The probability that a borrower will not pay in full promised interest, principal, or both. This characteristic of a credit market instrument influences its interest rate. (7)

Default-risk-free instruments Securities that guarantee that principal and interest will be repaid in nominal terms. For example, U.S. Treasury securities are default-risk-free. (7)

Defensive transactions Open market transactions used by the Fed to offset fluctuations in the monetary base arising from disturbances in portfolio preferences of banks and the nonbank public, financial markets, and the economy. (20)

Defined benefit pension plan A common pension plan in which the employee is promised an assigned benefit based on earnings and years of service, and payments may or may not be indexed for inflation. (12)

Defined contribution pension plan A pension plan in which contributions are invested for employees, who own the value of the funds in the plan. (12)

Definitive money Money that does not have to be converted into a more basic medium of exchange, such as gold or silver. (2)

Deflation A condition in which falling prices cause a given amount of money to purchase more goods and services. (2)

Demand deposit An account against which checks convertible to currency can be written. (13)

Demand for money A decision by the public concerning how much of its wealth to hold in money balances, which is affected by current and anticipated future changes in output. (23, 26)

Demand-pull inflation Price increases resulting from policymakers' attempts to increase aggregate demand for current output above the full-employment level. (28)

Depository institutions Commercial banks, savings and loan institutions, mutual savings banks, and credit unions that accept deposits and make loans, acting as intermediaries in the saving-investment process. (3, 12)

Depository Institutions Deregulation and Monetary Control Act of 1980 (DIDMCA) Regulatory reform eliminating interest rate ceilings, providing for uniform reserve requirements, and broadening the scope of permissible activities by S&Ls. (15)

Depreciation A decrease in a currency's value against another currency. (8, 22)

Derivative instrument An asset, such as a futures or option contract, that derives its economic value from an underlying asset such as a stock or bond. (9)

Derivative market Markets in which such claims as futures or option contracts—that derive their economic value from an underlying asset such as a stock or bond—are traded. (9)

Determinants of portfolio choice The key factors affecting a saver's portfolio allocation of assets. They are a saver's wealth, expectations of return on assets, degree of risk of assets, liquidity of assets, and the cost of acquiring information about assets. (5)

Devaluation The lowering of the official value of a country's currency relative to other currencies, thereby resetting the exchange rate. (22)

Direct finance A form of financing wherein an individual saver holds financial claims issued directly by an individual borrower. (3)

Discount bond A credit market instrument in which the borrower repays the amount of the loan in a single payment at maturity but receives less than the face value initially. (4)

Discount loan A loan made by the Federal Reserve System (central bank) to a member bank. (14, 17)

Discount policy The oldest of the Federal Reserve's principal tools for regulating the money supply. It includes setting the discount rate and terms of discount lending. (20)

Discount rate The interest rate specified by the Fed for loans to depository institutions. (17)

Discount window The means by which the Fed makes discount loans to banks, serving as a channel for meeting the liquidity needs of banks. (20)

Discretion strategy An attempt by the central bank to adjust monetary policy as it sees fit to achieve its goals. (28)

Disinflation A policy-induced decline in long-run inflation. (28)

Disintermediation An exit of savers and borrowers from banks to financial markets. (15)

Diversification Splitting wealth among many different assets to reduce risk. (3, 5)

Dividends Periodic payments (usually once each quarter) that owners of equities generally receive from the firm. (3)

Dual banking system The system in the United States in which banks are chartered by either the federal government or a state government. (14)

Duration For an asset or liability, the responsiveness of the percentage change in the asset's or liability's market value to a percentage change in the market interest rate. (13)

Duration gap A bank's exposure to fluctuations in interest rates, measured as the difference between the average duration for bank assets and the average duration for bank liabilities. (13)

Dynamic transactions Open market operations aimed at achieving desired changes in monetary policy indicated by the Federal Open Market Committee. (20)

Economic growth A goal of monetary policy, seeking increases in the economy's output of goods and services over time. (21)

Economies of scale A fall in the transactions costs per dollar of investment as the size of the transactions increases. (11)

Edge Act corporations Special subsidiaries of U.S. banks that conduct only international banking services, as provided in the Edge Act of 1919. (16)

Efficient financial market A market in which all information that is available to market participants is reflected in market prices. (10)

Efficient markets hypothesis A proposition that applies rational expectations to the pricing of assets. It says that when traders and investors use all available information in forming expectations of future rates of return and the cost of trading is low, the equilibrium price of the security is equal to the optimal forecast of fundamental value based on the available information. (10)

Electronic funds transfer systems Computerized payment clearing devices, such as debit cards and automated teller machines. (2)

Equation of exchange An equation stating that the quantity of money times the velocity of money equals nominal spending in the economy. (23)

Equilibrium real interest rate The interest rate at which desired lending and desired borrowing are equal. It is determined by the intersection of the demand curve and the supply curve for loanable funds in a closed economy. (6)

Equity A claim to a share in the profits and assets of a firm. (3)

Eurobonds Obligations that are denominated in a currency other than that of the country where they are sold, usually in U.S. dollars. (3)

Eurocurrency deposits Time deposits that are denominated in a currency other than that of the issuing domestic financial center (for instance, dollar deposits at a French bank). (16)

Eurodollars A deposit denominated in dollars in a bank or bank branch outside the United States. (3, 16)

Euromarkets Relatively unregulated banking centers in which funds are raised in a currency other than that of the issuing domestic financial center. (16)

European Central Bank A European-wide monetary institution that has been proposed to conduct monetary policy and, eventually, to control a single currency. (22)

European Monetary System A monetary agreement by a number of EC nations to limit exchange rate fluctuations. (22)

European Monetary Union A plan drafted as part of the 1992 single European market initiative, in which exchange rates are fixed (as of 1999), ultimately by using a common currency. (22)

Excess reserves Reserves that depository institutions elect to hold that are greater than the reserves required by the Fed. (13, 17)

Exchange rate The price of one country's currency in terms of another, such as yen per dollar or francs per pound. (1, 8)

Exchange rate mechanism A device used by a group of EC nations to limit fluctuations in the values of their currencies relative to one another. (22)

Exchange rate regime A system of adjusting currency values and flows of goods and capital among countries. (22)

Exchange rate risk The potential fluctuations in an asset's value because of increases or decreases in exchange rates. (16)

Exchanges Auction markets at which buyers and sellers of securities trade, such as the New York and American Stock Exchanges. (3, 12)

Expectations-augmented Phillips curve An expanded Phillips curve relationship in which the Phillips curve shifts with changes in expected inflation. (28)

Expectations theory of the term structure of interest rates The proposition that investors view assets of all maturities as perfect substitutes, given the same levels of default risk, liquidity, information costs, and taxation. (7)

Expected real interest rate The nominal interest rate minus the expected rate of inflation. (4)

Extended credit Longer-term discount loans extended to a bank by the Fed under exceptional circumstances to alleviate severe liquidity problems. (20)

Fads Overreaction to good or bad news about an issue or a class of assets. (10)

Federal deposit insurance A federal government guarantee of certain types of bank deposits for account balances of up to $100,000. (13, 14, 15)

Federal Deposit Insurance Corporation Improvement Act of 1991 (FDICIA) Regulatory reform in which the bank supervisory framework connected enforcement actions to the bank's level of capital. (14)

Federal funds instruments ("Fed funds") Overnight loans between banks of their deposits with the Fed. (3)

Federal funds rate The interest rate charged on the overnight loans among banks. (3, 13, 20)

Federal Open Market Committee (FOMC) The Federal Reserve System committee, with 12 members, that gives directions for open market operations. Members include the Board of Governors, the president of the Federal Reserve Bank in New York, and the presidents of four other Federal Reserve banks. (19)

Federal Reserve bank A district bank of the Federal Reserve System that, among other things, conducts discount lending. (19)

Federal Reserve float The difference between cash items in the process of collection and deferred availability cash items reported in the Fed's balance sheet. (18)

Federal Reserve System (the Fed) The central bank in the United States, which promotes price stability in the banking industry and issues currency. (1, 14, 17, 19, 20, 21)

Fiat money Money authorized by central banks as the definitive money, which does not have to be exchanged by the central bank for gold or some other commodity money. (2)

Finance company Intermediaries that raise funds in large amounts through the sale of commercial paper and securities to make (generally smaller) loans to households and businesses. (12)

Financial distress A situation in which households or firms must sell illiquid assets, possibly at a loss, to meet current obligations. (27)

Financial futures (contracts) Claims that imply settlement of a purchase of a financial instrument at a specified future date, though price is determined at the outset. (3, 9)

Financial innovation Alterations in the operation of financial markets and institutions caused by changes in costs of providing risk-sharing, liquidity, or information services, or changes in demand for these services. (3, 15)

Financial institutions Go-betweens for savers and borrowers, such as banks or insurance companies. (1, 3, 12)

Financial Institutions Reform, Recovery, and Enforcement Act of 1989 (FIRREA) The regulatory reform that eliminated the FSLIC and formed the Resolution Trust Corporation to clean up the thrift crisis. (15)

Financial instruments IOU notes created by financial institutions, which are assets for savers and liabilities for (claims on) borrowers. (1, 3)

Financial integration The way in which financial markets are tied together geographically—domestically and internationally. (3)

Financial intermediaries Institutions such as commercial banks, credit unions, savings and loan associations, mutual savings banks, mutual funds, finance companies, insurance companies, and pension funds that borrow funds from savers and lend them to borrowers. (1, 3)

Financial intermediation Indirect finance through institutions that raise funds from savers and invest in debt or equity claims of borrowers. (3)

Financial markets Places or channels for buying and selling newly issued or existing bonds, stocks, foreign exchange contracts, and other financial instruments. (1, 3)

Financial panics Periods characterized by violent fluctuations in financial markets, bank runs, and bankruptcies of many firms. (14, 27)

Financial structure The mix of finance between equity and debt, as well as the source of funds (direct finance through financial markets or indirect finance through financial intermediaries). (11)

Financial system A network of markets and institutions to transfer funds from individuals and groups who have saved money to individuals and groups who want to borrow money. (1, 3)

Fisher hypothesis A proposition stating that the nominal interest rate rises or falls point-for-point with expected inflation. (4)

Fixed exchange rate system A system in which exchange rates are set at levels determined and maintained by governments. (22)

Fixed payment loan A credit market instrument that requires the borrower to make a regular periodic payment (monthly, quarterly, or annually) of principal and interest to the lender. (4)

Flexible exchange rate system An agreement among nations in which currency values are allowed to fluctuate freely. (22)

Floating rate debt Loans whose interest payments vary with market interest rates. (13)

Foreign bank branch A full-service affiliate of a foreign financial institution, bearing its name, accepting deposits, and making loans. (16)

Foreign-exchange market intervention Deliberate action by the central bank to influence the exchange rate. (22)

Foreign-exchange market stability A goal of monetary policy to limit fluctuations in the foreign-exchange value of the currency. (21)

Forward transactions Agreements to exchange currencies, bank deposits, or securities at a set date in the future. They provide savers and borrowers the ability to conduct a transaction now and settle it in the future. (8, 9)

Free cash flow Funds that represent the difference between the firm's cash receipts and cash disbursements, including payments to equityholders and debtholders. (11)

Free reserves The difference between excess reserves and borrowed reserves (discount loans) in the banking system. (21)

Free-rider problem A situation in which individuals obtain and use information that others have paid for. (11)

Frictional unemployment Unemployment caused by searches by workers and firms for suitable matches of workers to jobs. (28)

Full-employment (*FE*) line A vertical line depicting the economy's production level achieved by the use of all available production factors, regardless of the real rate of interest. (24)

Full-employment output The production level achieved by using all available factors of production in place in the economy in the current period, irrespective of the real rate of interest. (24, 25, 28)

Fully funded pension plan A pension plan in which the contributions, together with the projected future earnings, are sufficient to pay the projected assigned benefits. (12)

Fundamental value The present value of an asset's expected future returns, which equals the market price of the asset in an efficient financial market. (10)

Futures contract An agreement that specifies the delivery of a specific underlying commodity or financial instrument at a given future date at a currently agreed-upon price. (10)

Garn-St. Germain Act of 1982 Regulatory reform authorizing banks to issue money market deposit accounts and broadening the permissible activities of S&Ls. (15)

GDP deflator An index of prices of all goods and services included in the gross domestic product, which is the final value of all goods and services produced in the economy. (2)

General Account The U.S. Treasury's deposit account with the Federal Reserve. (18)

General directive A summary of the Federal Open Market Committee's overall objectives for monetary aggregates and/or interest rates. (20)

General equilibrium Outcome in which all markets in the economy are in equilibrium at the same time. (24)

Gold standard A fixed exchange rate system in which the currencies of participating countries are convertible into an agreed-upon amount of gold. (22)

Goods market The market for trade in all goods and services that the economy produces at a particular point in time. (24)

Government allocation Distribution of goods and services by which a central authority collects the output of producers and distributes it to others according to some plan. (2)

Government budget constraint An equation depicting the relationships among federal spending and tax decisions, sales of securities by the Treasury, and changes in the monetary base. (18)

Gradualism A policy, recommended by new Keynesian economists, in which the rate of growth of the money supply is slowly reduced so that the inflation rate can adjust slowly, with smaller losses of output and jobs. (28)

Hedge fund A largely unregulated speculative investment vehicle for high-net-worth individuals and institutional investors. (12)

Hedging Reducing one's exposure to risk by receiving the right to sell or buy an asset at a known price on a specified future date. (9)

High employment A goal of monetary policy emphasizing a low rate of unemployment. (21)

Hyperinflation Rapid inflation in excess of hundreds or thousands of percentage points per year for a significant period of time. (2, 28)

Hysteresis A situation in which unemployment rates can be higher than those associated with full employment for extended periods of time. (25)

Idiosyncratic risk (unsystematic risk) A unique risk that assets carry that does not affect the market as a whole. For example, the price of an individual stock is influenced by factors affecting the company's profitability, such as a strike or the discovery of a new product. (5)

Income The flow of earnings over a period of time. (2)

Indicator A financial variable whose movements reveal information to the central bank about present or prospective conditions in financial markets or the economy. (21)

Inflation A condition in the economy in which rising prices cause a given amount of money to purchase fewer goods and services, thus decreasing the purchasing power of money. (2, 28)

Inflation target A goal for inflation announced by the central bank and pursued by using its policy tools. (21)

Information Facts about borrowers and about expectations of returns on financial assets. (3)

Information costs The costs that savers incur in finding out the creditworthiness of borrowers and monitoring how borrowers use the funds acquired. (3, 11)

Information lag A condition that makes it impossible for the Fed to observe instantaneously movements in GDP, inflation, or other goal variables. (21)

Insider information Facts that are known to a firm's management but are not available to other investors or prospective investors in the firm. (10)

Insurance company Financial intermediaries that specialize in writing contracts to protect their policyholders from the risk of financial loss associated with particular events. (12)

Interest A rental fee for using borrowed funds. (4)

Interest rate The cost of borrowing funds, usually expressed as a percentage of the amount borrowed. (1, 4)

Interest rate risk The risk that the value of financial assets and liabilities will fluctuate in response to changes in market interest rates. (13)

Interest rate stability A goal of monetary policy focusing on reducing fluctuations in interest rates. (21)

Interest rate swap An agreement to sell the expected future returns on one financial instrument for the expected future returns on another. (9, 13)

Intermediaries See *Financial intermediaries*.

Intermediate targets Objectives for financial variables—such as the money supply or short-term interest rates—that the Fed believes will directly help it to achieve its ultimate goals. (21)

Intermediate-term debt A debt instrument that has a maturity between 1 and 10 years. (3)

International banking facilities (IBFs) Institutions within the United States that cannot conduct domestic banking business but can take time deposits from and make loans to foreign households and firms. They are exempt from reserve requirements, federal restrictions on interest payments to depositors, and, in some states, state and local taxation. (16)

International banks Financial institutions that provide risk-sharing, liquidity, and information services to firms and individuals engaged in international trade and finance. (16)

International capital market The market for lending and borrowing across national boundaries. (1, 5)

International capital mobility The ability of investors to move funds among international markets. (8)

International Monetary Fund (IMF) The multinational lender of last resort, created by the Bretton Woods agreement to help countries make short-run economic adjustments to a balance of payments deficit or surplus while maintaining a fixed exchange rate. (22)

International reserves A central bank's assets that are denominated in a foreign currency and used in international transactions. (22)

International transactions currency The currency of choice in settling international commercial and financial transactions. (16)

Investment banks Securities market institutions that assist businesses in raising new capital and advise them on the best means of doing it (issuing shares or structuring debt instruments). (12)

Investment institutions Financial institutions (mutual funds and finance companies) that raise funds to invest in loans and securities. (12)

IS curve The negative relationship between the real interest rate and the level of income, all else being equal, that arises in the market for goods and services. (24)

Junk bonds Corporate bonds issued by lower-quality and thus riskier firms. (3, 7)

L The broadest monetary aggregate, including *M3* short-term Treasury securities, commercial paper, savings bonds, and bankers' acceptances. (2)

Lags in policymaking and implementation process Delays in deciding upon and carrying out monetary policy. (26)

Large open economy The economy of a country whose domestic saving and investment shifts are large enough to affect the real interest rate in the international capital market. The United States, Japan, and Germany are examples of countries with large open economies. (5)

Law of one price A theory stating that if two countries produce an identical good, profit opportunities should ensure that the price of the good is the same around the world, no matter which country produces the good. This law assumes that the goods are tradeable and allows differences that reflect transportation costs. (8)

Legal tender The requirement that a particular currency be acceptable in the settlement of commercial and financial transactions. (2)

Lemons problem An adverse selection problem in which individuals do not know the quality of asset choices (for example, of used cars), so they average quality, overvaluing some assets and undervaluing others. At the average price, owners of the undervalued assets are less likely to sell, but owners of the overvalued assets are more likely to sell. (11)

Lender of last resort The ultimate source of credit to which banks can turn during a panic. (14)

Leveraged buyout (LBO) A type of restructuring in which external equity is replaced by debt. (11)

Liabilities Sources of funds and claims on future income of borrowers. (3)

Life insurance company A firm that sells policies to protect households against a loss of earnings from disability, retirement, or death of the insured person. (12)

Liquidity The ease with which one can exchange assets for cash, other assets, or goods and services. (1, 3, 7)

Liquidity of balance sheet positions The quantity of liquid assets that households and firms hold relative to their liabilities, which is a determinant of spending on business investment, housing, and consumer durables. (27)

Liquidity preference theory A proposition, developed by John Maynard Keynes, that emphasizes the sensitivity of money demand to changes in interest rates. (23)

Liquidity risk The possibility that depositors may collectively decide to withdraw more funds than the bank has on hand. (13)

LM **curve** The positive relationship between the real interest rate and the level of income, all else being equal, that arises in the market for real money balances. (24)

Load fund A mutual fund that charges commissions for purchases and/or sales. (12)

Loan A transaction in which the borrower receives funds from a lender and the borrower agrees to repay funds with interest. (4)

Loan commitment An agreement by a bank to provide a borrower with a stated amount of funds during some specified period of time. (13)

Loan sale A financial contract in which a bank agrees to sell the expected future returns from an underlying bank loan to a third party. (13)

Loan syndicate An arrangement in which a loan is arranged and managed by a lead bank; other banks hold fractions of the loan. (16)

Long-run aggregate supply curve (*LRAS***)** The graph of the relationship of firms' output to price level in the long run. It is vertical at the full-employment output. (25)

Long-term debt A debt instrument that has a maturity of 10 years or more. (3)

Luxury asset An asset for which the wealth elasticity of demand exceeds unity. (6)

M 1 The narrowest monetary aggregate, which measures money as the traditional medium of exchange, including currency, traveler's checks, and checkable deposits. (2)

M 2 A monetary aggregate that includes the components of *M1* plus short-term investment accounts that could be converted to definitive money, but not as easily as the components of *M1*. *M2* now includes money market deposit accounts, noninstitutional money market mutual fund shares, and other very liquid assets of firms such as overnight repurchase agreements and overnight Eurodollars. (2)

M3 A monetary aggregate that includes *M2* plus some less liquid assets, including large-denomination time deposits, institutional money market mutual fund balances, term repurchase agreements, and term Eurodollars. (2)

Main bank In Japan, a large bank within a finance group that owns some equity in member firms, is a big source of credit for group firms, and monitors activities of member firms. (14)

Management buyout (MBO) A form of restructuring in which a firm's managers acquire a greater stake in the firm by buying back shares from other shareholders. (11)

Market risk (systematic risk) A risk that is common to all assets of a certain type, such as potential general fluctuations in economic conditions that can increase or decrease returns on stocks collectively. (5)

Marketable securities Liquid assets that banks hold and can trade in secondary markets. (13)

Matched sale-purchase transactions (reverse repos) Agreements that are often used by the Fed Trading Desk for open market sales, in which the Fed sells securities to dealers in the government securities market and the dealers agree to sell them back to the Fed in the very near future. (20)

Maturity The length of time before a debt instrument expires. The maturity can be a very short period of time (30 days or even overnight) or a long period of time (30 years or more). (3)

Medium of exchange A term that economists use to describe money. (2)

Member banks Banks that are members of the Federal Reserve System. (19)

Menu costs Costs to firms that are caused by changing prices because of inflation (reprinting price lists, informing customers, and so on). (28)

Misperception theory Propositions about the effects of imperfect information on the part of firms on aggregate supply. (See also *New classical view*.) (25)

Monetary aggregates Measures of the quantity of money that are broader than currency. They include *M1*, *M2*, *M3*, and *L*. (2, 23)

Monetary base All reserves held by banks as well as all currency in circulation. (17)

Monetary neutrality The proposition that money has no effect on output in the long run because an increase (decrease) in the nominal money supply raises (lowers) the price level in the long run but does not change equilibrium output. (25)

Monetary policy The management of the money supply and its links to prices, interest rates, and other economic variables. (1, 21, 26)

Monetary policy goals Objectives set by the central bank in carrying out monetary and regulatory policy. (21)

Monetary theory The area of study concerning the relationships linking changes in the money supply to changes in economic activity and prices in the economy. (1)

Monetizing the debt The Fed's purchasing of Treasury securities to finance budget deficits. (18)

Money Anything that is generally accepted as payment for goods and services or in the settlement of debts. Money acts as a medium of exchange, is a unit of account and a store of value, and offers a standard of deferred payment. (1, 2)

Money center banks Large, established national banks. (14)

Money channel The path through which monetary policy affects output through effects on interest-sensitive spending. (27)

Money demand function A function relating the demand for real money balances to its underlying determinants. (23)

Money market deposit account (MMDA) Federally insured bank deposit accounts that provide services similar to those of money market mutual funds. (15)

Money market mutual funds Funds that issue shares to savers backed by holdings of high-quality short-term assets. (12)

Money markets Financial markets that trade assets used as the medium of exchange, such as currency or shorter-term instruments with a maturity of less than one year. (3, 12)

Money multiplier The number that indicates how much the money supply changes in response to a given change in the monetary base. (17)

Money supply The stock of the medium of exchange supplied by the central bank. (17)

Money supply process The means by which actions of the central bank, the banking system, and the nonbank public determine the money supply. (17)

Moral hazard The lender's difficulty in monitoring borrowers' activities once the loan is made. (11)

Mortgages Loans, usually long-term, to households or firms to purchase buildings or land. The underlying

asset—house or factory or piece of land—serves as collateral. (3)

Multiple deposit contraction The process by which a decrease in bank reserves reduces the volume of checkable deposits in the banking system. (17)

Multiple deposit expansion Part of the money supply process in which funds are deposited and redeposited in banks. Banks serve as a link between the central bank and the nonbank public, taking increases in reserves from the central bank and funneling them to the nonbank public by making loans. (17)

Municipal bonds Obligations of state and local governments that are exempt from federal, state, and local income taxes. (7)

Mutual funds Financial intermediaries that raise funds by selling shares to individual savers and investing them in diversified portfolios of stocks, bonds, mortgages, and money market instruments. (3, 12)

Narrow banking Deposit insurance reform in which only deposits in safe assets would be insured. (15)

National banks Federally chartered banks supervised by the Office of the Comptroller of the Currency, a department of the U.S. Treasury. Originally, national banks were allowed to issue bank notes as currency. (14)

Natural rate of unemployment The rate of unemployment that exists when the economy produces the full-employment level of output. (28)

Negotiable certificate of deposit A large-denomination fixed-maturity instrument that is sold by a bank to investors and can be traded in a secondary market. (3, 13)

Negotiated Order of Withdrawal (NOW) Effectively, a bank checking account that pays interest. (15)

Net worth (equity capital) The difference between a firm's current and expected future holdings (assets) and its debts (liabilities). (11, 13)

Neutrality of money The absence of an effect of change in the nominal money supply on output and the real interest rate. (24, 26)

New classical view A theory stating that for short-run aggregate supply, there is a positive relation between aggregate supply and the difference between the actual and the expected price level. (25)

New Keynesian view Economic explanations for price stickiness in the short run, based on features of many real-world markets: the rigidity of long-term contracts and imperfect competition among sellers in the goods market. (25)

No-load funds Funds that earn income only from management fees (typically about 0.5% of assets), not from sales commissions. (12)

Noise traders Relatively uninformed traders who pursue trading strategies with no superior information and who may overreact. (10)

Nominal exchange rate The value of one currency in terms of another currency. (8)

Nominal interest rate An interest rate that is unadjusted for changes in purchasing power. (4)

Nominal interest rate parity condition The market equilibrium condition in which domestic and foreign assets have identical risk, liquidity, and information characteristics, so their nominal returns—measured in the same currency—also must be identical. (8)

Nonbank banks Financial institutions that take demand deposits but do not make loans. (14)

Nonbank office Affiliates of bank holding companies that do not accept demand deposits but do make loans. (14)

Nonmoney asset market A market that handles trading in assets that are stores of value, including stocks, bonds, and houses. (24)

Nontransaction deposit Claims on banks including savings deposits and time deposits. (13)

Off-balance-sheet lending Bank lending activities in which the bank does not necessarily hold as assets the loans that it makes, including standby letters of credit, loan commitments, and loan sales. (13)

Official reserve assets Assets held by central banks that can be used in making international payments to settle the balance of payments. (22)

Official settlements balance The net increase in a country's official reserve assets. (22)

Offshore markets International financial centers that are located in unregulated areas with low tax rates on banks—for example, in the Caribbean (the Bahamas and Cayman Islands) and in Hong Kong and Singapore. (16)

Okun's law A statistical relationship identified by Arthur Okun between changes in output and the unemployment rate. (28)

Open economy An economy in which borrowing and lending take place in the international capital market. (5)

Open-end mutual funds Mutual funds that issue redeemable shares at a price tied to the underlying value of the assets. (12)

Open market operations The purchase and sale of securities in financial markets by the Federal Reserve System. Open market operations are its most direct route for changing the monetary base. (17, 20)

Open market purchase The buying of government securities by the Fed, with the intent of raising the monetary base. (17)

Open market sale The sale of government securities by the Fed, with the intent of reducing the monetary base. (17)

Open Market Trading Desk A group of traders at the Federal Reserve Bank of New York who buy and sell securities for the Fed's account. (20)

Operating targets Variables directly under the Fed's control that are closely related to the intermediate targets of monetary policy. Operating targets include the federal funds rate and nonborrowed reserves. (21)

Options contract A right (option) conferred upon a trader to buy or sell a particular asset (shares of stock, a bond, or unit of foreign currency, for example) within a predetermined time and at a predetermined price. (3, 9)

Outright purchase or sale The Fed's buying securities from or selling securities to dealers. (20)

Over-the-counter (OTC) markets Secondary financial markets for broker-dealers that are organized via telephone and computer, with no centralized place for auction trading. (3, 12)

Payments system A mechanism for conducting transactions in the economy. Commercial banks play a key role in this system by clearing and settling transactions in the economy. (2, 13)

Payments system factors Substitutes for money in transactions that affect the demand for money. (23)

Pension fund Financial institutions that invest contributions of workers and firms in financial assets o provide retirement benefits for workers. (12)

Phillips curve A relationship, found by A. W. Phillips, in which high unemployment was associated with a low rate of wage inflation, and vice versa. (28)

Plan funding A method by which pension assets accrue to finance retirement benefits. (12)

Political business cycle model The theory that the policymakers will urge the Fed to try to lower interest rates to stimulate credit demand and economic activity prior to an election. (19)

Portfolio A collection of assets. (3, 5)

Preferred habitat theory of the term structure of interest rates Proposition that investors care about both expected returns and maturity, viewing instruments with different maturities as substitutes, but not perfect ones. (7)

Present value (PV, present discounted value) A concept that is used to evaluate credit marked instruments by placing all payments in terms of today's dollars so that they can be added together. (4)

Price controls Official government restrictions on price changes. (28)

Price index A summary statistic that incorporates changes in the price of a set of goods relative to the price in some base year. (2)

Price level The average price of a market basket of goods and services in the economy. (1)

Price stability A goal of monetary policy to stabilize the purchasing power of the currency. (21)

Primary markets Financial markets in which newly issued debt or equity claims are sold to initial buyers by private borrowers to raise funds for durable-goods purchases or new ventures and by governments to finance budget deficits. (3)

Prime rate Traditionally, the interest rate charged on six-month loans to high-quality borrowers. (13)

Principals Owners (but not direct managers) of a firm or organization. (11)

Principal-agent problem The type of moral hazard that may arise when managers (agents) who control a firm's assets do not own very much of the firm's equity and therefore do not have the same incentive to maximize the firm's value as the owners (principals) do. (11)

Principal-agent view A theory of central bank decision making implying that officials maximize their per-sonal well-being rather than that of the general public. (19)

Producer price index (PPI) An index of the prices that firms pay in wholesale markets for crude materials, intermediate goods, and finished goods. It is a commonly used measure to calculate inflation. (2, 28)

Productivity growth A measure of the growth of output in a country relative to the growth of inputs. (8)

Program trading Using computer-generated orders to buy or sell many stocks at the same time, causing rapid adjustments of institutional portfolios. (10)

Property and casualty insurance company A firm that sells policies to protect households and firms from risks of illness, theft, accident, or natural disasters. (12)

Public interest view A theory of central bank decision making implying that officials act in the interest of citizens' well-being. (19)

Purchasing power The ability of money to be used to acquire goods and services. (2)

Purchasing power parity (PPP) theory of exchange rate determination The proposition that changes in the nominal exchange rate between two currencies are accounted for by differences in inflation rates in the two countries. This theory assumes that real exchange rates are constant. (8)

Put option The right to sell an underlying asset, which is obtained by buying the put option. Sellers of put options have an obligation to buy the asset. (10)

Quantity theory of money demand A theory, developed by Irving Fisher and others, that states that the determinant of the demand for real balances is the real volume of transactions. (23)

Quota A common trade barrier that limits the volume of foreign goods that can be brought into the country. (8)

Rate of capital gains The percentage change in the price of a financial asset. (4)

Rational expectations The assumption in the model of an efficient market that participants will use all available information in estimating the expected price level or change in the money supply so that the market price equals the present value of expected future returns. (10, 26)

Real business cycle view The theory that changes in aggregate demand have no effect on output, even in the short run, assuming perfect information and perfectly flexible prices. Short-term changes to output are primarily temporary shocks to productivity, such as changes in the availability of raw materials. (25)

Real exchange rate The purchasing power of a currency relative to the purchasing power of other currencies. (8)

Real interest rate An interest rate that is adjusted for changes in purchasing power caused by inflation. (4)

Real money balances The value of money balances adjusted for changes in purchasing power. (23)

Recession A contraction in current output in the business cycle. (26)

Regulation Q The regulation, authorized by the Banking Act of 1933, that placed ceilings on allowable interest rates on time and savings deposits and prohibited the payment of interest on demand deposits (then the only form of checkable deposits). (15)

Repurchase agreements (repos or RPs) Very short-term loans that are used for cash management by large corporations. Maturities are typically less than two weeks and often the next day. (3, 13)

Required reserve ratio The percentage of deposits that banks must hold as reserves, as specified by the Fed. (17)

Required reserves The minimum amount that depository institutions are compelled to hold as reserves by the Federal Reserve System. (13, 17)

Reserve requirement The requirement that banks hold a fraction of checkable deposits as vault cash or deposits with the central bank. (17)

Reserves A bank asset consisting of vault cash (cash on hand in the bank) plus deposits with the Federal Reserve. (13)

Restrictive covenants Limits on the actions of a borrower or insured person made by a lender or insurer. For example, a lender may restrict risk-taking activities of the borrower, require the borrower to maintain a certain level of net worth, or require the borrower to maintain the value of collateral offered to the lender. (11, 12)

Restructuring Rearranging the financial structure of a firm to shift control over the resources of the firm and to provide incentives for managers to maximize the firm's value. (11)

Revaluation Raising the official value of a country's currency relative to other currencies, thereby resetting the exchange rate. (22)

Riegle-Neal Interstate Banking and Branching Efficiency Act of 1994 A regulatory reform providing for a consistent nationwide standard for bank expansion. (15)

Risk The degree of uncertainty of an asset's return. (1)

Risk-averse Characteristic of savers who desire to minimize variability in return on savings. (5)

Risk-based premiums A fee for insurance that is based on the probability of the insured individual's collecting a claim. (12)

Risk-loving Characteristic of savers who actually prefer to gamble by holding a risky asset with the possibility of maximizing returns. (5)

Risk-neutral Characteristic of savers who judge assets only on their expected returns. (5)

Risk premium The difference between the yield on a financial instrument and the yield on a default-risk-free instrument of comparable maturity. It measures the additional yield a saver requires in order to be willing to hold a risky instrument. (7)

Risk sharing Services provided by the financial system wherein savers and borrowers spread and transfer risk. (3)

Risk structure of interest rates The differences in risk, liquidity, information costs, and taxation that result in differences in interest rates and yields across credit market instruments of the same maturity. (7)

Rules strategy An attempt by the central bank to follow specific and publicly announced guidelines for policy. (28)

Savers Suppliers of funds, providing funds to borrowers in the anticipation of repayment of more funds in the future. (3)

Saving curve A graph that illustrates the relationship between aggregate saving and the expected real rate of interest. (5)

Saving-investment diagram A graph that shows the relationship between the saving and investment curves. It is used to determine the equilibrium real interest rate. (24)

Savings institution A category of banking firms including S&Ls and mutual savings banks. (12)

Seasonal credit Discount lending to satisfy geographically specific seasonal liquidity requirements. (20)

Secondary markets Financial markets in which claims that have already been issued are sold by one investor to another. (3)

Securities market institutions Financial institutions (investment banks, brokers and dealers, and organized exchanges) that reduce costs of matching savers and borrowers. (12)

Segmented markets theory The proposition that yields on each financial instrument are determined in a separate market, with separate market-specific demand and supply considerations. (7)

Shoe leather costs The cost to consumers and businesses of minimizing currency holdings due to inflation. (28)

Short-run aggregate supply (SRAS) curve A plot of the relationship between aggregate output supplied and the price level. (25)

Short-term debt A debt instrument that has a maturity of less than one year. (3)

Simple deposit multiplier The reciprocal of the required reserve ratio. (17)

Simple loan A credit transaction in which the borrower receives from the lender an amount of funds called principal and agrees to repay the lender principal plus an additional amount called interest (as a fee for using the funds) on a given date (maturity). (4)

Simple Phillips curve The statistical relationship between inflation and the difference between unemployment and the natural rate of unemployment. (28)

Small open economy An economy in which total saving is too small to affect the world real interest rate, so the economy takes the world interest rate as a given. (6)

Special Drawing Rights (SDRs) Paper substitute for gold, issued as international reserves by the International Monetary Fund in its role as lender of last resort. (22)

Specialist   A broker-dealer on the floor of the exchange who makes a market in one or more stocks and matches buyers and sellers. (12)

Specialization   A system in which individuals produce the goods or services for which they have relatively the best ability. (2)

Speculation   The attempt to profit from disagreements among traders about future prices of a commodity or financial instrument by anticipating changes in prices. (10)

Speculative attack   The sale of weak currencies or purchase of strong currencies by market participants who believe a government will be unable or unwilling to maintain the exchange rate, in an attempt to force a devaluation or revaluation of the currency. (22)

Spot transactions   Transactions in which trade and settlement occur at the same time. (9)

Stabilization policies (activist policies)   Public policies designed to smooth short-run fluctuations in output involving shifts of the *AD* curve by changes in government purchases or taxes or by changes in the nominal money supply. (26)

Standard of deferred payment   The feature of money by which it facilitates exchange over time in credit. (2)

Standby letter of credit (SLC)   A promise that a bank will lend the borrower funds to pay off its maturing commercial paper if necessary. (13)

State and local government bonds (municipal bonds)   Intermediate and long-term bonds issued by municipalities and state governments that are exempt from federal income taxation and allow governmental units to borrow the funds to build schools, roads, and other large capital projects. (3)

State banks   Banks that are chartered by a state government. (14)

Statistical discrepancy   An adjustment to the capital account in the balance-of-payments accounts to reflect measurement errors and omissions. (22)

Sterilized foreign-exchange intervention   A transaction in which a foreign-exchange intervention is accompanied by offsetting domestic open market operations to leave the monetary base unchanged. (22)

Stock market   A market in which owners of firms buy and sell their claims. (1)

Stocks   Equity claims issued by corporations. They represent the largest single category of capital market assets. (3)

Store of value   A function of money; the accumulation of value by holding dollars or other assets that can be used to buy goods and services in the future. (2)

Subsidiary U.S. bank   Affiliate of a foreign bank that is subject to domestic banking regulations and need not bear the name of its foreign parent. (16)

Supply shocks   Shifts in the price or availability of raw materials or in production technologies that affect production costs and the aggregate supply curve. (25)

Syndicate   See *Loan syndicate*. (16)

T-account   A simplified accounting tool that lists changes in balance sheet items as they occur. (13)

Takeover   A struggle for corporate control in which a group of current or new shareholders buys a controlling interest in a firm, reshapes the board of directors, and even replaces managers. (11)

Targets   Variables that a central bank can influence directly and that help to achieve monetary policy goals. (21)

Tariff   A common trade barrier consisting of a tax on goods purchased from other countries. (8)

Term premium   The additional yield that investors require for investing in a less preferred maturity. (7)

Term structure of interest rates   The variation in yields for related instruments differing in maturity. (7)

Theory of portfolio allocation   A statement that predicts how savers allocate their assets on the basis of their consideration of their wealth, expected return on the assets, degree of risk, liquidity of the assets, and the cost of acquiring information about assets. (5)

Time deposits   Accounts with a specified maturity, which could range from a few months to several years. (13)

Total rate of return   The sum of the current yield of a credit market instrument and the rate of capital gain or loss on it. (4)

Trade balance   The component of the current account that equals the difference between merchandise exports and imports. (22)

Transactions costs   The cost of trade or exchange; for example, the brokerage commission charged for buying or selling a financial claim like a bond or a share of stock. (3, 11)

Treasury tax and loan accounts   U.S. Treasury's deposit accounts with commercial banks. (18)

Underfunded   A term used to describe a defined benefit plan when contributions, together with the projected future earnings, are not sufficient to pay off projected defined benefits. (12)

Underground economy   Economic activity that is not measured in formal government statistics. (17)

Underwriting A way in which investment banks earn income; in the simplest form, they guarantee a price to an issuing firm that needs capital, sell the issue at a higher price, and keep the profit, known as the "spread." (12)

Unit of account A function of money; the provision of a way of measuring the value of goods and services in the economy in terms of money. (2)

Universal banking Allowing banks to be involved in many nonbanking activities with no geographic restrictions. (14)

Unsterilized foreign-exchange intervention A transaction in which the central bank allows the monetary base to respond to the sale or purchase of domestic currency. (22)

U.S. government agency securities Intermediate or long-term bonds issued by the federal government or government-sponsored agencies. (3)

U.S. Treasury bills (T-bills) Debt obligations of the U.S. government that have a maturity of less than one year. (3)

U.S. Treasury bonds Securities issued by the federal government to finance budget deficits. (3)

U.S. Treasury securities Debt obligations issued by the federal government to finance budget deficits. (3)

Vault cash The cash on hand in the bank. (13, 17)

Velocity of money The average number of times a unit of currency is spent each year on a purchase of goods and services in the economy. (23)

Venture capital firm A firm that raises equity capital from investors to invest in emerging or growing entrepreneurial business ventures. (11)

Wealth The sum of the value of assets. (2)

Wealth elasticity of demand The relationship of the percentage change in quantity demanded of an asset to the percentage change in wealth. (5)

World Bank (International Bank for Reconstruction and Development) The bank created by the Bretton Woods agreement to grant long-term loans to developing countries for their economic development. (22)

World real interest rate The real interest rate determined in the international capital market. (6)

Yield curve A graph showing yields to maturity on different default-risk-free instruments as a function of maturity. (7)

Yield to maturity The interest rate measure at which the present value of an asset's returns is equal to its value today. (4)

ANSWERS TO SELF-TEST

True or False

1. True.
2. False. The sale of consumer durable goods is more dependent on the availability of bank credit than is the sale of groceries.
3. True.
4. True.
5. False. The likelihood of experiencing financial distress falls.
6. True.
7. False. The bank lending channel works in addition to the money channel.
8. True.
9. True.
10. False. According to the balance sheet channel, businesses with weak balance sheets are more sensitive to changes in monetary policy.

Fill in the Blank

1. decrease
2. Disintermediation
3. Credit controls
4. increase; right
5. money
6. bank lending
7. money
8. Regulation Q
9. credit crunch
10. Low-net-worth

Multiple Choice

1.	a	2.	b
3.	b	4.	a
5.	a	6.	a
7.	d	8.	c
9.	b	10.	c
11.	b	12.	a
13.	b	14.	d